More Praise for

Getting the Love You Want

"What a treasure this book is, full of the insight, wisdom, and empathy that enriches loving relationships, even those that may seem worn at the seams or beyond hope. Harville and Helen bring fresh ideas, kind hearts, and deep humanity to everything and everyone they encounter."

—Diane Ackerman, *New York Times* bestselling author of
A Natural History of Love

"In this new edition of *Getting the Love You Want*, after having sold an amazing 4 million books, Helen and Harville show their readers how to create safety with an interactional structure that allows two lovers to turn escalating conflicts into a win-win dialogue that is enriched by partners' differences. Readers will benefit from the new wisdom of these two pioneers in understanding relationships."

—Julie Schwartz Gottman and John Gottman, author of
The Seven Principles for Making Marriage Work

"In this thirtieth-anniversary edition of their timeless classic, *Getting the Love You Want*, Helen Hunt and Harville Hendrix have teamed up to provide couples with a time tested strategy to improve their relationships. By combining Imago Therapy with a new scientific understanding of how brain and behaviors change, *Getting the Love You Want* will help couples untangle the deep and confusing mysteries of love and connection and help them harvest the joy and healing power present in healthy, mutual, intimate relationships."

—Amy Banks, M.D., senior scholar at the Wellesley Centers
for Women and author of *Wired to Connect: The Surprising
Link Between Brain Science and Strong, Healthy
Relationships*

"*Getting the Love You Want* is one of the most important relationship books of all time. It is a classic. Harville and Helen's insight that we are attracted to mates that are similar to our caregivers is one of the most important revelations in the field of relationship psychology. Millions have benefited from this book, and so will you."

—Douglas Abrams, coauthor of *The Book of Joy,*
and Rachel Abrams, M.D., author of *BodyWise*

"*Getting the Love You Want* is an awesome book. Relationships are the key to life, and this book is a key to getting it right. This book has stood the test of time to be one of the best, and the updates are timely and relevant. We are total fans of Harville and Helen, and love this book."

—Scott and Theresa Beck, cofounders of Gloo, LLC

"Where would we be without *Getting the Love You Want*? This articulate, wisdom-drenched, and profoundly knowledgeable book has given us tangible relational support when we've needed it most. More than just advice, this soulful and practical handbook has helped us build a foundational template for our marriage. We are forever grateful to Helen and Harville for sharing what is certainly among the greatest contributions to relational healing and harmony. Now, more than ever, its pages offer guidance, vision, rituals, insights, and illumination for cultivating and maintaining a healthy and vibrant partnership."

—Grammy Award–winning singer and songwriter
Alanis Morissette and rapper Souleye

"This superb updated revision of *Getting the Love You Want* will inspire you to create a deeper, more loving connection. The exercises alone are powerful reminders of how to love more elegantly."

—Ellyn Bader, Ph.D., founder of The Couples Institute and
creator of the Developmental Model of Couples Therapy

"Helen LaKelly Hunt and Harville Hendrix have done it again! Their powerful approach to bringing love alive in a couple's relationship through the creation of safety, trust, and connection enables us to let go of the common images of what we've longed for in our past in order to become fully present for our partner right now. Science affirms what these two pioneers in loving relationships have taught for decades: By taking practical steps to increase our self-understanding and cultivate clear communication, we can achieve the kind of intimacy and connection we've often longed for. By teaching us how to create safe conversations that open us to the true person in front of our eyes, we are literally able to get the love we want—and then some! Take in these time-tested practical steps to love and enjoy the freedom and closeness you deserve."

—Daniel J. Siegel, M.D., executive director of the Mindsight Institute and *New York Times* bestselling author of *Aware: The Science and Practice of Presence*

"Harville and Helen have been a force in the world of relationships for decades, and their work has inspired so many. Imago theory and therapy help set a foundation for couples to know themselves, and each other, in ways that will serve them for a lifetime."

—Scott Kriens, cofounder of 1440 Multiversity

"If you were to read one book that would change the way you relate to the most important people in your life, this is that book. When published in 1988, *Getting the Love You Want* was the first book to stress the importance of loving partnership for emotional well-being. The messages in it are still most important for anyone, male or female, gay or straight, who wants to be in a healthy, happy relationship."

—Marion Solomon, Ph.D., coauthor of *Love and War in Intimate Relationships: Connection, Disconnection, and Mutual Regulation in Couple Therapy*

"Learn: how the imprints of the past unconsciously eclipse the present. Learn: how safety is fundamental to illuminating relationships. Learn: to practice conscious partnership to brighten your future together. The goal of living is enriching connection. There are no better relationship experts from which to learn than Harville Hendrix and Helen LaKelly Hunt."
    —Jeffrey K. Zeig, Ph.D., founder and CEO of the
    Milton H. Erickson Foundation

"The world has changed drastically since the first edition of *Getting the Love You Want* thirty years ago, and so have many of the dynamics we see between partners. Fortunately, our knowledge about how to help couples improve their relationships has expanded alongside these changes. Harville Hendrix and Helen LaKellyHunt have kept pace with the times. Their new edition provides guidance for couples who are 'doubly challenged'—both from childhood wounding and also from the cultural reward system in which they operate. At the same time, readers still receive all the many effective exercises from the last edition."
    —Stan Tatkin, Psy.D., MFT, developer of a Psychobiological
    Approach to Couple Therapy® (PACT) and founder of the
    PACT Institute

GETTING THE

LOVE YOU WANT

a guide for couples

FULLY REVISED AND UPDATED

Harville Hendrix, Ph.D.,
and Helen LaKelly Hunt, Ph.D.

St. Martin's Griffin
New York

The Library of Congress Cataloging-in-Publication Data
is available upon request.

ISBN 978-1-250-31053-8 (trade paperback)
ISBN 978-1-250-31054-5 (ebook)

Our books may be purchased in bulk for promotional, educational, or
business use. Please contact your local bookseller or the Macmillan
Corporate and Premium Sales Department at 1-800-221-7945, extension
5442, or by email at MacmillanSpecialMarkets@macmillan.com.

Originally published in hardcover in 1988 by Henry Holt and Company.

Fully Revised and Updated Edition: January 2019

2 3 4 5 6 7 8 9 10

Contents

PART III: THE EXERCISES

In Appreciation of Jo Robinson

THIRTY YEARS AGO, we were introduced to Jo Robinson. She understood immediately what we were attempting to do. At that time, Jo was the author of *Unplug the Christmas Machine* and *Full House*. In the years that followed, Jo Robinson became a *New York Times* bestselling author and coauthor of many books, including *Hot Monogamy, The Omega Diet, When Your Body Gets the Blues,* and *Pasture Perfect*. Her most recent book is *Eating on the Wild Side: The Missing Link to Optimum Health*.

For the first edition of this book, Jo took a lengthy rough manuscript and many transcriptions of lectures and workshops and worked tirelessly to transform a badly organized and somewhat opaque manuscript and much supplementary material into a well-organized and finely polished product. In our second and third editions, Jo again answered the call to help us organize our new ideas, working tirelessly to integrate them into a heavily revised edition. As she did in the beginning, Jo immersed herself in the material by attending a couples' workshop and extensively interviewing us throughout the writing process. For this last edition, she conscientiously helped us formulate a vision and began the extensive editing process.

We owe her a debt of gratitude for her long-term devotion to this project and for her friendship over the past thirty years. Without her intelligence and writing skill, we would all have a difficult time indeed getting the love we want. Thanks, Jo.

Acknowledgments

IN THE PROCESS of writing this book and its various evolutions, we have become acutely aware of a truth so aptly stated by the poet John Donne that "no man is an island," and by Walt Whitman, who said, "I contain multitudes." Pulling together the new material in this fully revised and updated edition has deepened our awareness of our dependence upon many others in our circle. The new vistas would not have been possible were it not for the contributions of many colleagues, students, trusting couples, friends, and family that have supported us.

Our first appreciation goes to Sanam Hoon. About twenty-five years ago, she came into our lives as staff and eventually executive director of the Institute for Imago Relationship Therapy (currently Imago Relationships International). She became indispensable, managing projects, handling legal and publication issues, and overseeing aspects of our professional lives. Sanam was essential in this edition, taking over where Jo left off and completing this revision with polish and perfection. We owe her an unpayable debt of gratitude and look forward to continuing our journey.

Our indebtedness to Oprah Winfrey is unlimited. She first exposed Imago to millions of people in 1988, putting *Getting the*

Love You Want on the *New York Times* bestseller list. Repeated invitations to be on her show have returned this book to the bestseller list eleven times, and she has rated the second appearance on her show in 1989 among her top twenty shows in her twenty years on television.

We deeply appreciate Alanis Morissette for her enthusiastic support of Imago over the years, speaking about it in many public appearances and in her conversation with Oprah. Her endorsement of this edition is a great honor.

The board of Imago Relationships International (IRI) and the Imago faculty members have been unambivalent in their dedication to Imago and have shepherded its expansion internationally. We gratefully acknowledge all the Imago therapists and educators who have helped to develop and deepen Imago Relationship Therapy and make it available in this country and in over fifty countries around the world. We especially want to recognize Wendy and Bob Patterson for their heroic commitment to the sustainability of IRI and its global footprint for so many years and Dave Green and Christine Petrik, who exemplify joyful connecting and are deeply involved in ensuring Imago's future. Bruce Crapuchettes and Francine Beauvoir, long-standing faculty members, have spread this work through Imago training and workshops and are Imago authors in their own right. Melva and Jesse Johnson did phenomenal work stepping up with the IRI community when it was just founded and decades following. Gene Shelly and Nedra Fetterman were the first co-deans of the Imago faculty and, with others, innovatively helped bring Imago training to the digital era with the clinical online training. Brenda Rawlings and Ben Cohen were also strong co-deans of the faculty representing our global outreach.

Plus, we want to acknowledge two of our daughters. Kimberly Miller recently became a licensed marriage and family therapist in California, and in addition to several trainings she's pursued, two years ago, also went through the Imago training and is now a Certified Imago Therapist. Yeah, KJ! Additionally, our daughter and son-in-law Drs. Kathryn and Ron Rombs knew that the Catholic Church needed the wisdom of Imago Therapy, and while we were offering Imago in ways to other houses of worship, they put together an outreach to couples in the Catholic Church. The support of all three of you meant the world to us!

We want to acknowledge and thank Dave and Jessica Lindsey, a visionary couple who followed their intuition on how this work could save countless marriages and pledged a profound commitment to alleviate the unnecessary suffering in relationships, and strengthen countless families throughout the country.

In the second edition in 2001, we included our appreciation to Barney Karpfinger, who had become our new agent. His support was invaluable for that edition and for all other books published before and after that revision. And for more than two decades, he has been a champion for the development of our careers.

Our appreciation also goes to the people at Henry Holt and Company who supported the publishing of this newest edition and worked so patiently with us on the revision. We are especially thankful for Ryan Smernoff and Madeline Jones, our editor, and Maggie Richards, deputy publisher and VP director of sales and marketing.

For this edition, we appreciate the founding members of Relationships First (RF) for their support and their dedication to make relationship education available for everyone. We especially want to recognize Dan Siegel and Caroline Welch for their leading contributions in interpersonal neurobiology, and encouragement of RF. Special thanks to Christi Carter, who has steadfastly held the reins on our nonprofit work to spread safe conversations everywhere.

We are deeply indebted to all the couples who have read this book and passed it on to others and to other professionals and friends who have recommended the book.

Finally, we also want to thank our six children and our six

grandchildren for their support. We appreciate the lessons we have learned, and continue learning, from them over the years. They have helped us live the ideas and become a more integrated and authentic couple, walking the talk.

Deep appreciation to each and every one!

Preface

WELCOME TO THE fully revised and updated edition of *Getting the Love You Want: A Guide for Couples.* By purchasing this book, you are continuing to circulate a classic with a thirty-year history of transforming relationships all across the globe! We're glad you're a part of a new consciousness, that of couples everywhere committing to strengthening their relationships at home.

Here is something about the book you may not know. A few weeks after its publication in 1988, Oprah Winfrey featured it on her show, winning her an Emmy. For the next twenty-three years, she created over a dozen shows featuring the book, which helped to put it on the *New York Times* bestseller list eleven times. This massive visibility attracted around four million readers globally. Approximately 2,500 therapists have become Imago Trained and practice Imago Couples Therapy in over fifty countries, making it among the largest and most popular mainstream couples' therapy in the world.

But that is the old news. Here is the new. On the cover, you will notice that this edition has two authors. In all preceding editions, I (Harville) am the only author. In the 2008 edition, Helen, my partner in life and work, appeared on the cover as cowriter of the new preface. That started something that this edition completes, which I feel most passionate about: the public recognition of Helen as cocreator of Imago Relationship Therapy.

Why now, why not then? you might ask. Well, it was discussed as an option in 1988, but I (Helen) firmly declined. It was a chance to make Harville distinctly visible in important ways he deserved, so Harville was willing to agree with me. Supporting the book as it was being written was a tremendous honor. Not only was this a chance for Harville's distinct visibility, but I needed to spend time with issues around my Dallas family business, with our own new blended family, and I was very happy to be a behind-the-scenes support. It was Harville's talent that went into the writing and executing of this beautiful vision. Contributing to the content was different from writing it down, and in that regard, Harville was clearly the author. This continued with the second book, *Keeping the Love You Find: A Personal Guide,* but with the third book on parenting, I became a visible partner, Harville fully including me as coauthor, which set the pattern for the future. But Harville and I were conflicted around how to talk about my role in and my original contribution to Imago.

Now let's regress to see how this story began. We met in 1977. We both were divorced, and we began dating. After several months, as we discovered so many interests in common, I asked Harville what his dream future might look like. Since he was leaving his teaching job at Southern Methodist University's Perkins School of Theology, and had no specific plans going forward, he shared with me a few options he was considering. One was to write a book. I asked him what the focus of the book would be. And he said, "I'm curious: Why do couples fight? Why does the dream become the nightmare?" I began to ask him what he thought was the answer, and a conversation grew out of that evening with each of us helping to finish each other's sentences. This continued throughout our dating years, and six years after we married, the manuscript *Getting the Love You Want: A Guide for Couples* was finished and then published in 1988. Harville and I have continued to talk about couples' theory most days in our lives, the forty-plus years we've known each other!

As we have reflected upon *how* we co-created Imago theory and therapy, I (Harville) discovered a basic and productive complementary: Helen is right-brain dominant, which means she accesses information through her feelings and senses, intuits subtle qualities, and sees the connections. I am left-brain dominant, which means I access information through observation and logical thinking and construct wholes out of parts. Helen is the creative source, and I the architect and contractor. Between us, raw content derived through these different mental operations has been transformed into the publication of ten books on intimate relationships, a global organization of Imago therapists, Imago Educators, plus relational social activists who are zealously committed to healing couples and creating a relational culture.

Even though we were cocreators of Imago theory for over forty years in all its forms, my name was the only one on the book, so I was considered its sole author. And since I was the solo Imago professional trainer and couples' workshops presenter for the first ten years after publication, I was seen by the public as sole creator of Imago Relationship Therapy. When a brand is established with high-profile status, it gets quite solidified in public opinion.

Although Helen was inducted into the National Women's Hall of Fame for her work in the women's movement, her motivation was helping women have equal voices in society but to also have equal relationships at home, too. While I (Harville) was a marriage therapist in the office, we both saw Helen as being a marriage therapist in the culture. Couples had been her soul calling a decade before we met. After we became partners, creating, developing, and teaching Imago ideas was clearly a part of her DNA. And while we won't go into too many details here, we will summarize by saying people logically saw me as the creator of Imago and Helen in the shadows as my supportive partner. Over the years, as our children were leaving home and our marriage became more connected, Helen turned fully to what she really loves to do professionally and began to regularly colead couples' workshops, copresent at national and international conferences, and coauthor books and articles on Imago Relationship Therapy.

Then a series of serendipitous things began to happen that led to a profound awareness: our issue was an instance of a world historical problem, the historical second-class status of women, and the unconscious bias against women's equality. And both Helen and I were unconsciously complicit in it.

Here's one way we moved to consciousness. I (Helen), published a book called *And the Spirit Moved Them* through the Feminist Press. It is about a group of women whose contributions to the origins of the women's movement in the United States were omitted. My book restored them to their rightful place in early feminist history. At the same time these women came out of the shadows of history into the light, the *Hidden Figures* movie appeared. This movie valorized the African American women whose contributions to the success of the space program had never been imagined or acknowledged. At the same time, we became aware of other books about women in politics and in the medical professions, a sort of zeitgeist of bringing other women out of the shadows of the men around them.

Helen's place in Imago was a women's issue, and thus a man's issue and a human issue. It dawned on me (Harville) that we were unconsciously participating in a cultural dynamic of which we consciously disapproved—the second-class status of women. Helen's living in the shadow of recognition for her contributions to Imago was an instance of this world historical situation that is just now beginning to right itself. This awareness was shocking on the one hand and liberating on the other.

At the moment of that insight, all barriers to sharing authorship melted. Receiving rightful and unrestrained recognition brought tears to Helen's eyes and joy to my heart. The timing of the publication of the revised version of *Getting* and Helen's pivotal contributions to its inception and publication thirty years ago made it a vehicle to correct the issue of her visibility and, simultaneously, to contribute to the project of women's equality across the world. So, this fully revised and updated edition, with us as coauthors, is not only a celebration of a durable book; it is participation in a world historical process of bringing social justice and equality to women, and thus to everyone. While its processes have created relational equality for women in the couples who have used it, they are now creating equality for its coauthors. It's about time!

And there's more! The theory keeps evolving. In the years of our struggle with professional equality in our relationship and personal equality at home, we were also observing relational inequality as a chronic dynamic for couples. But this was not surprising, since women's social, economic, and political equality has been an issue since the dawn of civilization.

Our new awareness was that couples are doubly challenged. First, the source of the most obvious challenge comes from childhood wounding that leaves most of us so self-absorbed that we are unaware of the inner world of others. Therefore, we think we are alike in significant ways, and when that does not check out, we object to our partners, or the world, being different from how we see it. That leads to conflict and polarization, the ingredients of misery.

The second challenge comes from the fact that couples are soaking in a cultural value system that rewards competition, being "the best," and winning at all cost. When this value system interfaces with the need for control that comes from our childhood history, the relationship becomes toxic and often unsustainable—hence, a 50 percent divorce rate and 75 percent unhappiness rate for couples who do not divorce. This complex issue makes it hard for couples, because the way they understand their emotional needs and try to get them met is dictated by the competitive value system in which they live. The outside shapes the inside.

The traditional therapy process has been to explore the inner world of each partner: their feelings, thoughts, and memories, with the goal of helping them deepen their understanding of their inner world. The guiding assumption was that insight would free them to relate in a healthier way. But they did not. The success rate of that method was about 25 percent.

So, we (Harville and Helen) shifted the focus of Imago from exploring what was going on *inside* couples to what was going on *outside* and *between* them—another contribution by Helen, bequeathed from Martin Buber. We discovered that when we help couples change their interactive behaviors—rather than how they feel, think, or remember—they feel connected and begin to have new thoughts and create new memories. The primary interactive behavior is *how* couples talk to each other, not *what* they talk about, which we came to call Imago Dialogue. This shift, which gave birth to the Imago Dialogue process, was initiated by Helen in 1977, who one day, early in our relationship, when we were in a deep conflict, shouted, "Stop! Let's one of us talk and the other listen." We did. To our surprise, we calmed down and began to talk without shouting. This was one of the first times, followed by many, that I (Harville) incorporated one of Helen's contributions into a therapeutic process. In this case, it became the primary therapeutic tool and is used by every Imago therapist in the world. The target of therapy became the interactions of partners between each other, essentially their outside world rather than their inside world. It became apparent that not only is *how* partners talk to each other more important than *what* they talk about, it is also more important than what they remember from childhood or understand about the *whys* of their behavior.

That's not all. The rest is amazing. Therapy becomes simple, precise, and effective, but not easy. When partners use Imago Dialogue, a three-step structured process, to talk to each other, they experience *safety* in the relationship. Safety is nonnegotiable, and it is created by structure. Safety makes it possible for couples to be vulnerable with each other, drop their guards, open up, and become what we call *present* to each other. Effectively, when one really listens while the other is talking and removes all forms of negativity about what they are hearing, they create an environment in which the wounds of childhood are healed in their current intimate relationship, and they do not have to do the exploration of their memories, feelings, and thoughts as has been thought in the past one hundred years since therapy was founded. Not only is the inside changed when changes occur on the outside, the past is also healed in the present. And being present to each other without judgment creates emotional equality that contributes to changing the competitive culture in which they were wounded. The personal becomes social and political. Everything is connecting to everything, all the time.

Finally, all this helped us refine the answer to the questions we asked at the beginning of our relationship: Why do couples fight? Why the nightmare? And what to do about it? It turns out not to be complicated. We believe that couples fight because they "object to difference." And they put each other down emotionally, and sometimes physically, because they are unconsciously competitive. This comes from the cultural value system that directs them to compete for the emotional resources in the relationship and to be the one that is "right." Their fight also turns into competition for equality, and that becomes the problem. Fighting for equality is an indication of inequality, and that creates anxiety, and anxiety strengthens their defenses. When partners are anxious and defensive, they either withdraw from the scene and disappear emotionally or compete with each other, until the death of their relationship or themselves.

So, we insist that safety is nonnegotiable. It is the necessary first step to the Imago Dialogue template for all conversations. The three-step process enables partners to talk with each other about anything without polarizing and to connect with each other about anything beyond their differences. Such talking integrates the brain and reduces the tendency to overreact when triggered. The second step is a pledge to remove all negativity so that safety can become predictable. This is also nonnegotiable. The third step is partners flooding each other with all sorts of affirmations on a daily basis, to increase positive connecting.

When safety in the relationship is achieved and maintained, the inner world changes. Anxiety goes down. Defenses relax. Perceptions of the other change from negative to positive. Interactive pleasure increases! Spontaneous play appears with its daily laugh. The sensation of being fully alive returns, and we feel at home in a connecting universe. That is what we humans felt when we started out in our vibrant universe. Everyone and everything pulsated, feeling connected, curious and joyful. It was the time before our caregivers put out the lights and everything turned to shades of gray with patches of black. When connecting is restored, the colored lights turn on again, and the partner and the world are bathed in wonder. We have returned to where we started—fully alive and joyfully connecting—a state of being only available in a relationship with a significant person where the Space Between is reliably and predictably safe.

We hope to meet you again on the inside and guide you to your promised land. And we wish you happy reading and a wondrous relationship.

Harville and Helen
May 2018

part I

THE UNCONSCIOUS PARTNERSHIP

LOVE, LOST AND FOUND

IN THE THIRTY-FIVE years that we have been helping people get the love they want, we've witnessed many changes in the outward appearance of love relationships. For example, we've seen a dramatic increase in the age at which people marry. When we first worked with couples, the median marriage age for first-time marriages was twenty-three years for men and twenty-one years for women. By 2017, that had risen to thirty years for men and twenty-seven for women.[1] Today, people in their twenties are just as likely to be in school, working, or exploring the world as getting married and starting a family. Many marry later, if at all. And young people are suspicious of marriage and have given up on the institution, since they have seen so few marriages they would want to emulate.

Three decades ago, most of the couples we saw were spending too little time together, which redirected energy away from their relationship. Today, the digital world has shrunk that time even more. A 2016 survey[2] reported that adults are now spending five hours a day on their portable devices, and that's in addition to the time they spend watching TV, playing DVDs, and working on their laptops and personal computers. Apple's digital devices—the iPhone and the iPad—are aptly named: they all strengthen the "I" and not the relationship we most care about.

Another twenty-first century phenomenon is the growing reliance on the Web. In the 1970s and '80s, most couples met each other at school, work, or social events. Today, millions of people meet their matches on internet dating sites. For a monthly fee, a computer will scrutinize your personality and preferences and churn out a list of people who come closest to your ideal. With luck, you'll find a 100 percent match! Matches are no longer made in heaven—they're made by computer algorithms.

The Truths that Endure

AMID ALL THE changes in the way we meet and mate, two truths endure. First, people everywhere still seek lasting love. We all long to feel the deep sense of connection and joy that floods us when love is new. A man who attended a recent workshop said that "falling in love with my wife made me feel loved and accepted for who I was for the very first time. It was intoxicating." Nineteenth-century romantic poet John Keats put it this way: "My creed is Love and you are its only tenet—You have ravished me away by a Power I cannot resist." You are in love. You are no longer alone. The sensation of being fully alive and joyfully connecting is running through your nervous system. You feel at home in the universe itself. You have been captured by the power and wonder of romantic love.

The second truth is that when love flounders, people experience the same heartache that couples reported since the age of Cleopatra and Antony when suicide was the best answer. One client said as his girlfriend was leaving him, "I can't sleep or eat. My chest feels like it's going to explode. I cry all the time, and I don't know what to do." Indeed, this is the same trauma that has been described throughout recorded history. An ancient medical text from the Middle East, written more than three thousand years ago, described a condition called "lovesickness."[3] According to the text, you know a patient is lovesick when he is "habitually depressed, his throat tight, finds no pleasure in eating or drinking, and endlessly repeats, with great sighs, 'Ah, my poor heart!'"

It Gets Personal

WE KNOW THE pain of lost love because both of us had first marriages that ended in divorce. For me (Harville), my first wife and I began having marriage difficulties when our two children were young. We were deeply committed to our relationship and went through eight years of intensive examination, working with several therapists. Nothing helped, and ultimately, we filed for divorce.

As I sat in the divorce court waiting my turn to see the judge, I felt like a double failure, a failure as a husband and as a therapist. That very afternoon, I was scheduled to teach a course on marriage and the family, and the next day, as usual, I had several couples to counsel. Despite my professional training, I felt just as confused and defeated as the other people who sat beside me, waiting for their names to be called.

In the year following my divorce, I woke up each morning with an acute sense of loss. When I went to bed at night, I stared at the ceiling, trying to find some explanation for our failed marriage. Sure, my wife and I had our ten rational reasons for divorcing, just like everyone else. I didn't like this about her; she didn't like that about me; we had different interests and goals; we had grown apart. But beneath our list of complaints, I could sense that there was a central disappointment, an underlying cause of our unhappiness that had eluded eight years of probing.

Time passed, and my despair turned into a compelling desire

to make sense out of my dilemma; I was not going to walk away from the ruins of my marriage without gaining some insight. I met Helen two years later.

I (Helen) also had two young children, and like Harville, I was deeply sorrowful and also puzzled by the failure of my first marriage. I was aware that a distance had grown between my husband and me, and I thought his long hours at work contributed to the problem. When he was unavailable, I felt lonely and sad. But I grew to wonder if there were other, more hidden causes of our growing distance. Why hadn't we been able to identify those deeper issues and solve the problems?

IMAGO THERAPY

FROM THE DAY we (Harville and Helen) met, we discovered that we shared the same intense interest in the psychology of relationships. Harville was a clinical pastoral counselor, and Helen was working on her master's in counseling degree at Southern Methodist University. During our courtship, we spent much of our time gathering insights from wide-ranging fields, including philosophy, religion, feminism, and physics. We spent our "dates" sharing what we were discovering.

Imago (i-MAH-go) Therapy, the ideas and techniques you will be reading about in this book, was born out of our decades-long collaboration and refined in the crucible of our own marriage. In the past thirty-five years, we have used our insights to counsel thousands of couples, some in private practice and some in the group workshops that we now colead.

Working with so many people has deepened our understanding of how marriages work, why they break down, and how couples can learn to reconnect and experience the joy and wonder that was there when they first fell in love. Drawing on these insights, we have been able to make Imago Therapy more and more effective. Today, we can help couples get the love they want more quickly than we had in the past, and with even better results.

CORE IDEA

ONE OF THE core ideas of Imago Therapy is that the underlying cause of most couples' discontent lies buried beneath the surface. Superficially, partners argue about household chores, money, parenting styles, their next vacation, or who is spending too much time on their cell phones. Outside of their awareness, however, each one is being compelled by an unwritten agenda that was formed early in life: to recover the sensations of being fully alive and joyfully connecting with which we came into the world. Although the specifics of each person's agenda are unique, the overriding goal is the same: to experience with the partner the same sensations they experienced with their caretakers. And they assign their partner the task of making it happen! "Partner, I expect you to satisfy the unmet emotional needs that I brought from childhood."

Most of us vastly underestimate the scope of the unconscious mind. There is an analogy that might give a better appreciation for its pervasive influence. In the daytime, we can't see the stars. We talk as if they "come out" at night, even though they are there all the time. We also underestimate the sheer number of stars. We look up at the sky, see a smattering of dim stars, and assume that's all there is. When we travel far away from city lights, we see a sky strewn with stars and are overwhelmed by the brilliance of the heavens. But it is only when we study astronomy that we learn the whole truth: the hundreds of thousands of stars that we see on a clear, moonless night in the country are only a fraction of the stars in the universe, and many of the points of light that we assume to be stars are in fact entire galaxies. So it is with the unconscious mind: the orderly, logical thoughts of our conscious mind are but a thin veil over the unconscious, which is active and functioning at all times. When we fall in love, this unconscious, trapped in the eternal now and having only a dim awareness of the outside world, is trying to re-create the environment of childhood. And the reason the unconscious is trying to resurrect the past is not a matter of habit or blind compulsion but of a compelling need to heal old childhood wounds.

Few people are aware of this agenda, and many would deny it. "What does my childhood have to do with my partner's drinking problem? I want to deal with the here and now." They do not know that their being unavailable to their partner may be the source of their partner's drinking problem, which in turn feeds their unavailability to connect in the here and now. Nor do they know that the mutual experience of ruptured connecting is a replay of each partner's childhood. While each partner contributes to the complaint of the other, on an unconscious level, we expect our partners to intuit our unmet needs and satisfy them without asking for anything in return. Additionally, we picked that partner to reexperience these old feelings so that we could then heal the sadness and pain from the past.

YOUR WONDROUS BRAIN

HOW CAN YOU satisfy your needs from the past if you are not aware of them? Learning a few facts about your brain will give you a better understanding of the potential we all have to recover our original joy.

Let's take a brief look at the physical structure of the brain, that mysterious and complex organ with many different subdivisions. For simplicity's sake, we divide the brain into three concentric layers.[4]

The brain stem, which is the inner and most primitive layer, oversees the flow of messages between the brain and the rest of the body. It also controls such basic functions as breathing, swallowing, heart rate, blood pressure, and other vital body functions. Located at the base of the skull, it is sometimes referred to as the "reptilian brain," because all vertebrates from reptiles to mammals share this portion of the anatomy.

Flaring like a wishbone around the top of the brain stem is the layer of the brain called the limbic system, which stores long-term memory and can generate strong emotions. Scientists can surgically stimulate the limbic system of lab animals and create spontaneous bursts of fear and aggression. In your partnership, you may have been the sender or the recipient of similar impulsive eruptions!

In this book, we will use the term *old brain* to refer to both the brain stem and the limbic system. Think of your old brain as being hardwired and determining most of your automatic reactions.

The third area of the brain on top of and surrounding the two other inner layers is the cerebral cortex, a much larger, convoluted mass of brain tissue. This portion of the brain, which is most highly developed in *Homo sapiens*, is the site of most of your cognitive functions. We will refer to the cerebral cortex as the *new brain* because it appeared most recently in evolutionary history.

Your prefrontal cortex of the new brain is the part of you that is conscious, alert, and in contact with your daily surroundings. It's the part of you that makes decisions, thinks, observes, plans, anticipates, responds, organizes information, and creates ideas. The new brain is inherently logical and tries to find a cause for every effect and an effect for every cause. By and large, this analytical, probing, questioning part of your mind is the part that you think of as being "you." When you and your partner are operating out of your new brain, you can help manage and quell some of the emotional responses coming from your old brain.

OLD-BRAIN LOGIC

IN CONTRAST TO your new brain, you are unaware of most of the functions of your old brain. They operate unconsciously. Scientists who study the brain tell us that its main concern is self-preservation. Ever on the alert, the old brain asks the primeval question: "Is it safe or dangerous?"

As it goes about its job of ensuring your safety, your old brain operates in a fundamentally different manner from your new brain. One of the crucial differences is that the old brain has only a hazy awareness of the external world. Unlike the new brain, which relies on direct perception of the outside world, your old brain gets its incoming data from the images, symbols, and thoughts produced by the new brain.

This data is sorted into very broad categories. For example, while your new brain easily distinguishes John from Suzy from Roberto, your old brain segregates all people into six categories. Is this someone to: (1) nurture, (2) be nurtured by, (3) have sex with, (4) run away from, (5) submit to, or (6) attack.[5] Subtleties such as "this is my neighbor," "my cousin," "my mother," or "my husband" slide right on by.

The old brain and the new brain, different in so many ways, are constantly exchanging and interpreting information. Understanding this fact about the nature of your brain helps explain why you can have feelings about your partner that seem out of proportion to the events that triggered them.

Let's suppose that you are a middle-aged man, a middle manager in a medium-size company. After a hectic day at work, where you manage to placate an important client and put the finishing touches on a multimillion-dollar budget, you leave for home, eager to share your successes with your wife. Just before you get to the house, she sends you a text saying that she is still at work and won't be home for several hours. You had counted on her being there! You park in the garage and walk into an empty house. Do you recover from your disappointment and relish the time to yourself? Do you use the time to do a final check on the budget? Yes. But not before you head straight for the freezer and dish out a bowl of vanilla ice cream, your go-to comfort food, to help subdue your anger and disappointment.

When your wife finally gets home, you feel cool and distant toward her. You continue to be reserved the following day. You bring your work to the dinner table and barely glance up at her. You spend the evening watching sports on TV.

Days later, you might become puzzled by your reaction. You know that your wife has a demanding job just like you do. She, too, has to work overtime. Why were you so upset at her? Why did you feel betrayed? Outside your awareness, her absence triggered feelings you had decades ago when you were being raised by working parents. When you were in grade school, you stayed after school in a day care program and were picked up by your mother just before dinner. You envied friends who went straight home at the end of the school day. As a young teen, you walked home from school to an empty house and spent hours watching TV, waiting for your parents to come home. When they did come home, they were often too stressed from work to spend relaxed time with you.

Decades later, your past would worm its way into your present, making you overreact to your wife's late homecoming. To your old brain, you were experiencing the same sense of abandonment you had felt growing up.

CREATING NEW PATHWAYS

IF YOU COULD become conscious of and begin to regulate these unwelcome, unconscious intrusions from your past, you and your partner would be less reactive and have fewer arguments. You would be able to stay in your new brain and interact more rationally. Your stress level would go down, and you would be more open to spending enjoyable time with each other once again.

But how can you accomplish this feat? How can you diminish these subterranean intrusions if you're unaware of many of the painful episodes from your own past and even less familiar with your partner's emotional childhood wounds?

Several of the exercises in Imago Therapy are designed to help you fill in these gaps. In a surprisingly short amount of time, you will be able to identify key issues that are interfering with your efforts to have a safe, loving partnership. (You'll find these exercises in part 3 of this book. We recommend that you read all of parts 1 and 2 before you begin working on the exercises.) This new awareness will enhance your sensitivity to each other's unmet needs and motivate you to be more willing to satisfy them.

If the core idea of our work is about understanding how the unconscious purpose of marriage is to finish childhood, the core practice is learning a new skill. Imago Dialogue introduces a radically new way of talking that makes all conversations safe. As you practice this essential exercise, you will create a safe environment in which you can begin to understand each other on a deeper level than ever before. The important thing to remember is that safety is the key. When you and your partner learn to create safety in your relationship, you will also be able to talk about sensitive issues without slipping into an argument or feeling frustrated or hopeless. Another fundamental exercise, Behavior Change Request, shows you how to convert a frustration into a request and turn the request into a simple, doable behavior. Removing the criticism embedded in a frustration keeps the space between you safe.

As you work your way step by step through Imago Therapy, you will be creating a zone of safety between you—a sacred space we call the Space Between—that is essential for getting the love you want. You might liken this zone to a river that runs between you. You both drink from the river and bathe in it, so it's important that it be free from garbage and toxins. Your interactions in the Space Between determines what you experience inside. To keep the water running clean and pure, you must stop filling it with criticisms and hurtful comments and replace them with respectful, safe interactions. You must move from self-care to caring for this Space Between.

New Findings About the Brain

AS THE NEUROSCIENCES advanced in the 1990s, I (Helen) became fascinated by the concept of neuroplasticity, which states that our brains are impacted and changed by the experiences we have with others and the outside world. We have "social brains" that are influenced by our relationships. Prior to this discovery, brain scientists assumed the brain was unchanged by its interaction with other people and the outside world. This discovery helps explain why the exercises in Imago Therapy can be so transformative. Your brain is changed every time you interact with others.

Through animal experiments and sophisticated brain imaging techniques, neurologists have discovered that experiences from your childhood are recorded in your brain as chemical pathways linking individual nerve cells. Painful experiences from your past are recorded in extra-strong pathways, their strength caused by a stronger flow of chemical messengers. Each time you have a similar painful experience, the pathway becomes stronger still. Later in life, when you have a conflict with your partner, the intensity of your response can be amplified by this hidden pathway. We call this PFSD (post-family stress disorder), the mental condition that can develop during highly stressful relationship situations. Few people recognize that relational stress is similar to PTSD (post-traumatic stress disorder) that results from military combat, a natural disaster, or living in a war zone, among other situations. Long after the stressful interaction, people with PFSD find that interactions in their present life can trigger episodes of intense anxiety, especially events that are reminiscent of the original relational trauma. This phenomenon is much less intense when it is caused by the relatively mild interpersonal distress that most people experience during childhood, but if "emotional baggage" from your past amplifies a conflict you are having with your partner, it can rupture the connection between you and trigger anxiety similar to the original rupture in childhood.

Imago Therapy can short-circuit this unwanted turbulence from your past by helping you create and strengthen new neural pathways. When you have a positive experience with your partner, your old brain encodes it by creating new connections between brain cells. When you have more and more positive interactions, the pathway intensifies. Meanwhile, the old and disruptive pathway that was created in your childhood loses its strength (fewer chemical messengers flow between the cells). It no longer has the same capacity to intrude into your relationship.[6]

We liken this process to building a new freeway beside an old highway—once people travel on the freeway, they spend less time on the old, narrow road. And when they do wander over to the old road, they recognize it immediately and know they have the option of a new response to an old stimulus. Over time, the old road is no longer maintained and becomes cracked and overgrown with weeds. Meanwhile, the freeway has become the road more traveled.

We have witnessed this transformation in the many couples who have taken part in Imago Therapy and Education. As negative experiences from the past become less intrusive in a couple's day-to-day life, there are fewer misunderstandings between them. They respond to what's happening between them in more appropriate ways. They have fewer flare-ups in temper and begin to spend more relaxed time together. This safer, more connecting relationship begins to be a source of joy and rejuvenation.

CHILDHOOD WOUNDS

Everything else you grow out of,
but you never recover from childhood.
— BERYL BAINBRIDGE

GAINING MORE INSIGHT into each other's childhood wounds is a key part of Imago Therapy, but you don't have to spend weeks psychoanalyzing each other or years paying someone else to help you explore what is out of your awareness in the unconscious part of your mind. We have learned over the years of helping couples that just spending quality time talking about each other's pasts can be very helpful. We've seen how effective this can be in our couples' workshops. Years ago, we devoted half the workshop time to helping couples learn more about each other's pasts. Now, we spend a fraction of that time and get the same results. There is a concept informally called *woundology*, where couples spend too much time dwelling on the past, which should be avoided.

Nonetheless, spending some time sharing your childhood experiences is vital because it gives you a better understanding of your partner's inner reality and helps you shift from judgment to curiosity and empathy. There are times in most relationships when one partner is mystified by the other's behavior: "You're crazy. You keep doing the same things over and over, and it's totally unproductive!" Or, "I am totally confused by you. You make no sense." "I'm surprised that you're going to accept that promotion. You are far too busy already." There are also times when you are triggered by something your partner does or by your partner's repetitive behavior. Knowing something about your childhoods will help you understand that. Exercises 2–7 in part 3 of this book will help you uncover some of the unconscious or barely conscious struggles of your past and then share them with each other. When you've expanded your understanding of each other's inner world, you will seem less confusing to each other and be able to validate and be more empathic with each other. "Oh, so now I get why you want to spend time by yourself when you get home from work. Your father left you very little free time. That makes sense to me. And I can imagine that you feel anxious when I don't allow that and grateful when I do." You also become less of a puzzle to yourself and can cut yourself some slack. "So when you are late to an appointment and I get anxious and angry, I get it that my father never kept his word, was usually late, and never seemed sorry about it."

Also, the more you know about each other's emotional histories, the less likely you are to see your partner as your adversary. Instead, you will begin to see that you are partners suffering from past hurts and also partners in the project of helping each other create safety in your relationship and respond to each other's needs. This way, you both can experience the sensations of feeling fully alive and joyful connecting. You are allies on this journey, not competitors. You create a conscious partnership and have each other's back.[1] We will talk more about this later.

There's a three-word sentence that we use to describe this phenomenon: "Energy follows attention." In other words, what you focus on is what you get. If you keep focusing on the way your partner frustrates you, that's what you will see. But if you temper your view with the knowledge of your partner's struggles and your own, you will feel more compassionate for your partner and accepting of yourself. Compassion, the experience of co-feeling, is an essential component of love. Both of you accepting each other's challenges from the past is a precondition of the ability to receive the love you want.

INSATIABLE BEINGS

WHAT ARE SOME of the most common childhood issues? When many people first hear the words *childhood wounds*, they think we're talking about major traumas such as physical abuse, the loss of a parent early in life, or having parents who were addicted to drugs or alcohol. For all too many people, this is the tragic reality of childhood.

But even if you grew up in a relatively nurturing environment, you may still bear invisible scars from childhood that can frustrate your wish to have a loving and lasting relationship. To give you an understanding of these early relational stresses, we want to take you on a brief journey through childhood.

Let's start at the beginning. There have been no miracle babies born with the ability to reveal the dark mysteries of life before birth, but we do know something about the physical reality of the fetus. We know that its biological needs are taken care of instantly and automatically by an exchange of fluids between itself and its mother. We know that a fetus has no need to eat, breathe, or protect itself from danger and that it is constantly soothed by the rhythmical beat of its mother's heart.

From these simple biological facts, we can surmise that the fetus lives a tranquil, floating, effortless existence. It has no awareness of boundaries, no sense of itself, and no recognition that it is encased in a sac inside its mother. There is a widely held belief that when a baby is inside its mother's womb, it experiences a sense of oneness, an Edenic experience free from desire. The Jewish theologian Martin Buber put it this way: "In fetal existence, we were in communion with the universe."[2] This idyllic existence comes to an abrupt end as the mother's contractions expel the baby from the womb. For the first time, the baby needs to be fed, burped, soothed, and have its diapers changed.

We reflected on this knowledge when our daughter Leah was in this stage. When all her physical needs were taken care of, she would nestle in our arms and look around her with the contentment of a Buddha. She was born about three hours after she first indicated she was ready to join the human race. I (Harville) had the privilege of helping extract her from the womb, cutting the umbilical cord and holding her for about thirty minutes. I expected to see a groggy face, unfocused eyes, an involuntary smile, and other instinctive reactions, like burping or crying. Instead, what I saw clashed with my expectations and with the textbook descriptions I had read. She locked eyes with me, and when I smiled, she smiled, which shocked me. I moved my fingers in front of her eyes, and she followed them. I smiled again, and she smiled back. She mirrored my opening and closing my mouth and became attentive to my voice. In contrast to the science of the infant as having no sense of separateness, Leah came into the world as a social being, interacting with me and others upon arrival. To check our perceptions, we went to the research journals to see if we could find any explanation for what we were experiencing. What we learned was newly discovered and not common knowledge, even in developmental psychology, but is now common knowledge.

The bottom line is this: if a baby is drugged by the pain medications the mother received, the baby makes no distinction between itself and the rest of the world. This is a developmental mental state called *symbiosis*. The infant interacts as if it is merged with the mother and has no separate reality. However, if babies are not drugged, they are alert and clearheaded, curious about their surroundings, and instantly start interacting with the outside world as social beings. Leah's impatience to show up did not give me (Helen) time to receive any pain medication. Leah started life drug-free with an awareness of herself as a separate being who began interacting with us upon arrival.

Although she was immature and utterly dependent on us for survival, she was nonetheless a lively, curious, and interactive human being. Those first moments with her established a special bond between us that has survived into her adulthood, which others can sense when we are together.

Now that we are grandparents, we've had the privilege of seeing our grandchildren dwell in this idyllic experience. I (Harville) had a similar opportunity to hold one of our granddaughters, Clare, moments after her birth. Our daughter had had a difficult delivery and needed to sleep, so I was able to hold Clare for the first six hours of her new life. She slept most of the time, and I cradled her head next to my heart. All that time, I was acutely aware that I was holding a wondrous being full of life and joy. When she awakened, she and I repeated the dance I had with Leah many years prior, and we share a similar bond.

As adults, we seem to have a fleeting memory of this state, which we call *original connecting*. It appears that we recall a distant time when we were connecting with others and to the world. Like Buber said, through connecting with others, we simultaneously connect to the universe. And we want that experience again. It is a vibrant world full of wonder and joy that is so compelling that it becomes a life agenda for everyone. This feeling is described in the myths of many cultures around the world, as if words could lend it more reality. It is the story of a primordial paradise—the biblical Garden of Eden, the golden age story of the Greek poet Hesiod, the Hindu concept of Purusha, or the Sumerian recount of Dilmun—and it strikes us with compelling force.

The bliss of the newborn does not last forever. Freud correctly labeled us "insatiable beings," and no parents, no matter how devoted, can respond perfectly to all these changing needs. When a baby wakes up in the morning, she begins interacting with her world. She cries to be fed. Then her diapers are wet, and she cries to be changed. Then she wants to be held, a physical craving as powerful as the need for food. A bubble of gas forms in her stomach, and she signals distress the only way she knows how—with an undifferentiated cry.

If her caregivers are perceptive enough, she is fed, changed, held, and rocked and experiences momentary satisfaction. But if her caregivers can't figure out what is wrong, or if they withhold their attention for fear of spoiling her, or if they're too busy or distracted, she experiences disconnecting and becomes anxious. The world is not a safe place to be. The vibrant and joyful world turns to dismal shades of gray. Since she has no way of taking care of herself and no sense of delayed gratification, getting the outside world to respond to her needs is a matter of life and death. The painful sensation of anxiety is triggered. and simultaneously, the desire to recapture her earlier sense of perfect union is activated.

A term that describes this yearning for connecting is *eros,* a Greek word that we normally equate with romantic or sexual love but that originally had the broader meaning of "the life force."[3] When the caregiver stays present to and resonates with the child, this life force is directed not only to the caregivers but also to siblings, relatives, and the world around her. However, if the primary caregiver is not emotionally available, the connection between them is ruptured, and eros is turned inward. Even a few minutes of unresponsiveness can make a child feel anxious, isolated, and become panicked and deregulated, thus losing awareness that it is connected to others and the universe.

STILL FACE EXPERIMENT

A CLASSIC INSTANCE of this reality was brought home to us when we watched a short video titled "The Still Face" produced by child development specialists at a major university in Massachusetts. The video documented one of their studies of parent-child bonding, and from our perspective, it is the template of the three stages of the human journey: it starts out well; it goes bad; we spend the rest of our lives trying to get back where we started.

The opening scene is the first stage. In it, you see a happy baby sitting in a high chair. Her smiling mom is sitting in a chair in front of her, giving the baby her full attention. The mom is leaning toward her child so that their faces are about two feet apart. Whenever the baby makes a sound, her mother mirrors that sound. When the baby points around the room, the mom turns around to see where she is pointing. When the mother points, the baby points. This is connecting in its primal form.

The second stage in the human journey is prefigured in the second scene, when it all goes bad. This happens when the re-searchers ask the mom to "turn away" and then turn back with a still, blank face and stop responding to her child in any way. When the baby sees her mom's expressionless face, she senses at once that something is wrong, and she tries to regain her mother's attention. She smiles up at her mom, but her mother does not respond. She points around the room, but her mother does not look where she is pointing. She holds up her arms, asking to be picked up, but her mother does not move. Now the baby becomes visibly distraught. She pushes back into her high chair and turns her head side to side. Then she makes a high-pitched shrieking sound and puts a fist into her mouth. She does every-thing she has experienced in the past to reengage her mother. But her mother remains mute and still, and the baby breaks down in tears.

The transition from being a smiling, engaged baby to a crying, distraught baby took less than two minutes. Losing the experi-ence of primal connecting, the baby was overwhelmed with anx-iety about the loss and began trying desperately to reengage the mother.

The third stage of the human journey starts when the mom is instructed by the researchers to respond to her child once again with a smile and gestures that resonate with her baby. The infant takes a moment to adjust, but then she brightens up and all is well. Crisis averted. Connecting is restored, and joy returns. But now the baby has a memory of the pain of disconnecting that will influence her in the future. Since the rupture was minimal, the impact is minimal, but since memory is permanent, a negative expectation has been set.

If the parent-child connection is ruptured time and again, however, emotional damage begins to occur. The child learns that the world is unreliable and thus not always receptive to her needs. Having overly busy, unpredictable, or neglectful caregivers when you are very young will leave emotional scars that follow you into adulthood.

From our view, these scars are very active in adult intimate relationships and show up constantly when a partner turns away or shows a still face when the other is trying to engage. An instance of this in our relationship occurred in a hotel room overlooking a Florida beachfront. I (Helen) woke up early, looked out the window at the rising sun over a glowing beach, and then turned to my work. When Harville awakened, he looked at the same scene with a loud and appreciative exclamation. I was tempted to explain to him that I had already seen the beautiful view and was now working on an important email. But I recalled the "Still Face" video and moved to the window to join Harville's enthusiasm for the rising sun and shining beach, rather than be a still face. If I had not joined him, his excitement would have had no echo. The power of this experience led us to include it as a technique we recommend to couples in our workshops and therapy, to cultivate curiosity and wonder by echoing the joy (or the sadness) in their partners.

THE PERILOUS PILGRIMAGE

AS A CHILD grows out of infancy, new needs emerge, and each new need defines a potential area of wounding. A toddler, for instance, develops a growing interest in exploring the world beyond the boundaries of home. She discovers there is a wondrous world of others and things that stir her curiosity, and she begins interacting with this larger world. We call this the stage of exploration. If a little boy had an adult's command of language, he would say something like this: "I'm ready to walk away from you now. I'm ready to spend some time by myself. I'm a little insecure about leaving you, however, so I'll be back in a few minutes to make sure you are still here." Since the child has only a limited vocabulary, he simply climbs down from his mother's lap, turns his back, and toddles out of the room.

Now, ideally, the mother or father smiles and says something like this: "Bye-bye! See you later!" When the toddler comes back, suddenly aware of how dependent he really is, his parent says, "Hi! Did you have fun?" They let the child know that it is OK to leave their side and venture off on his own, yet they are available whenever he needs them. The boy has internalized the caregiver's reliable presence and learned that the world is a safe, exciting place to explore. Connecting to others is possible and fun if the home base is safe.

But some children are frustrated at this stage of development. The mother or father is the one who feels insecure when the child is out of sight, not the child. For some reason—one that is rooted in the parent's own childhood—some parents need the child to remain dependent. When a little girl wanders out of the room, her insecure parent might call out, "Don't go into the next room! I won't be able to see you!" The child dutifully comes back to her parent's side. If her parent continues to be overprotective during her early years, she becomes angry and anxious. Her inner drive to explore and be autonomous is being denied. She is afraid that if she stays too close to her caregiver, she will be engulfed; she will be trapped in a symbiotic union forever.

Throughout the developmental stages—from infancy to young adulthood—additional needs emerge along with more opportunities for parents to support or rupture connection. All of us had imperfect parenting, including our parents, who also are products of imperfect parenting. But what we have discovered in our years of working with couples is that, generally speaking, there are two simplified categories that parenting falls into: intrusive or neglectful caretaking. Parents were either overinvolved—telling us what to do, think, and feel—or they were underinvolved—physically or emotionally absent. These challenges are across the spectrum from subtle to severe. As a response, we become anxious and self-absorbed, losing our capacity for empathy. We become the walking wounded in a battlefield of injured soldiers.

For the child who experienced intrusive parents, in later years, she becomes an *isolator,* a person who unconsciously pushes others away. She keeps people at a distance because she needs to have "a lot of space" around her; she wants the freedom to come and go as she pleases; she thinks independently, speaks freely, processes her emotions internally, and proudly dons her self-reliant attitude. All the while underneath this cool exterior is a two-year-old girl who was not allowed to satisfy her natural need for independence. When she marries, her need to be a distinct "self" will be on the top of her hidden agenda.

For the child who experienced neglectful parents, ones who push them away when they come running to them for comfort: "Go away. I'm busy." "Go play with your toys." "Stop clinging to me!" The caregivers are not equipped to handle any needs but their own, and their children grow up feeling emotionally abandoned. Eventually they grow up to become *fusers,* people who seem to have an insatiable need for closeness. Fusers want to "do things together" all the time. If people fail to show up at the appointed time, they feel abandoned. The thought of divorce fills them with terror. They crave physical affection and reassurance, and they often need to stay in constant verbal contact. Underneath all this clinging behavior is a young child who needed more time on a parent's lap.

Ironically, for reasons we will explore in later chapters, fusers (who experienced neglectful caretaking) and isolators (who experienced intrusive parenting) tend to grow up and marry each other, thus beginning an infuriating game of push and pull that leaves neither partner satisfied.

When our daughter Leah was three years old, she wanted to explore everything around her. She had so much energy that she could run all day long and not be tired. "Run with me, Daddy! Somersault!" She twirled in circles and got so dizzy that she would fall down and laugh and laugh. She would chase fireflies, talk to leaves, swing from her knees on the monkey bars, and wanted to pet every dog she saw. She enjoyed naming objects and developed a keen ear for words. When we looked at Leah, we saw a fountain full of joy and wonder that made us envy her and yearn for what we had lost.

We worked hard to keep eros alive in Leah, to sustain the brightness of her eyes and the thrill of her contagious laughter. But despite our best intentions, she had anxious moments. Once, she was frightened by a large dog and became wary of strange animals. One day, she slipped into a pool and developed a fear of water. Sometimes we were more directly to blame. We had five other children besides Leah, and there were times when she felt left out. There were days when we came home from work too tired to listen to what she was saying, too distracted to give her our full attention.

Regrettably, we also wounded her by unwittingly passing on our own childhood challenges, the emotional inheritance of generations. We either overcompensated for what we didn't get from our own parents or blindly re-created the same painful situations. We call this the *legacy of wounding*.

For whatever reason, when Leah's bids for connecting were ignored, a questioning look would come over her face. She would be less aware of the beauty of the world around her. Her vibrant and joyful world would turn to varying shades of dismal gray. During those times, her contagious sensation of being fully alive would be replaced with the sensation of anxiety, and she would withdraw into herself and become absorbed by her pain.

THE LOST SELF

WE HAVE NOW explored one important feature of the vast hidden world we call the *unconscious partnership*, and that is our storehouse of unmet childhood needs, our unfulfilled desire to be nurtured and protected and allowed to proceed unhindered along a path to maturity. Now we will turn to another kind of childhood wound, an even subtler kind of psychic injury called *socialization*, all those messages we receive from our caretakers and from society at large that tell us who we are and how we have to behave. These, too, play a compelling but hidden role in our relationships with our partners.

At first, it may seem strange to equate socialization with emotional injury. To help explain why this is so, we want to tell you about Sarah. (As is true for most of the people we mention in this book, names and certain identifying characteristics have been changed to preserve anonymity.) Sarah is an attractive, personable woman in her midthirties. A main concern in her life is her apparent inability to think clearly and logically. "I can't think," she says over and over again. "I just can't think." She is a lower-level manager in a computer firm, where she has worked diligently for fifteen years. She would have advanced much further in the company if she were an effective problem-solver, but whenever she is presented with a difficult situation, she panics and runs to her supervisor for support. Her supervisor gives her sage advice, reinforcing Sarah's belief that she is incapable of making decisions on her own.

It didn't take much probing to discover part of the reason for Sarah's anxiety. From a very early age, she received from her mother the explicit message that she was not very intelligent. "You're not as smart as your older brother," her mother would say, and "You'd better marry a smart man, because you're going to need a lot of help. But I doubt if a smart man would marry you." As blatant as these messages were, they didn't fully account for Sarah's perceived inability to think. Amplifying her mother's message was the prevalent view of the 1950s that little girls were sweet, pretty, and compliant and their career goals were limited to the helping professions; the girls in Sarah's grade school dreamed of being wives, nurses, and teachers, not executives, astronauts, and doctors.

Another influence on Sarah's problem-solving capacity was the fact that her mother had very little confidence in her own reasoning ability. She managed the house and took care of her children's needs, but she deferred all major decisions to her husband. This dependent, passive model defined "womanhood" for Sarah.

When Sarah was fifteen, she was fortunate enough to have a teacher who recognized her natural abilities and encouraged her to work harder on her schoolwork. For the first time in her life, Sarah came home with a report card that was mostly As. She will never forget her mother's reaction: "How on earth did that happen? I bet you can't do that again." And Sarah couldn't, because she finally gave in and put to sleep the part of her brain that thinks calmly and rationally.

The tragedy was not only that Sarah lost her ability to reason but also that she acquired the unconscious belief that thinking was dangerous. Why was that? Since Sarah's mother had strongly rejected her intellectual capabilities, she believed that if she were to think clearly, she would be defying her mother; she would be contradicting her mother's definition of her. She couldn't risk alienating her mother, because she was dependent on her mother for survival. It was dangerous, therefore, for Sarah to know that she had a mind. Yet she couldn't fully disown her intelligence. She envied people who could think, and when she married, she chose a man who was exceptionally bright, an unconscious ploy to make up for the psychological damage of childhood.

Like Sarah, we all have parts of ourselves that we have hidden from consciousness. We call these missing elements the *lost self.* Whenever we complain that we "can't think" or that we "can't feel anything" or "can't dance" or "can't have orgasms" or "aren't very creative," we are identifying natural abilities, thoughts, or feelings that we have surgically removed from our awareness. They are not gone; we still possess them. But for the moment, they are not a part of our consciousness, and it is as if they do not exist.

As in Sarah's case, our lost self was formed early in childhood—largely as a result of our caretakers' well-intentioned efforts to teach us to get along with others. Each society has a unique collection of practices, laws, beliefs, and values that children need to absorb, and mothers and fathers are the main conduit through which they are transmitted. This indoctrination process goes on in every family in every society. There seems to be a universal understanding that, unless limits are placed on the individual, the individual becomes a danger to the group. In the words of Freud, "The desire for a powerful and uninhibited ego may seem to us intelligible, but, as is shown by the times that we live in, it is in the profoundest sense antagonistic to civilization."

But even though our parents often had our best interests at heart, the overall message handed down to us was a chilling one. There were certain thoughts and feelings we could not have, certain natural behaviors that we had to extinguish, and certain talents and aptitudes we had to deny. In thousands of ways, both subtly and overtly, our parents gave us the message that they approved of only a part of us. In essence, we were told that we could not be accepted and exist in this culture.

A few parents take this invalidation process to the extreme. They deny not only their children's feelings and behaviors but the entire child as well. "You do not exist. You are not important in this family. Your needs, your feelings, your wishes are not important to us." The impact of these messages is devastating to the child, resulting in a lifelong struggle to feel worthy, valued, loveable. Frequently, they will pretend to be someone else, while repressing feelings of anger, fear, and/or depression or turn to addictions to soothe the psychic pain.

TOOLS OF REPRESSION

IN THEIR ATTEMPTS to repress certain thoughts, feelings, and behavior, parents use various techniques. Sometimes they issue clear-cut directives: "You don't really think that." "Big boys don't cry." "Don't touch yourself there!" "I never want to hear you say that again!" "We don't act like that in this family!" Or, they scold, threaten, or spank. Much of the time, they mold their children through a subtler process of invalidation—they simply choose not to see or reward certain things. For example, if parents place little value on intellectual development, they give their children toys and sports equipment but no books or science kits. If they believe that girls should be quiet and feminine and that boys should be strong and assertive, they only reward their children for gender-appropriate behavior. For example, if their little boy comes into the room lugging a heavy toy, they might say, "What a strong little boy you are!" But if their daughter comes in carrying the same toy, they might caution, "Be careful of your pretty dress."

The way that parents influence their children most deeply, however, is by example. Children instinctively observe the choices their parents make, the freedoms and pleasures they allow themselves, the talents they develop, the abilities they ignore, and the rules they follow. All of this has a profound effect on children: "This is how we live. This is how to get through life." Whether children accept their parents' model or rebel against it, this early socialization plays a significant role in mate selection and, as we will soon see, is often a hidden source of tension in married life.

A child's reaction to society's edicts goes through a number of predictable stages. Typically, the first response is to hide forbidden behaviors from the parents. The child thinks angry thoughts but doesn't speak them out loud. He explores his body in the privacy of his room. He teases his younger sibling when his parents are away. Eventually, the child comes to the conclusion that some thoughts and feelings are so unacceptable that they should be eliminated, so he constructs an imaginary parent in his head to police his thoughts and activities, a part of the mind that psychologists call the *superego*. Now, whenever the child has a forbidden thought or indulges in an "unacceptable" behavior, he experiences a self-administered jolt of anxiety. This is so unpleasant that the child puts to sleep some of those forbidden parts of himself—in Freudian terms, he represses them. The ultimate price of his obedience is a loss of connecting with all parts of himself and with being accepted for who he truly is, never fully developing the muscles that were prime for growing.

PLATO'S ALLEGORY

ONE DAY WHEN we were talking about all the splits in the psyche, I (Helen) recalled an allegory in Plato's *Symposium* that serves as a mythical model for this state of split existence.[4] Human beings, the story goes, were once composite creatures that were both male and female. Each being had one head with two faces, four hands and four feet, and both male and female genitals. Being unified and whole, these supposed ancestors of ours wielded tremendous force. In fact, so brazen were these androgynous beings that they dared to threaten the gods. The gods, of course, would not tolerate this insolence, but they didn't know how to punish the humans. "If we kill them," they said to one another, "there will be no one to worship us and offer up sacrifices." Zeus pondered the situation and finally came up with a solution. "Men shall continue to exist," he decreed, "but they will be cut in two. Then they will be diminished in strength so we need not fear them." Zeus proceeded to split each being in two, asking

Apollo's help to make the wounds invisible. The two halves were then sent in opposite directions to spend the rest of their lives searching passionately for the other half-creature, the reunion with whom would restore their primal connection.

Just like Plato's mythical creatures, we, too, seem to go through life truncated, cut in half. We cover our wounds with healing ointment and gauze in an attempt to heal ourselves. But despite our efforts, an emptiness wells up inside us. We try to fill this emptiness with food and drugs and activities, but what we yearn for is the joyful connection and the sensation of feeling fully alive that we experienced as very young children. This becomes a spiritual yearning for connecting, and, as in Plato's myth, we develop the profound conviction that finding the right person—that perfect mate—will complete us.

Plato's story is our story. Connecting was our primal experience and the basis of our eagerness for life's adventures, but the outside world did not meet our needs all the time. We may have forgotten most of our early struggles, but our old brains kept a careful record of them, especially experiences that triggered strong emotions, such as anger, fear, or despair. Although we are now adults, capable of keeping ourselves fed, warm, and dry, the most primitive part of our brains still expect people around us to be mindful of our unmet needs and do what they can to satisfy them.

At the end of his career, Freud asked the now famous question: "What do women want?" We, too, have been struggling to answer the question: "What do men and women want from their love relationships?" We now believe that the answer to Freud's question and our question—indeed, all of humanity's yearning—is one and the same. Above all else, we seek the sensation of feeling fully alive that is triggered when we experience connecting. To us, it is more than a psychological term. From our extensive reading in other disciplines, we have come to believe that "connecting" describes the universe. As all things are interconnected, so are we; it is our nature to be connected.

This responsibility is not distributed uniformly among your friends and family, however. No, indeed! Your old brain is seeking one particular person to be the primary source of your salvation—the person with whom you fell in love. That person is the conduit for reexperiencing full aliveness and joy, or not. Curiously, for reasons we will explore in the next chapter, the person you are most likely to fall in love with is someone who has both the positive and the negative traits of your parents! Your capricious old brain is seeking reparation from someone who resembles the very people who were the source of most of your childhood challenges in the first place. Outside of our awareness, we enter marriage with the expectation that our partners will magically restore this original state of connecting. It is as if they hold the key to a long-ago kingdom, and all we must do is persuade them to unlock the door.

YOUR IMAGO

In literature, as in love, we are astonished
at what is chosen by others.
— ANDRÉ MAUROIS

MANY COUPLES HAVE a hard time believing that they se-
lected a partner who resembled their caregivers, especially their
negative traits. Not so, they tell us. They were looking for people
who had only positive traits—people who were, among other
things, kind, loving, financially secure, good looking, and intelligent. In fact, people with the most traumatic upbringing said
they searched for people who were dramatically different from
their caregivers. They told themselves, "I'll never marry a drunk-
ard like my father," or "There's no way I'm going to marry a
tyrant like my mother," or "I'm going to marry someone who
knows how to handle money, not like my parents." But no
matter their conscious intent, most people are attracted to people
who have many of the same negative and positive traits as their
parents and with whom they are just as frustrated and disappointed.

We came to this stark conclusion only after listening to
hundreds of couples talk about their partners. At some point
during the course of therapy, just about every person would
turn to his or her partner and say, "You treat me just like my

self-absorbed mother!" or "You make me feel just as bad as my stepfather did! You two are just the same!"

This idea gained further validity when we assigned couples an exercise that had them compare the personality traits of their partners with the personality traits of the people who raised them. In most cases, there was a close correlation between the two, and, shockingly, *the traits that matched up the most closely were the negative traits!* (You will find this exercise in part 3.)

Why do negative traits have such an appeal? If we chose mates on a logical basis, we would look for partners who *compensated* for our parents' inadequacies, not duplicated them. If your parents wounded you by being unreliable, for example, the sensible course of action would be to marry a dependable person, someone who would help you feel more secure. If your parents wounded you by being overprotective, the logical solution would be to look for a partner who allowed you plenty of space so that you could overcome your fear of being engulfed. The part of your brain that played the role of matchmaker, however, was not just your logical, orderly new brain but your time-locked, myopic old brain as well. And your old brain was trying to return you to the scene of your childhood so you could get back to your unfinished business.[1] It is the attempt to re-create the early experiences for the sole purpose of healing, to finally get what you needed in childhood.

SEARCH FOR THE LOST SELF

WHAT ABOUT YOUR other unconscious drive, your need to recover your lost self, those thoughts and feelings and behaviors that you had to repress to adapt to your family and to society? What kind of person would help you regain these birthright abilities? Would it be someone who actively encouraged you to develop these missing parts? Would it be someone who shared your weaknesses and therefore made you feel less inadequate? Or, on the other hand, would it be someone who complemented your weaknesses? To find the answer, think for a minute about some part of your being that you feel is deficient. Maybe you feel that you lack artistic talent, or strong emotions, or, like Sarah in the last chapter, the ability to think clearly and rationally. Years ago, when you were around people who were especially strong in these areas, you probably were even more aware of your shortcomings. But if you managed to form an intimate relationship with one of these "gifted people," you experienced quite a different reaction. Instead of feeling awestruck or envious, you suddenly felt more complete. Being emotionally attached to this person—this is "my" boyfriend or "my" girlfriend—made his or her attributes feel a part of a larger, more fulfilled you. It was as if you had merged with the other person in order to feel whole.

Look around you, and you will find ample evidence that people choose mates with complementary traits. Dan is glib and talkative; his wife, Gretchen, is thoughtful and introverted. Janice is an intuitive thinker; her husband, Patrick, is very logical. Rena is a dancer; her boyfriend, Matthew, has a stiff and rigid body. What people are doing in these yin-yang matches is trying to reclaim their lost selves by proxy. Opposites, indeed, attract.

Your Imago

TO GUIDE YOU in your search for your ideal mate, someone who both resembled your caretakers and compensated for the lost parts of yourself, you relied on the storehouse of information that you had been gathering from your interactions with the most important people in your childhood. This might have been your mother or father, one or more siblings, or maybe a nanny, grandparent, or family friend. Whoever they were, a part of your old brain recorded every experience you had with them—the sound of their voices, the amount of time they took to answer your cries, the color of their skin when they got angry, the way they smiled, the way they moved their bodies, their characteristic moods, and their talents and interests. Your brain recorded your significant interactions with them, especially those that were connected to feelings. Your brain didn't interpret this data; it simply etched them onto a template.

It may seem improbable that you have such a detailed record of people inside your head when you have only a dim recollection of your early years. In fact, many people have a hard time remembering anything that happened to them before the age of five or six—even traumatic events that should have made a lasting impression. But scientists report that we have incredible amounts of information stored in our brains that are not available to conscious memory. Neurosurgeons discovered this fact accidentally while performing brain surgery on patients who were under local anesthesia and therefore were able to talk and answer questions.[2] When stimulating portions of the brain with weak electrical currents, the patients were suddenly able to recall forgotten episodes from childhood. The memories were vivid, often in color, and included details such as the clothes that people were wearing, the sound of their voices, and exactly what they were doing at the time. There are those who suggest that everything we have ever experienced is encoded somewhere in the recesses of our old brains.

As you were collecting all this data about your caregivers, your old brain filed the information under one heading: *the people most responsible for my survival.* We named this composite image the *Imago,* which is the Latin word for *image.*[3] You might think of your Imago as a silhouette with few distinguishing physical characteristics but with the combined character traits of your primary caregivers.

Romantic love is correlated to the degree to which a person matches your Imago. When you first met someone, a hidden part of your brain ticked and hummed, coolly analyzing that person's traits and comparing them with your data bank of information. If there was little correlation with your Imago, you felt only minimal interest—even if an internet dating service pronounced you a 100 percent match! If there was a high degree of correlation, you found the person highly attractive.

This Imago matching process resembles the way soldiers were trained to identify flying aircraft during World War II. The soldiers were given books filled with silhouettes of friendly and enemy aircraft. When an unidentified plane came into view, they hurriedly compared the plane with the images. If it turned out to be a friendly plane, they relaxed and went back to their posts. If it was an enemy aircraft, they leaped into action.

As with all aspects of your unconscious mind, you were not aware of this sorting mechanism. The only way you might glimpse your Imago is in dreams. If you reflect on your dreams, you may have noticed that some people were transformed into other people, even though the dream continued on the same course. You may even recall a dream in which your partner suddenly metamorphosed into your mother or father, or a dream in which your partner and a parent played such similar roles or treated you in such a similar manner that they were virtually indistinguishable.

This is the closest you will ever come to directly verifying the existence of your Imago. But when you do the exercises in part 3 of this book and have a chance to compare the traits of your mate with the traits of your primary caregivers, the similarities between the two will become clear.

THE IMAGO AND ROMANTIC LOVE

LET US GIVE you an illustration of how the Imago influences mate selection. One of my (Harville) clients, Lynn, is forty years old and has three school-age children. She lives in a New England town where she works for the city government. Peter, her husband, is a computer consultant.

In the initial sessions with Lynn and Peter, I learned that Lynn's father had had a profound influence on her. He was a good provider and kept the yard, house, and cars in good order, but he could be very insensitive to her needs. She told me about the relentless way he would tickle her, even though he knew she hated it. When she would finally break down and cry, he would laugh at her and call her a crybaby. She will never forget the time he threw her into a river to "teach her how to swim." When Lynn told me this story, her throat was tight and her hands gripped the arms of her chair. "How could he have done that to me?" she asked. "I was only four years old! I looked at my own daughter when she was four years old and was amazed that he could have done that to me. It's such a trusting, vulnerable age."

Although she wasn't aware of it, Lynn had much earlier images of her father stored in her unconscious, ones that also influenced her memories of him. Let's suppose that her father would neglect to warm the bottle when it was his turn to feed her, and she learned to associate lying in his arms with the shock of cold milk. Or maybe, when she was ten months old, he would toss her high into the air, not heeding her frantic cries.

Lynn's mother was an equally potent source of images. Her mother was generous with her time and attention and consistent with her discipline. Unlike Lynn's father, she was sensitive to her daughter's feelings. Lynn remembers being twelve years old and having her mom listen sympathetically to her problems at school. But Lynn's mother was also a perfectionist. Nothing Lynn said or did seemed to be quite good enough. Her mother was always correcting her grammar, combing her hair, criticizing her clothes, and double-checking her homework. Lynn felt as though she were a work in progress, and her mother was the one who determined what needed to change.

Another aspect of her mother's personality was that she was not comfortable with her own sexuality. Lynn remembers that her mother always wore long-sleeved blouses buttoned up to the top button and then covered the blouses with loose, concealing sweaters. She never allowed anyone in the bathroom with her, even though the house had only one bathroom. When Lynn was a teenager, her mother did not talk with her about menstruation, boyfriends, or sex. It's not surprising that one of Lynn's problems is that she is sexually inhibited.

Other people also had a strong influence on Lynn, especially her older sister. Judith, four years older, was Lynn's idol. Tall and talented, Judith seemed to succeed at everything she did. Lynn wanted to spend as much time as possible around her, but most of the time, her sister did not want her tagging along.

Gradually, the personality traits of these key people—Lynn's mother, her father, and her older sister—merged together in Lynn's unconscious to form her Imago. Her Imago was a picture of someone who was, among other things, affectionate, devoted, critical, insensitive, superior, and generous. The character traits that stood out in bold relief were the negative ones—the tendency to be critical, insensitive, and dismissive—because these were the ones that had wounded her; this is where she had unfinished business. She needed someone to match her Imago in order to re-create the early life scenario and finally get what she needed in childhood.

Lynn first met Peter at a friend's house. When she was introduced to him, she felt as though she already knew him. "It was a curious sensation." The next week, she kept finding excuses to go over to her friend's house, and she was glad when Peter was there. Gradually, she became aware of an even stronger attraction and realized that she wasn't happy unless she was around him. In these first encounters, Lynn wasn't consciously comparing Peter with anyone she knew—certainly not her parents or her sister—she just found him a wonderfully appealing person who seemed easy to talk to.

When Lynn and Peter came to me for counseling, I grew to appreciate what a comprehensive Imago match Peter was for Lynn. He was outgoing and confident, traits that he shared with

Lynn's father and sister. But he also had a critical nature, like Lynn's mother. He kept telling Lynn that she should lose weight, wear more appealing clothes, and be more playful—especially in bed. He also criticized her for being so subservient to her boss.

The parent trait that was most marked in him, however, was his lack of compassion for her feelings, just like her father. Lynn had frequent bouts of depression, and Peter's advice to her was: "Talk less and do more. I'm tired of hearing about your problems!" This was consistent with his own approach to unpleasant feelings, which was to cover them up with purposeful activity.

Another reason Lynn was attracted to Peter was that he was so at home in his body. When I looked at the two of them, I was reminded of the words of one of my professors: "If you want to know what kind of person a client is married to, imagine his or her opposite." Peter would sprawl in his chair with abandonment. Sometimes he would kick off his shoes and sit cross-legged. Peter wore loose-fitting corduroy pants, shirts open at the neck, and loafers without socks. Lynn wore tailored clothes buttoned to the top button or a business suit with a silk scarf wrapped around her neck. She sat with her legs crossed and her back straight. They were the perfect complementary couple sporting opposite traits looking for a fight.

Now we have a better understanding of why Lynn was attracted to Peter. Why was Peter attracted to Lynn? The fact that she had an emotional nature was one of the reasons. Although his parents had accepted Peter's body, they had rejected his feelings. When he was with Lynn, he felt more connected to his repressed emotions. In addition, she had numerous character traits that resembled his parents. Her sense of humor was like his father's, and her dependent, self-effacing manner was characteristic of his mother. Because Lynn matched Peter's Imago and Peter matched Lynn's, they had "fallen in love."

One of the questions that we are asked most frequently is this: How can people tell so much about each other so quickly?

While certain characteristics may be right on the surface—Peter's physical abandon, for example, or Lynn's sense of humor—others are not so apparent.

The reason that we are such instant judges of character is that we rely on what Freud called *unconscious perception*. We intuitively pick up much more about people than we are aware of. When we meet strangers, we instantly register the way they move, the way they seek or avoid eye contact, the clothes they wear, their expressions, the way they fix their hair, the ease with which they laugh or smile, their ability to listen, the speed at which they talk, the amount of time it takes them to respond to a question—we record all these traits in a matter of minutes.

When we lived in New York, I (Helen) would walk to work each morning and automatically appraise the people on the crowded Manhattan sidewalks. My judgment was quick: this person is someone I wish I knew; that person is someone I have no interest in. I found myself attracted, disinterested, or repulsed with only a few seconds of observation. Similarly, when I go to a party, it doesn't take me long to single out the people I want to talk to. Other people report similar experiences. A truck driver told me that he could tell whether or not he wanted to pick up a particular hitchhiker even though he was driving at sixty-five miles an hour. "And I'm rarely wrong," he said.

Our powers of observation are especially acute when we are looking for a mate because we are searching for someone to satisfy our fundamental needs, and we are drawn to what is familiar. Simultaneously, we are looking for someone who exhibits our lost selves. We unconsciously reconstitute our earliest family matrix. Our old brain scrutinizes all reasonable candidates: Is this someone who will nurture me and help me recover my lost self? When the old brain registers interest, we find ourselves instantly attracted. In all subsequent encounters, the unconscious mind is fully alert, searching for clues that this might indeed be a good Imago match. If later experiences are in line with our unconscious expectations, our interest climbs even higher.

Not everyone finds a mate who conforms so closely to his or her Imago. Sometimes only one or two key character traits match up, and the initial attraction is likely to be mild. Such a relationship is often less passionate and less troubled than those characterized by a closer match. The reason it is less passionate is that the old brain is still looking for the ideal gratifying object: this is close but not the One. The reason it tends to be less troubled is that fewer childhood struggles are being triggered. When couples with weak Imago matches stop seeing each other, it's often because they feel little interest in each other, not because they are in great pain. "There wasn't all that much going on," they say. Or "I just felt restless. I knew that there was something better out there."

At this point in our discussion of love relationships, we have a better understanding of the mystery of romantic attraction. More than we realize, we are searching for a person who has similar traits to the people who raised us. Our underlying wish is that this Imago match will satisfy our unconscious, unmet needs.

We also have new insight into marital conflict: if the primary reason we select our mates is that they have traits that resemble our caretakers' traits, both positive and negative, it is inevitable that they are going to open up some painful memories from childhood. But we picked them because we needed their exact character traits to activate the earliest memories of our primary caretakers.

But before we sink into this quagmire of conflict and confusion we call the *power struggle*, let's focus on the ecstasy of romantic love, those first few months or years of a relationship when we are filled with the delicious expectation of feeling fully alive and joyful on a regular basis.

ROMANTIC LOVE

We two form a multitude.

—Ovid

WE KNOW FROM our own relationship and from listening to others that most lovers believe that their time falling in love was an extraordinary and unique experience, different from the experiences of all the other people of the world. Unbeknownst at the time, we are reexperiencing our true nature—joyful connecting—which we lost awareness of in childhood. Because we are addicted to this authentic experience, we return to it in our memories again and again. When we ask couples to describe their idyllic first weeks, they describe a perfect world. People seemed friendlier, colors were brighter, food tasted better—everything around them shimmered with a pristine newness.

They also felt better about themselves. They had more energy and a more positive outlook on life. They felt wittier, more playful, more optimistic. When they looked in the mirror, they had a new fondness for the face that looked back at them—maybe they were worthy of their lover's affection, after all! Some people felt so good about themselves that, for a time, they were able to give up their substitute sources that triggered the sensation of connecting and feeling fully alive. They no longer felt the need to indulge themselves with sweets or drugs or alcohol or tranquilize themselves with video games or TV reruns to compensate for its absence. Working overtime lost its appeal, and scrabbling after money and power seemed rather pointless. The experience of being in love left them with little need for anything and an interest in everything. Life was joy and they were the One.

At the peak of a love relationship, these intense good feelings radiate outward, including everyone and everything. People feel more loving and connected with those around them. Some are blessed with a heightened spiritual awareness, a feeling of inner unity and a sense of being connected with nature that they hadn't experienced in a long time. They are seeing the world not through the fractured lens of their wounded self, but through the polished lens of their original nature of joyful connecting.[1]

Lynn and Peter, the couple introduced to you at the end of the previous chapter, said that when they were newly in love, they spent a day sightseeing in New York City. After dinner, they impulsively took the elevator to the top of the Empire State Building so they could see the sunset from the observation deck. They held hands and looked down on the thousands of people milling below them with a feeling of compassion—how tragic that these people were not sharing their feelings of ecstasy.

This timeless sentiment is beautifully expressed in a letter from Sophia Peabody to Nathaniel Hawthorne, dated December 31, 1839.[2] They would marry three years later.

Best Beloved,
. . . What a year has this been to us! My definition of Beauty is, that it is love, and therefore includes both truth and good. But those only who love as we do can feel the significance and force of this.

My ideas will not flow in these crooked strokes. God be with you. I am very well and have walked far in Danvers this cold morning. I am full of the glory of the day. God bless you this night of the old year. It has proved the year of our nativity. Has not the old earth passed away from us? Are not all things new?

Your Sophie

THE CHEMISTRY OF LOVE

WHAT CAUSES THE rush of good feelings that we call romantic love? Scientists who study natural hormones and chemicals tell us that lovers are literally high on drugs—substances that flood their bodies with a sense of well-being.[3] During the attraction phase of a relationship, the brain releases more dopamine and norepinephrine, two of the body's neurotransmitters. These chemicals help contribute to a rosy outlook on life, a rapid pulse, increased energy, and a sense of heightened perception.

Oxytocin is enhanced as well. It is a potent hormone that plays a role in many aspects of our lives, including childbirth, nursing, orgasm, the bonding of mother and child, and social connections between individuals. Some refer to it as "the love-sex hormone." During the phase when lovers want to be together every moment of the day, the brain also ramps up its production of endorphins and enkephalins, natural narcotics that enhance the sense of security and comfort. Dr. Michael R. Liebowitz, associate professor of clinical psychiatry at Columbia University, suggests that the mystical experience of oneness that lovers undergo may be caused by an increase in the production of serotonin—the hormone boosted by many antidepressant medications.

But as intriguing as it is to look at love from a neurochemical point of view, scientists can't explain what triggers the release of these potent chemicals or what causes them to diminish. All they can do is document the fact that romantic love is an intense emotional experience with measurable biological components— heart palpitations, sweating, sleeplessness, and impaired ability to concentrate. To gain additional insight, we need to return to the field of psychology and to the view that romantic love is a creation of the unconscious mind, a reexperiencing of the joyful connecting experienced in childhood in the present.

THE UNIVERSAL LANGUAGE OF LOVE

IN THE PREVIOUS chapter, we talked about the joy that accompanies falling in love, which is due in part to the deep-seated belief that love will give us a chance to be nurtured once again and reexperience the felt sense of connecting with which we began our lives.

We can find plenty of evidence that this is indeed what happens. One place to look is in the universal language of lovers. By listening to popular songs; reading love poems, plays, and novels; and listening to thousands of couples describe their relationships, we have come to the conclusion that all the words exchanged between lovers can be reduced to four basic sentences—the rest is elaboration. These four sentences offer a glimpse into the unconscious realm of romantic love as reexperiencing original connecting.

The first of these sentences occurs early in a relationship, maybe during the first or second encounter, and it goes something like this: "I know we've just met, but somehow I feel as though I already know you." This isn't just a line that lovers say to each other. For some unaccountable reason, they feel at ease with each other. They feel a comfortable resonance, as if they had known each other for years. We call this the *phenomenon of recognition*.

Somewhat later, lovers get around to the second significant exchange of information. "This is peculiar," they say to each other, "but even though we've only been seeing each other for a short time, I can't remember when I didn't know you." Even though they met only a few weeks or months ago, it seems as though they've always been together; their relationship has no temporal boundaries. We call this the *phenomenon of timeless-ness.*

When a relationship has had time to ripen, lovers look in each other's eyes and proclaim the third meaningful sentence: "When I'm with you, I no longer feel alone; I feel whole, complete." Patrick, another of our clients, expressed the feeling to us in these words: "Before I knew Diane, I felt as though I had been spending my life wandering around in a big house with empty rooms. When we met, it was like opening a door and finding someone at home for the very first time." Being together seemed to put an end to his relentless search for restored connecting. He felt a sense of belonging to and being a part of everything. We call this the *phenomenon of reunification.*

Finally, at some point, lovers utter a fourth and final declaration of love. They tell each other, "I love you so much, I can't live without you." They have become so involved with each other that they experience connecting as their essence, something they cannot lose. We call this the *phenomenon of necessity.*

Whether lovers say words like these or merely experience the feelings behind them, they underscore what we have been saying so far about romantic love and the nature of the unconscious.

The first sentence—in which lovers report an eerie sense of recognition—loses some of its mystery when we recall that the reason people "choose" their lovers is that the lovers have traits that are similar to the caregivers with whom they experienced the original connecting. No wonder they have a sense of déjà vu, a feeling of familiarity. On an unconscious level, they are connecting once again with the people who raised them, only this time they believe their deepest, most fundamental, most infantile yearnings are going to be satisfied. Someone is going to show up and be present to them always; they are no longer going to have to feel alone and empty.

The second statement, "I can't remember when I didn't know you," is a testimony to the fact that romantic love is an old-brain phenomenon. When people fall in love, their old brain fuses the image of their partners with the image of their parents and they enter the realm of the eternal now. To the unconscious, being in an intimate love relationship is very much like being an infant in the arms of a resonating mother.

In fact, if we could observe a pair of lovers at this critical juncture of their relationship, we would make an interesting observation: the two of them are taking part in an instinctual bonding process that mimics the way mothers bond with their babies. Researchers suggest that oxytocin is fueling the behaviors of both partners.[4] New lovers coo, prattle, and call each other diminutive names that they would be embarrassed to repeat in public. They stroke, pet, and delight in every square inch of each other's bodies — "What a cute little navel!" "Such soft skin!" "I want to kiss your toes!" — just the way a mother adores her baby. Meanwhile, they add to the illusion that they are going to be each other's surrogate parents by saying, "I'm going to love you the way nobody ever has," which the unconscious mind interprets to mean "more than Mommy and Daddy."

Needless to say, the old brain revels in all this delightfully regressive behavior. The lovers believe they are going to be transformed — not by hard work or painful self-realization but by the simple act of connecting with someone the old brain has confused with their caretakers.

What about the third sentence — that feeling of joyful connecting and oneness that envelops lovers? When lovers tell each other, "When I'm with you, I feel whole, complete," they are acknowledging that they have unwittingly chosen someone who manifests the very parts of their being that were cut off in childhood; they have rediscovered their lost self. A person who grew up repressing his or her feelings will choose someone who is unusually expressive. A person who was not allowed to be at ease with his or her sexuality will choose someone who is sensual and free. When people with complementary traits fall in love, they feel as if they've suddenly been released from repression. Like Plato's truncated, androgynous beings, each of them had been half a person; now they are whole. Together, they feel complete. They have everything they want because they are experiencing the original condition of connecting.

And what about the fourth sentence—the declaration that lovers feel that they might die if their relationship were to end? What can this tell us about the nature of romantic love? First, it reveals the fear that not being together would extinguish their sense of being loved. Loneliness and anxiety would well up inside them again, and they would no longer feel at one with the world around them. On a deeper level, it shows that they unknowingly transferred responsibility for their very survival from their parents to their partners. This same marvelous being who has awakened Eros is now going to protect them from Thanatos, the ever-present fear of death. By attending to their unmet childhood needs, their partners are going to become allies in their struggle to experience safety and belonging, which is essential for survival. On a deeper level, this sentence reveals the fear that, if the lovers were to part, they would no longer feel connected, and they'd lose a sense of belonging in the world.

A Brief Interlude

FOR A WHILE, however, these fears are held at bay, and the new lovers feel that being together is going to give them complete fulfillment. Companionship alone is a soothing balm. Because they are spending so much time together, they no longer feel lonely or isolated. As their level of trust increases, they deepen their intimacy. They may begin to talk about some of the pain and sorrow of their childhood years, and if they do, they are rewarded by their lover's heartfelt sympathy: "Oh, I feel so sad that you had to go through that." They feel as if no one, not even their own parents, has cared so deeply about their inner world.

As they share these intimacies, they may even experience

moments of empathic communion. During these rare moments, they aren't judging each other, or trying to interpret what each other is saying, or even comparing their various experiences. For a short time, they are letting go of their lifelong self-absorption and becoming curious about the reality of another human being.

But romantic love brings more than kind words and empathic moments to heal their wounds. With a sixth sense that can be lamentably lacking in later stages of a relationship, lovers seem to divine exactly what their partners are lacking. If the partner needs more nurturing, they gladly play the role of Mommy or Daddy. If the partner wants more freedom, they grant him or her more independence. If the partner needs more security, they become protective and reassuring. They shower each other with spontaneous acts of caring that seem to restore their early experience of connecting. Being in love is like becoming the favored child in an idealized family.

I'm Everything You Want Me to Be

ALMOST ALL COUPLES take part in a conscious subterfuge early in their relationship. Their goal is to appear to be less needy and more giving than they really are. If they don't seem to have many needs of their own, their partners are free to assume that their goal in life is to take care of *their* needs, and this makes them very desirable indeed.

One couple, Louise and Steve, described to us the efforts they went to enthrall each other. One day, a week after they'd declared their love for each other, Louise invited Steve over to her house for dinner. "I wanted to display my domestic talent," she confessed. "He saw me as a career woman—which I am—and I wanted him to see that I could cook, too. The truth is, I can cook, just not very well. And, although I didn't tell him at the time, I don't like doing it. Since my divorce, I've lived on prepared meals and restaurant food." To make her life seem as uncomplicated as possible, she arranged to have her eleven-year-old son from her previous marriage stay the night with a friend—no reason to have Steve witness the difficulties she was having with her rebellious son at this stage of the game. Then she thoroughly cleaned the house, planned the menu around the only two things she felt confident cooking—quiche and roasted vegetables—and arranged fresh flowers in the living room and dining room. When Steve walked into the house, dinner was ready, her makeup was fresh, and classical music was wafting through the house.

Steve, in turn, came as his most charming, helpful self. "I brought an expensive bottle of wine, one that was much pricier than I usually drink. I winced at the price. When dinner was over, I helped with the dishes and volunteered to replace the bulb in the porch light." He was demonstrating his worthiness as a provider and helpmate. For several months, they were able to orchestrate their lives so that they seemed to have few needs of their own.

Some lovers practice a deeper level of deception that disrupts their relationship. This was true for Brad, the boyfriend of Jessica. Jessica had a history of becoming involved with unreliable men. She had been divorced twice and had had two difficult relationships after that. When her relationship ended with Brad, a man who at first seemed totally devoted to her, she came to me (Harville) for counseling. Her love life seemed out of control, and she despaired of having a lasting marriage.

Jessica told me that when she first met Brad, she had been strongly attracted to him. As they spent more time together, she felt secure enough to tell him about her previous difficulties with men. Brad was sympathetic and assured her that he would never leave her. "If anyone leaves, it will be you," he said. "I will always be here." He seemed for all the world like the stable, trustworthy mate that Jessica had been searching for all her adult life.

The two of them were intimate friends for about six months,

and Jessica began to relax into the security of their relationship. Then one day, she came home from work, opened her computer, and found an email from Brad. He said that he had been offered a higher-paying job in Alaska and couldn't turn it down. He had wanted to tell her in person, but he had been afraid she'd be too upset. He wrote that he loved her and hoped that she would understand.

When Jessica recovered from shock, she called Brad's best friend and demanded that he tell her what he knew. He told her that Brad had never stayed in one place very long. In the fifteen years that he had known him, Brad had moved five or six times and had been married twice.

Our suspicion is that Brad's subterfuge was well intentioned at first. It's not likely that he began his relationship with Jessica with the purpose of gaining her affection and then leaving her, but as time went on, he discovered he couldn't keep up the charade. He could no longer pretend to be someone he was not.

DENIAL

TO SOME DEGREE, we all use denial as a coping tool. When life presents us with a difficult situation, we want to ignore reality and create a more palatable scenario. But there is no time in our lives when our denial mechanism is more fully engaged than in the early stages of a love relationship.

John, a man in his thirties, was particularly adept at denial. A computer programmer, he had designed an accounting software program that was so successful that he was able to start his own software company. For the first ten or fifteen minutes of each session, he would talk about his company and how it was doing. Then the conversation would grind to a halt, he would avert his eyes, and he would get around to the real topic of conversation, which was Cheryl, the woman he loved. He was utterly bewitched by her and would marry her in a second if she would only say yes, but Cheryl kept refusing to make a commitment.

When John first met Cheryl, she appeared to be everything he wanted in a woman. She was attractive, intelligent, and delightfully sensual. But a few months into the relationship, he began to be aware of some of her negative traits. When they went out to dinner, for example, she often criticized the food or the service. She would also complain about her job at great length but would do nothing to improve her working conditions.

To avoid being put off by these negative traits, John engaged in mental gymnastics. When he went out to dinner with her, he would focus on her discriminating tastes, not her critical attitude. When she ranted about her job, he thought about what a trooper she was to put up with such terrible working conditions. "Other people would have quit the job long ago," he told me with a note of pride.

The only thing that really bothered him about Cheryl was her unavailability. At times, he felt as though she was pushing him away. The situation worsened after they had been seeing each other for about ten months. Seemingly out of the blue, Cheryl asked that he not see her during the week so that she could have "a little breathing room." John reluctantly agreed to her terms, even though he feared that she would be using her freedom to see other men.

As compensation, John started spending time with a woman named Patricia, who was very unlike Cheryl. She was devoted and patient and crazy about him. "She'd marry me in a minute," John told me one day, "just the way I'd marry Cheryl in a minute. But I don't care that much about Patricia. Even though Patricia is more fun to be around, I never think about her when I'm away from her. It's almost as if she doesn't exist. Sometimes I feel that I'm taking advantage of her, but I don't like to be alone." Meanwhile, thoughts about unavailable, critical Cheryl filled his mind. "Whenever I'm not thinking about work," he said, "I'm daydreaming about Cheryl."

Why was John so immune to Patricia's charms and so willing to overlook Cheryl's faults? It should come as no surprise that John's mother had a critical, distant nature, somewhat like Cheryl's. As a young child, he remembers seeing a worried look come over his mother's face and knowing that it would be hard to get her attention. He had no idea what was going on in her mind. Like all children, he had no knowledge of—or interest in—his mother's reality. All he knew was that she was frequently unavailable to him, rupturing the connection between them. He would try to regain her attention by provoking her. When that didn't work, he would become angry. Then she would push him away and send him to his room.

Eventually, John learned to suffer in silence. He has a vivid memory of the day he adopted a stoical attitude. His mother had yelled at him and spanked him with a hairbrush. He doesn't remember what had made her so angry. All he remembers is that he had felt his punishment was unjustified and that he had run sobbing to his room. When he got to his room, he went into his closet and closed the door. The closet had a mirror on the inside of the door, and he remembers turning on the light and staring at his tear-streaked face. *Nobody cares that I'm in here crying,* he told himself. *What good is it to cry?* After a while, he stopped crying and wiped away his tears. John never cried again, even when his mother died. That very day, he began to cover his sadness and his anger with an unchanging mask.

John's childhood experiences help explain his intense attraction to Cheryl. When Cheryl ignored his advances by asking him not to call her for a few days, he was filled with the same yearning for connection that he had experienced with his mother. As far as his old brain was concerned, Cheryl *was* his mother, and his efforts to win her favor were a grown-up version of the crying and yelling he had done as a child.

Something else about Cheryl that attracted John—though he

would have vehemently denied it—was the fact that she had a caustic, critical nature. This appealed to him for two reasons. First, as we've already discussed, it reminded him of his mother, who was an angry, emotional person. Second, Cheryl's bad temper helped John get in touch with his own denied emotions. Even though he had just as much anger as Cheryl, he had learned to mask his hostility behind a compliant, accepting manner. In childhood, this had been a useful adaptation, because it protected him from his mother's temper. But now that he was an adult, without being able to feel and express strong emotions he felt empty inside. He discovered that by being with Cheryl, he didn't have to be angry himself. It was his unconscious way of being connected to his own repressed anger.

HOME MOVIES

PROJECTION IS THE term that describes the way John took a hidden part of himself—his anger—and attributed it to his lover. He projected his repressed anger onto Cheryl's visible anger. Although she was indeed an angry person, he was also seeing in her a part of his own nature, a part of his being that is incompatible with his self-image. Like John, we project whenever we deny or repress traits in ourselves and attribute them to others. We project all the time, not just in our primary love relationships. People in love are masters at projection. Some couples go through their whole marriages as if they were strangers sitting in a darkened movie theater, casting flickering images on each other. They don't even turn off their projectors long enough to see who it is that serves as the screen for their home movies.

We can also project positive traits onto others as well. For example, outside her awareness, Marta projected an image of her father onto her husband. Her father and her husband did have similar traits. They were both kind, affectionate, and unusually accepting of other people. There were major differences as well. Her father had been a steady worker, took few chances, and was always concerned about the family's safety. Marta liked these qualities because they had made her feel secure and cared for. Marta assumed that her husband had these qualities, too. She had projected some of her father's positive traits onto her partner. As time went on, Marta had to acknowledge that her husband was not the safety-conscious, conservative man she had pictured him to be. He drove too fast, he continued to be an artisan craftsman even though he was bringing in very little income, and he would not stay within their agreed-upon budget. Spending money on fine art, good meals, and fast cars was a source of pleasure for him—just as they had been for his own father.

It was hard for Marta to accept these qualities in her husband because they seemed so out of character. We helped her see that it would have been out of character for her *father* to have this devil-may-care attitude, but not her husband. Eventually, she realized she could no longer project her home movie onto her husband because it was so at odds with who he really was.

PSYCHE AND EROS

THE FLEETING, COMPLEX nature of romantic love is beautifully illustrated in the myth of Psyche and Eros, a legend from the second century AD.[5] According to the legend, the goddess Aphrodite was jealous of a mortal, a beautiful young woman named Psyche. In a fit of rage, Aphrodite decreed that Psyche be carried to the top of a mountain, where she was to become the bride of a horrible monster. Psyche's parents and the local villagers sadly escorted the young virgin up the mountain, chained her to a rock, and left her to her fate. Before Psyche could be claimed by the monster, the West Wind took pity on her and gently wafted her down the mountain to a valley that—surprise, surprise—happened to be the home of Aphrodite's son, Eros, the god of love.

Psyche and Eros fell in love immediately, but Eros did not want Psyche to know that he was a god because he was afraid that he would seem overpowering to her. He concealed his godlike nature by coming to her only in darkness. At first, Psyche agreed to this strange request and enjoyed her new love, his splendid palace, and the beautiful grounds. Then one day, her two sisters paid a visit and became envious of her good fortune. They began to ask prying questions. When Psyche couldn't answer them, they planted the suspicion in her mind that her lover might be a loathsome serpent intent on devouring her.

That night, before Eros came to her, Psyche hid a lamp and a sharp knife under the bed. If her lover turned out to be an evil creature, she would lop off his head. She waited until Eros was sound asleep, then quietly lit the lamp. But as she leaned over to get a closer look at him, a drop of hot oil spilled from the lamp onto his shoulder. Eros quickly awoke. When he saw the lamp and the knife, he flew out the open window, vowing to punish Psyche for her distrust by leaving her forever. In anguish, Psyche ran after him, calling out his name, but she couldn't keep up with him and tripped and fell. Instantly, the heavenly palace and the exquisite countryside vanished, and she was once more chained to a rock on the lonely, craggy mountaintop. Her world of joyful connecting was abruptly ruptured.

As with all fairy tales, there is much to be learned from this tale. During romantic love, many people don't want their partners to see them as they really are, and they don't have a realistic view of their partners. As long as lovers maintain an idealized, incomplete view of each other, they get to stay in their wondrous castle. When Psyche lit the lamp and saw Eros clearly for the first time, she discovered that he was a magnificent god with golden wings. When you and I lit our lamps and took our first objective look at our lovers, we discovered that they weren't gods at all—they were imperfect humans, full of warts and blemishes, all those negative traits that we had denied. The bliss of romantic love began to be replaced with the tension and demands of the power struggle that ruptured connecting and plunged our world into the darkness and misery, just like poor Psyche.

THE POWER STRUGGLE

I can't live either without you or with you.

— OVID

WHEN DOES ROMANTIC love end and the power struggle begin? For most couples, there is a noticeable change about the time they make a commitment to stay together. Once they say, "Let's get engaged," or "Let's get married," or "Let's not see anyone else for a while," the playful, inviting dance of courtship draws to a close, and they begin to want more than the *hope* of feeling joyfully connected and fully alive—which is responsible for the euphoria of romantic love—they want the reality as well. Their partners now must satisfy a hierarchy of expectations, some of them conscious, but most hidden from their awareness.

What are some of the conscious expectations? In traditional male-female partnerships, many of them are parental messages reinforced by cultural stereotypes. For example, a man may expect his new bride to do most of the housework, cook the meals, shop for groceries, wash the clothes, arrange most of the social events, be the family nurse, and buy everyday household items. In addition to these traditional roles, he has expectations that are specific to his upbringing. On Sundays, for example, he may expect his wife to cook a special breakfast and then join him on a leisurely stroll in the park. This is the way his parents spent their Sundays together, and the day wouldn't feel "right" unless it echoed these dominant chords.

Meanwhile, his wife has an equally long and sometimes conflicting set of expectations. In addition to wanting her husband to be responsible for most of the "manly" chores, she may expect him to help with the cooking, shopping, and laundry as well. Like many women today, she may also want him to play a significant role in raising the children. Or she may be a hedge fund CEO and anticipates a reversal of traditional roles.

Then she, too, has expectations that reflect her childhood history. An ideal weekend for her might include going to their house of worship and then having an elaborate dinner with members of their extended families. Since neither of them discussed all these expectations in advance, they can be the source of ongoing tension.

Far more important than these conscious or semiconscious expectations, however, are the unconscious ones people bring into the relationship. The primary expectation is that their partners are going to love and care for them the way their parents never did.[1] Their partners are going to help satisfy their unmet childhood needs and nurture them in a consistent and loving way.

These are the same expectations that fueled the excitement of romantic love, but now there is less desire to reciprocate. After all, people don't get involved in a love relationship to satisfy their *partner's* needs—they do so to further their own psychological and emotional well-being. Once a relationship seems secure, a switch is triggered deep in the old brain that activates their latent childhood wishes. It is as if the wounded child within takes over. Says the child, "I've been good enough long enough to ensure that this person is going to stay around for a while. It's time for the payoff." So the two partners take a big step back from each other and wait for the dividends to start rolling in. Primarily, they are seeking to free themselves of the self-absorbed anxiety that whispers deep inside.

The change may be abrupt or gradual, but at some point, they wake up to discover that their needs are *not* being met. They have many of the same anxieties and feelings of ruptured connection that they had before they fell in love. Confused and disappointed, they become less affectionate. Now there are fewer back rubs, fewer love notes, and less lovemaking. They stop looking for excuses to spend time together and begin to spend more time at work, visiting friends, or exploring the internet. It's as if they've migrated to a colder climate.

WHY HAVE YOU CHANGED?

THERE'S ANOTHER RUDE awakening. At some point in their relationships, many couples discover that a personality trait they once valued in their partners is beginning to annoy them. A man finds that his wife's conservative nature—one of the primary reasons he was attracted to her—is now making her seem staid and prudish. A woman discovers that her partner's tendency to be quiet and withdrawn—a trait she once thought was an indication of his spiritual nature—is making her feel lonely and isolated. A man finds his partner's outgoing personality—once so refreshing—is now making him feel invaded. A woman discovers that her husband's logical nature—which initially complemented her emotional side—has now made him into an unfeeling robot.

What is the explanation for these disturbing reversals? If you will recall, in our desire to be connected and as complete and perfect as we were in infancy, we chose partners who made up for the parts of our being that were split off in childhood. We found someone who compensated for our lack of creativity or inability to think or to feel or our repressed sexuality. Through union with our partners, we felt connected to a hidden part of ourselves. At first, this arrangement seemed to work. But as time passed, our partners' complementary traits began to stir up feelings and attributes in us that were still taboo.

To see how this drama plays out in real life, let's continue with the story of John, the successful businessman from the previous chapter who was spending time with Patricia but desperately wanted to be with Cheryl. John came in for a therapy session one day in an ebullient mood. This time, he didn't spend the customary fifteen minutes talking about his software business; he plunged right in with his good news. Cheryl, in a rare, conciliatory gesture, had decided to let him move in with her for a six-month trial period. This was the answer to his dreams.

John's euphoria lasted several months, during which time he decided that he no longer needed to come for counseling. (As is true for most therapeutic clients, he had little interest in working on his issues as long as he was happy.) One day, he called and asked for an appointment. When he came in, he reported that he and Cheryl were having difficulties once again. One of the things he mentioned was that Cheryl's vibrant personality was beginning to grate on him. He could tolerate her "emotional excesses" (as he now described them) when she directed them at others—for example, when she was berating a clerk or talking excitedly with a girlfriend—but when she beamed her high-voltage emotions at him, he had a fleeting sensation of panic. "I feel like my brain is about to short-circuit," he said.

The reason John was feeling so anxious around Cheryl was that she was beginning to stir his own repressed anger. At first, being around her had given him the comforting illusion that he was in touch with his feelings. But after a time, her free emotional state stimulated his own feelings to such a degree that they threatened to emerge. His superego, the part of his brain that was carrying out his mother's injunction against anger, sent out frantic error messages warning him to keep his repression intact. John tried to reduce his anxiety by dampening Cheryl's personality: "For God's sake, Cheryl! Don't be so emotional!

You're behaving like an idiot." And "Calm down, and then talk to me. I can't understand a word that you're saying." The very character trait that had once been so seductive to him was now perceived by his old brain as a threat to his existence.

In a similar way, there probably came a time in your relationship when you began to wish that your partner was less sexy or silly or spontaneous—somehow less whole—because these qualities called forth repressed qualities in you and your lost self was threatening to make an unscheduled reappearance. When it did, it ran headlong into the internal police force that had severed those self-parts in the first place, and you were filled with anxiety. This was such an unpleasant experience that you might have tried to repress your partner the same way your caregivers repressed you. In an effort to protect your existence, you were trying to diminish your partner's reality.

Your growing discomfort with your partner's complementary traits was only part of the rapidly brewing storm. Your partner's negative traits, the ones that you had resolutely denied during the romantic phase of your relationship, are beginning to come into focus. Suddenly, your partner's chronic depression or drinking problem or lack of responsibility are painfully evident. This gives you the sickening realization that your partner has the potential to turn your vibrant world, filled with wonder and joyful connecting, back into a dismal, ruptured experience, repeating what had happened to you in childhood.

A GLIMPSE AT A PAINFUL REALITY

I (HARVILLE) MADE this painful discovery early on in my first marriage—in fact, on the second day of our honeymoon. My new bride and I were spending a week on an island off the shores of southern Georgia. We were walking along the beach. I was poking through piles of driftwood, and my wife was down by the water, two or three hundred feet in front of me, head down, totally absorbed in the task of looking for shells. I happened to glance up and saw her silhouetted against the rising sun. To this day, I can remember exactly what she looked like. She had her back to me. She was wearing black shorts and a red top. Her shoulder-length blond hair was blowing in the wind. As I gazed at her, I noticed a droop to her shoulders. At that instant, I felt a jolt of anxiety. This was immediately followed by the sinking realization that I had married the wrong person. It was a strong feeling—I had to check an impulse to run back to the car and drive away. While I was standing there transfixed, my wife turned to me, waved, and smiled. I felt as though she had awakened me from a nightmare. I waved back and hurried up to meet her.

It was as if a veil had been lifted for a moment and then dropped back down. It took me years to figure out what had happened. The connection was finally made one day while I was in therapy. My therapist was guiding me through a regression exercise, an exercise that is designed to take people back to their childhood. Suddenly, I recalled an event that had happened to me when I was only a few years old. I was playing on the floor in the kitchen. I visualized my mother busy at the stove with her back to me. This must have been a typical scene, because I was her ninth child, and she probably spent four or five hours a day cooking and cleaning in the kitchen. I could see my mother's back quite clearly. She was standing at the stove wearing a print dress, and she had apron strings tied around her waist. Her shoulders sagged, and her head was cast down.

As an adult viewing this long-ago scene, I was flooded with the awareness that she didn't have any physical or emotional energy for me. My father had died only a few months before from a head injury, and she was left alone with her grief, very little money, and nine children to care for. I was too young to be aware of the nature of her difficulties, of course. All I knew is that I wanted more love and affection. In my adult mind,

I could see that she had been so overwhelmed by tragedy that she had little to give me. This was a new discovery for me. Until that point in my therapy, I had thought my recurring anxiety was due to the fact that both my parents had died by the time I was six years old. But during that therapy session, I learned that my feelings of abandonment had started much earlier.

Still in my regressed state, I called to my mother, but she would not answer. I sat in the psychiatrist's office and cried in deep pain. Then I had a second revelation. I suddenly realized what had happened to me that day on my honeymoon. When I had seen my wife so far away from me, so absorbed in herself, and with the same slump to her shoulders, I had had the eerie premonition that my marriage was going to be a repetition of my early days with a depressed mother. The emptiness of my early days was going to continue. It had been too much for me to absorb, and I had quickly drawn the curtain.

At some point, most people discover that something about their partner awakens strong memories of childhood pain. Sometimes the parallels are obvious. A young woman with abusive parents, for example, may discover a violent streak in her boyfriend. A man with alcoholic parents may find himself married to an incipient alcoholic or drug addict. A woman who grew up with an unfaithful father may discover that her partner is having an affair.

But we have observed that the similarities between parents and partners are often subtler. This was the case for Bernard and Kathryn, who had been married for twenty-eight years. Bernard was a manager of a public utility; Kathryn was going back to school to get a degree in counseling. They had three children and one grandchild.

One evening as they walked into the office for their weekly appointment, they both looked downtrodden and defeated. It was obvious that they recently had one of the "core" scenes, a fight that they had had over and over again during the last twenty years of their marriage in countless subtle variations. Most couples have such a core scene, a fight they have so many times that they know their parts by heart.

They said that their most recent fight had taken place while they were decorating the house for Christmas. Bernard had been characteristically quiet, absorbed in his own thoughts, and Kathryn had been issuing orders. All three of their children and their spouses were coming to stay for the holidays, and Kathryn wanted the house to look clean and festive. Bernard dutifully performed whatever task was asked of him and went on pondering his own thoughts. After an hour or so, his silence became deafening to Kathryn, and she tried to involve him in a conversation about their children. He volunteered only a few sentences. She became more and more annoyed with him. Finally, she lashed out at him for the way he was hanging the lights on the tree: "Why don't you pay attention to what you're doing? I may as well do it myself!" Bernard let her tirade wash over him, then calmly turned and walked out the back door. Kathryn went to the kitchen window. As she watched the garage door close behind Bernard, she was filled with two primal emotions: fear and anger. Anger was uppermost: this time she wasn't going to let him retreat. She marched out after him and threw open the door. "For God's sake! Why don't you help me? You never help me when I need you. You always find some way to disappear. What's the matter with you?" His old brain responded to her attack—which was nothing more than an adult version of the infant's cry—with a counterattack. "Maybe I'd help you more if you weren't so bitchy!" he retorted. "You're always hounding me. Can't I be alone for five minutes?" Now *he* was seething with anger, and Kathryn burst into tears.

From an outside perspective, it is easy to write the step-by-step evolution of their arguments. The trigger for the fights was almost always the fact that Bernard was withdrawn. Trying to get some response from him, Kathryn would try to engage him in conversation. Bernard would give a minimal response and continue whatever he was doing. When Kathryn still did not get his attention, her anger would escalate. Pushed to his limit, Bernard would respond in kind.

When they were through recounting this latest episode, Kathryn was asked to remember how she had felt when she had been working on the holiday preparations and Bernard had been so quiet. She sat quietly for a moment, struggling to recall her feelings. Then she looked up with a puzzled expression and said, "I felt scared. It scared me that he wouldn't talk to me." For the first time, she realized that she was afraid of his silences.

"What were you afraid of, Kathryn?"

She answered quickly, "I was afraid he was going to hurt me."

Bernard looked over at her with wide-open eyes.

"Let's check this out with Bernard," I (Harville) said. "Bernard, were you thinking about hurting Kathryn?"

"Hurting her?" he said, bewildered. "Hurting her?! I have never touched her in my life. I was just thinking my own thoughts. I was probably thinking about something mundane like the fact that the roof needed to be replaced or that I needed to put snow tires on the cars."

"Really?" asked Kathryn. "You weren't mad at me that day?"

"No! Sure, I got annoyed when you kept ordering me around and criticizing me, but all I wanted to do was get away. I kept thinking about how nice it would be to be out in the garage working on my own projects instead of being nagged at all the time."

"Well, the way I see it, you're always angry at me, and eventually, you can't hold it in any longer, so you blow up."

"I do blow up," Bernard acknowledged, "but it takes about two or three hours of you harping at me before I do! Anybody would get angry at that. I don't start out being angry at you."

This checked out with the observations in the office. Bernard did not seem to be an angry man. By guiding with prompts, attuned therapists know when a moment is ripe for deepening.

"Kathryn," I said, "for a moment, I want you to close your eyes and think some more about what makes you afraid when Bernard doesn't respond to you."

After half a minute, she replied, "I don't know. It's just the silence." She was having a hard time coming up with additional insight.

"Well, stay with that thought for a moment and try to recall something about silence in your childhood. Close your eyes."

The room was quiet. Then Kathryn opened her eyes and said, "It's my father! I've never seen that before. He was often depressed. In fact, he was later diagnosed with bipolar disorder. Sometimes his depression would last for weeks, and he would barely talk to anyone. When he was in one of those moods, I knew not to bother him because if I did one thing wrong, he would get very angry. Once, he slapped me across the face. Whenever I saw him start to sink into a depression, I would feel scared. I knew that we were all in for a hard time."

Kathryn's father and her husband shared a personality trait—they both were prone to long periods of silence—and this undoubtedly was one of the reasons that Kathryn was attracted to Bernard. She didn't marry a talkative, outgoing person—she found someone who had her father's negative traits so she could continue her struggle for consistent love and kindness. But Bernard resembled Kathryn's father only superficially. He was silent because he was an introvert, not because he was depressed and given to anger.

We have found this phenomenon in many of our couples. They react to their partners as if they were carbon copies of their parents, even though not all their traits are the same. In their compelling need to work on unfinished business, they project the missing parental traits onto their partners. Then, by treating their partners as if they actually had these traits, they manage to provoke the expected response. Our colleague claims that people either "pick Imago matches, project them, or provoke them."

OF TURTLES AND HAILSTORMS

WHILE READING ABOUT Bernard and Kathryn, you may have noticed another complementary trait about them: they both respond to anxiety in different ways. As their core scene unfolded, Bernard ultimately retreated to the garage with Kathryn stomping out soon after, hurling the "always" and "never" accusations. As mentioned earlier, a part of our old brain's sole purpose is survival. It constantly scans the environment, checking to see if something is safe or dangerous. If the environment is safe, it can eat, play, nurture, or mate. But if it perceives something in the environment as dangerous, an internal defense system goes into action: freezing ("Maybe it won't see me"), fleeing ("If I run/fly/swim fast enough, I can escape"), or fighting ("I can injure or kill my enemy"). It is this archaic "fight, flight, or freeze" defense system that keeps us alive. However, this part of the brain does not distinguish between past or present, nor does it differentiate between emotional or physical safety. It is all the same "code red" warning. It is why safety in the Space Between is essential in Imago Therapy.

Similarly, as we experienced challenges with intrusive or neglectful parenting in our childhood, we adapted defenses to protect ourselves from emotional injury by either minimizing our feelings (freeze or play dead) or maximizing our feelings (fight or flight). In Imago, we call the minimizer the Turtle and the maximizer the Hailstorm. This is the unconscious voice inside the Hailstorm: "I'm going to *make* my partner give me more attention and love by raising my voice and expressing my feelings and thoughts with a lot of energy." Simultaneously, the unconscious voice inside the Turtle says, "I'm going to *make* my partner honor my boundaries by retreating even further into my isolated shell, excluding them from my personal space, and figuring out things by myself." The Hailstorm-Turtle dynamic ends up perpetuating itself with drastic consequences: the more the Turtle retreats, the more the Hailstorm hails, and vice versa, exacerbating their mutual anxiety. And of course, true to the nature of the oscillating energy of opposites in a relational field, Hailstorms and Turtles fall in love.

Now we have defined the three major sources of conflict that make up the power struggle. As the sensation of feeling fully alive in romantic love slowly erodes, the two partners begin to:

1. Stir up each other's repressed behaviors and feelings.
2. Reinjure each other's childhood wounds.
3. Use opposing defenses to protect themselves from relational anxiety.

All these interactions are unconscious. All people know is that they are feeling disappointed, confused, angry, anxious, and unloved. It is only natural that they blame their unhappiness on their partners. They, of course, haven't changed—they're the same people they used to be! It's their partners who have changed!

WEAPONS OF LOVE

IN DESPAIR, PEOPLE begin to use negative tactics to force their partners to be more loving. They withhold their affection and become emotionally distant. They become irritable and critical. They attack and blame: "Why don't you . . . ?" "Why do you always . . . ?" "How come you never . . . ?" They fling these verbal stones in a desperate attempt to get their partners to be warm and responsive. If they give their partners enough pain, they believe, their partners will relent and return to their former loving ways. But to a therapist, global words like *always* and *never* are an indication of a childhood wound. These are clues that the "past injury" is activated in the present relating.

What makes people believe that hurting their partners will

make them more loving? Why don't people simply, quietly, and respectfully tell each other in plain English that they want more affection or attention or lovemaking or freedom or whatever it is that they are craving? We asked that question out loud one day as we were conducting a couples' workshop. It wasn't just a rhetorical question; we didn't have the answer. But it just so happened that, a few minutes before, we were talking about babies and their instinctual crying response to distress. All of a sudden, the answer became clear. Once again, our old brains were to blame. When we were infants, we didn't smile sweetly at our mothers to get them to feed us. We didn't pinpoint our discomfort by putting it into words. We simply opened our mouths and cried. It didn't take long to learn that the louder we screamed, the quicker they came. The success of this tactic leaves an "imprint," a part of our stored memory about how to get the world to respond to our needs: "When you are frustrated, provoke the people around you. Be as unpleasant as possible until someone comes to your rescue."

This primitive method of signaling distress is characteristic of most couples immersed in a power struggle, but there is one example that stands out in our minds with a couple who had been married about twenty-five years. The husband, Zachary, was convinced that his wife, Tina, was not only selfish but vindictive. "She never thinks of me," he complained, listing numerous ways his wife ignored him. Meanwhile, Tina sat in her chair and shook her head in mute disagreement. As soon as he was through, she leaned forward in her chair and said in a strong and earnest voice, "Believe me, I do everything I can to please him. I spend more time with him; I spend less time with him. I even learned how to ski this winter, thinking that would make him happy—and I hate being out in the cold! But nothing seems to work."

To help end the stalemate, we asked Zachary to tell his wife one specific thing that she could do that would make him feel better—one practical, doable activity that would help him feel more loved. He hemmed and hawed and then said, "If she's been married to me for twenty-five years and still doesn't know what I want, she hasn't been paying attention!"

This man, like the rest of us, was clinging to a primitive view of the world. When he was an infant lying in the cradle, he experienced his caregiver as a large creature leaning over him, responding to all his needs. He was fed, clothed, bathed, and nurtured, even though he could not articulate a single need. A crucial lesson learned in the preverbal stage of his development left an indelible imprint on his mind: other people were supposed to figure out what he needed and give it to him without his having to do anything more than cry.[2] Whereas this arrangement worked fairly well when he was a child, in adulthood, his needs were far more complex. Furthermore, his wife was not a devoted mother hovering over his crib. She was his partner, and she had needs and expectations of her own. Although she wanted to make him happy, she didn't know what to do. Lacking this information, she was forced to play a grownup version of pin the tail on the donkey: "Is this what you want? Is this?"

When partners don't tell each other what they want and constantly criticize each other for not giving it to them, it's no wonder that a rupture forms in the relationship. The river that flows between them—the Space Between—has become clogged with debris, and their love begins to falter. In its place comes the grim determination of the power struggle as they try to force each other to be more responsive. Even though these maneuvers provoke further hostility, the partners persevere. This is a classic example of what Freud called the *repetition compulsion,* the tendency of human beings to repeat ineffective behaviors over and over again.

Another example of this power struggle comes from our own relationship. We had a challenging issue that repeatedly showed up: deciding where and how to spend our vacations together. It's an area where we are polar opposites. I (Helen) am a homebody, and since our work and family require us to travel a great deal of the time, I prefer spending our vacations at home. Harville, however, is passionate about traveling. So our vacation planning time was full of conflict. Whoever "won" the argument would feel self-righteous while the "defeated" one would feel resentful and invisible. This battle of the wills repeated for years. It wasn't until we engaged in the principles we will describe in later chapters that we were able to equally honor each other's voices and cocreate an elegant solution: a motorhome allowed Harville to travel the open road, while surrounding me with the chance to cook and leisurely do my needlepoint for hours, which was paradise for me.

Some couples stay in this hostile state all their lives. (We personally moved in and out of this ruptured state for more than three decades.) As time goes on, couples hone their ability to pierce each other's defenses and damage each other's psyches. Rob, for example, described a scene he had witnessed between his aging parents. His mother had multiple sclerosis and was confined to her bed. She entertained herself by reading and watching TV. One day, he walked into their bedroom and saw that his father was playing keep-away with the TV remote, preventing his mother from changing the channel. His mother had tears of frustration running down her face. Rob said that his parents' power struggle had gone on for at least forty years.

STAGES OF THE POWER STRUGGLE

WHEN YOU AND your partner are immersed in a power struggle, you have little sense of when it all started or how it will end. But from an outside perspective, the power struggle has a predictable course, one that parallels the well-documented stages of grief in a bereaved person.[3] First comes the shock, that moment of truth when a window opens and a troubling thought enters your consciousness: *This is not the person I thought I married. They tricked me!* At that instant, you realize your married life is not going to be what you'd hoped.

After the shock comes denial. Your disappointment is so great that you do your best to see your partner's negative traits in a positive light. "My partner does not lack compassion. She is simply preoccupied with her own needs." But eventually, the denial can no longer be sustained, and you feel angry. Either your partner has changed drastically since the days when you were first in love, or you have been deceived all along about your partner's true nature. You are in pain, and the degree of your pain is the degree of the disparity between your earlier view of your partner and your partner's emerging reality.

If you stay together beyond the angry stage of the power struggle, some of the venom drains away, and you enter the fourth stage, bargaining. This stage goes something like this: "If you stop drinking so much, I'll be more interested in sex." Or "If you make an effort to treat my mother more kindly, I'll go on more fishing trips with you." Relationship therapists can unwittingly prolong this stage of the power struggle if they spend their time helping couples negotiate behavioral contracts without getting to the root of their problems.[4]

The last stage of the power struggle is despair. When couples reach this final juncture, they have no hope of finding joy and happiness within the relationship; the pain has gone on too long. At this point, approximately half of all couples abandon the relationship. Most of those who stay together create what is called a *parallel* relationship and try to find their happiness outside the partnership.

Summary of the First Five Chapters

FOR THE SAKE of clarity, we would like to reduce the discussion in this first part of the book to its simplest form. First of all, we are drawn to our partners for two basic reasons: (1) they have both the positive and the negative qualities of the people who raised us, and (2) they compensate for positive parts of our being that were cut off in childhood. We enter the relationship with the unconscious assumption that our partners will become a surrogate parent and make up for all the deprivation of our childhood. All we have to do to feel connected and fully alive once again is to fall in love.

After a time, we realize that our dreams are not being fulfilled. We believe that our partners are willfully ignoring our needs. They know exactly what we want and when and how we want it, but for some reason, they are refusing to cooperate. This makes us angry, and for the first time, we begin to see our partners through a darker lens, and the traits that once were attractive (our "lost parts") now grate on us.

As conditions deteriorate, we decide that the best way to get our partners to satisfy our needs is to be unpleasant and irritable, just as we did in the cradle. If we yell loud enough and long enough, we believe, our partners will come to our rescue.

What may not be apparent in this summary is this: there is little difference between romantic love and the power struggle. On the surface, of course, these two stages are worlds apart. A couple's delight in each other has turned to antagonism, and their desire to please each other has been replaced by a battle of wills.

Despite these apparent differences, the underlying motivation remains the same. In both stages, people are searching for a way to overcome their emotional difficulties and their deep-seated feelings of being unloved and unworthy of love. Another similarity is that people believe their partners have the power to provide the experience of feeling joyfully connected and fully alive.

What is the way out of this labyrinth? What lies beyond the power struggle? In the next part, we will talk about a new kind of relationship, the *conscious partnership,* and explain how partners who are entangled in a power struggle can reconnect and experience love and joy once again.

part II

THE CONSCIOUS
PARTNERSHIP

BECOMING CONSCIOUS

*Seldom or never does a marriage develop into
an individual relationship smoothly without crisis.
There is no birth of consciousness without pain.*
— CARL JUNG

SCANNING THE FIRST five chapters, one might get the impression that the old brain is the cause of most of our relationship problems. It's the old brain that prompts us to choose partners who have our caregivers' positive and negative traits. It's the old brain that is the source of our elaborate Turtle and Hailstorm defenses that spontaneously turn on when we don't feel safe. And it's the old brain that is responsible for our infantile response to frustration, the self-defeating "fight, flight, or freeze" response.

But the old brain also plays a positive role in love relationships. First of all, our unconscious mind is ever on the alert and is committed to keeping us alive. It also seeks to restore the connection and sense of joy we had as young children. And when we're drawn to a person who becomes our partner, even though our projections may temporarily blind us to our partners' reality, they're also what bind our partnerships together, setting up the preconditions for future growth.

The problem with the old brain is that it's reactive. It's hard to control its responses to the environment. To achieve the important objectives of the old brain, we need to enlist the aid of the new brain—the part of us that makes conscious choices, exerts will, knows that our partners are not our parents, that today is not always, and that yesterday is not today. We need to take the thoughtful, rational skills that we use in other parts of our lives and enlist them into caring for our love relationships. When we forge a working alliance between the powerful, instinctual drives of the old brain and the strategic, cognitive strengths of the new brain, we can begin to get the lasting love we want. Through the marriage of old-brain instincts and new-brain savvy, we can leave the frustrations of the power struggle behind us.

NEW BRAIN–OLD BRAIN MERGER

WHAT DO LOVE relationships look like when the new brain plays a more active role? Here's a typical interaction between a couple and how it might be handled in an unconscious partnership—a typical love relationship dominated by the old brain— and in a conscious partnership, a relationship in which the old brain is tempered by reason.

Imagine that you are happily eating breakfast and your partner loudly criticizes you for burning the waffles: "You do this time and time again!" Your old brain, the perpetual guardian of your safety, feels under attack. It cares not that the person who criticized you is your partner; all it cares about is that you're being bombarded. Unless you buffer your old brain's reactivity, you will respond with a fitting rejoinder—"Well, cook it yourself next time!" Or you might attempt to avoid the skirmish altogether by burying your head in your cell phone. Depending on your approach, your partner will feel either attacked or deflected and will want to strike out again. A perpetual-emotion machine is set in gear, and you will have prevented what the two of you really want, which is to have an enjoyable breakfast together.

Time to press the new brain into service. A more rational

approach is to acknowledge your partner's anger in a neutral tone of voice and not rush to your own defense. For example, you might say something like this: "So I get it that you're really upset that I burned the waffles again." Your partner might then respond, "Yes, I am! I'm tired of all the wasted food around here. Next time be more careful!" And, still relying on new-brain tact, you could say, "Well, that makes sense. Food does get wasted around here." Then, because you are not up in arms, you could offer a solution: "I'll get an extension cord and bring the waffle iron into the dining room so we can keep a closer eye on it." Your partner, disarmed by your rational tone of voice and your ability to think of an alternative solution, will probably become more tractable: "Good idea. And thanks for not getting upset. I'm a little edgy this morning. I'm behind at work, and I don't know how I'm going to manage." Because you were willing to risk a rational, creative response to your partner's anger, you are regarded as a trusted confidant, not a sparring partner. By relying on your new brain, which, unlike your old brain, recognizes that being criticized for burning the waffles is not the same thing as being attacked with the bread knife, you learn to moderate your instinctual "fight, flight, or freeze" response.

TEN CHARACTERISTICS OF A CONSCIOUS PARTNERSHIP

LET'S MOVE ON to the larger picture to see what we mean by *a conscious partnership.* First, a definition: a conscious partnership is a relationship that is mutually supportive and fosters the psychological and spiritual growth of both individuals; it's when both partners focus on the relationship as primary, the essential care of the Space Between.

What are some of the characteristics of a conscious partnership? The following list itemizes some of the key differences in attitude and behavior:

1) **You realize that your love relationship has a hidden purpose—to help you overcome the limitations of your childhood.** Instead of focusing on surface needs and desires, you learn to recognize the unresolved childhood issues that underlie them. When you look at relationships with this x-ray vision, your daily interactions take on more meaning. Puzzling aspects of your relationship begin to make more sense to you, and you have a greater sense of safety and control. To sum up this one core idea: the unconscious purpose of marriage is to finish childhood.

2) **You create a more accurate image of your partner.** At the very moment of attraction, you begin fusing your lover with your primary caregivers. Later in the relationship, you start denying your partner's negative traits, further obscuring your partner's reality. As you move toward a conscious relationship, you gradually let go of these illusions and begin to see more of your partner's truth. You see that your partner is neither your savior nor your adversary but another human being, struggling to be happy and connected.

3) **You learn to ask for what you want using Sender Responsibility[1] for communicating your needs and desires to your partner.** Sender Responsibility means you say things in a concise way, with a kind tone of voice, a soft look in your eyes, and with using "I" messages. In an unconscious partnership, you cling to the idea that your partner is a mind reader who can intuit your needs. In a conscious partnership, you realize that you have to develop clear channels of communication so that both you and your partner can get the specifics of the love you both want.

4) **You move from "reactive living" to "proactive living."** In an unconscious partnership, you often react without thinking, allowing your old brain to dictate your behavior. In a

conscious partnership, you employ new-brain responses by becoming intentional in your interactions and practice behaving in a more constructive and effective manner.

5) **You learn to value your partner's needs and wishes as well as your own.** In an unconscious partnership, you assume that your partner's role in life is to take care of your needs. In a conscious partnership, you divert more of your energy to meeting your partner's needs.

6) **You focus on keeping the relationship safe at all times.** In a conscious relationship, you acknowledge the negative effects of criticism, blame, and shame and therefore remove all negativity from the interactive space—the Space Between. You replace negativity with affirming, positive behaviors to establish the safety necessary for growth and healing.

7) **You find new ways to satisfy your basic needs and desires.** During the power struggle, people cajole, harangue, and blame their partners to coerce them to meet their needs. When you create a more conscious partnership, you discover that your partner can indeed be a resource for you once you abandon your self-defeating tactics.

8) **You shift from judgment to curiosity about your partner in order to discover their unique internal world.** In an unconscious relationship, you insist your partner be more like you. In a conscious relationship, you move away from assumptions and judgment and toward curiosity and wonder to discover who your partner is, accept that they are not you, and revel in the fact that that's OK.

9) **You become more aware of your drive to be loving and united with the connecting energies of the universe.** When Harville was discussing the Imago with me, I (Helen) suggested

that beneath the Imago was the Imago Dei,[2] the "image of God" that we each have the choice to cultivate. It is the capacity to love someone else unconditionally, without expecting something in return. We practice this as we seek to heal each other's childhood wounds, focusing for a while on just our partners, and helping them feel they can depend on us to be their advocate.

10) **You accept the difficulty of creating a lasting love relationship.** In an unconscious partnership, you believe that the way to have a good relationship is to fall in love with the perfect mate. In a conscious partnership, you realize you must *be* the right partner. As you gain this more realistic view, you acknowledge that creating a good relationship requires commitment, discipline, and the courage to change.

Let's take a closer look at number ten, the need to accept the difficulty of creating a conscious partnership, because none of the other nine characteristics will come to fruition unless you first cultivate your willingness to grow and change.

BECOMING A LOVER

WE ALL HAVE an understandable desire to live life as children. We don't want to go to the trouble of raising a cow and milking it; we want to sit down at the table and have someone hand us a cool glass of milk. We don't want to plant seeds and tend a grapevine; we want to walk out the back door and pluck a handful of grapes. This wishful thinking finds its ultimate expression in love relationships. We don't want to accept responsibility for getting our needs met; we want to "fall in love" with the ideal mate and live happily ever after. The psychological term for this childlike view is *externalization,* and it is the cause of much of the world's unhappiness.

Before I (Harville) worked with couples, Walter came in for his appointment with drooping shoulders and a sad expression.

"What's the matter?" I asked Walter. "You look very unhappy today."

"Harville," he said to me as he slumped into the chair, "I feel terrible. I just don't have any friends."

I was sympathetic. "You must be very sad. It's lonely not having any friends."

"Yeah. I can't seem to . . . I don't know. There are just no friends in my life. I keep looking and looking, and I can't find any."

He continued in a morose, complaining voice for some time, and I had to suppress a growing annoyance with his regressed, childlike state. He was locked into a view of the world that went something like this: wandering around the world were people on whose foreheads were stamped the words *Friend of Walter*, and his job was merely to search until he found them. "Walter," I said with a sigh, "do you understand why you don't have any friends?"

He perked up. "No. Tell me!"

"The reason you don't have any friends is that there aren't any friends out there."

His shoulders dropped once again.

I was relentless. "That's right," I told him. "What you want does not exist." I let him stew in this state for a few seconds. Then I leaned forward in my chair and said, "Walter—listen to me! All the people in the world are strangers. If you want a friend, you're going to have to go out and make one!"

Walter was resisting the idea that creating a lasting friendship takes time and energy. Even though he was responsible and took initiative in his job, he retained the childlike notion that all he had to do to establish intimacy was to bump into the right person. Because he hadn't acknowledged that a friendship evolves slowly over time and requires thoughtfulness, sensitivity, compassion, and patience, he had been condemned to a lonely life.

The passive attitude Walter brought to his friendships was even more pronounced in his love life: he couldn't seem to find the ideal woman. Recovering from a painful divorce (in a bitter legal battle, his wife had gotten custody of their son), he was desperately trying to find a new mate.

Another reason that Walter had difficulty with love relationships was that he was repressing most of his feelings. He hid his vulnerability behind his formidable intellect, which prevented genuine intimacy. He had been coming to group therapy sessions for about six months, and members of the group had given him the same message he had been hearing from his ex-wife — that he wasn't sharing his feelings, that he was emotionally distant. One evening, a member of the group finally broke through to him. "When you talk about your pain," she said, "I can't see any suffering. When you hug me, I can't feel your hugs." Walter finally realized that there was some basis to his ex-wife's complaints. "I thought she was just being bitchy and critical," he confessed. "It never occurred to me that maybe she was right. That I could learn something about myself from listening to her."

When Walter had time to absorb this awareness, he developed more enthusiasm for the therapeutic process and was able to work on dismantling his emotional barriers. As he became more emotionally alive, he was able to have a satisfying relationship with a new woman friend. During his last session, he shared his feelings about therapy. "You know," he said, "it took me two years to learn one simple fact: that, in order to have a good relationship, you have to be willing to grow and change. If I had known this ten years ago, I would still be living with my wife and son."

Walter can't be blamed for wanting to believe that relationships should be easy and "natural." It's human nature to want a life without effort. When we were infants, the world withheld and we were frustrated; the world reached out to us and we were satisfied. Out of thousands of these early transactions, we fashioned an infantile model of the world, and we cling to this out-dated model even at the expense of our relationships. We are slow to comprehend that in order to be loved, we must first become lovers. And we don't mean this in sentimental or phys-ical terms. We don't mean sending flowers, writing love notes, or learning new lovemaking techniques—although any one of these activities might be a welcome part of a relationship. To be-come lovers, we must first abandon the self-defeating tactics and beliefs that we've discussed in the first five chapters and re-place them with more constructive ones. We must change our ideas about love relationships, about our partners, and, ulti-mately, about ourselves.

The Fear of Change

A FEAR OF change is basic to human nature. Even when we're facing a positive change, such as getting promoted, moving into a new home, or going on vacation, we can feel anxious. Any-thing that breaks us out of our customary routines sets off an alarm in the old brain. The old brain is alerting us to the fact that we are entering foreign territory that has not been mapped or surveyed and that danger may lurk around every turn in the road.

We see a wish to cling to well-worn paths even in young children. When our daughter Leah was two and a half years old, her younger brother, Hunter, had outgrown his cradle. We de-cided it was time to move Leah into a youth bed so that the baby could have the crib. The youth bed had a six-inch rail going half-way down the bed to keep her from rolling off in the middle of the night, but the bottom half had no rail. The first morning that Leah awoke in her new bed, we heard her familiar wake-up cry: "Daddy! Daddy! Mommy! Mommy!" We went into her room, and there she was, on her knees, with her hands on the little rail, saying, "Pick me up!"—just as she had done in her old crib with the two-foot sides. We were taken aback by her helplessness. She could easily have climbed over the bar or scooted down a few feet to the part of the bed that had no railing at all. "Leah," we said with enthusiasm, "you can get out of your new bed all by yourself!"

"I can't," she said, sticking out her lower lip. "I'm stuck."

"Leah, look down here," we implored, patting the part of the bed without rails. "You can climb down right here!" She continued kneeling, frozen in place. Finally, we had to get up on the bed with her and show her how to do it. With our encouragement, she was able to follow close behind, overcome her resistance to change, and get out of bed.

We saw a more dramatic demonstration of the fear of change while watching the evening news. A local TV station carried a story about a little boy who had been born with severe immune deficiency, a disease that had crippled his immune system and left him defenseless against bacteria and viruses. Since the time he was three months old, he had spent his life encased in a plastic bubble, sealed off from life-threatening germs. His devoted mother and father were in the room most days, but they were separated from him by the plastic. The only way they could touch him was to put on long sterile gloves that were permanently inserted into the bubble.

Shortly after the boy's fifth birthday, he was given a successful bone-marrow transplant. After extensive testing, the doctors determined that his immune system was sufficiently developed to allow him to leave his sterile world.

On the day he was scheduled to come out, the bubble was slit open, and his overjoyed mother and father held out their arms to him. This was the first time in five years that they would be able to kiss and hug their son. To everyone's surprise, the boy cowered in the back of the bubble. His parents called to him, but he wouldn't budge. Finally, his father crawled inside and carried him out. As the little boy looked around the room, he started to cry. Because he had lived all his life in an eight-by-ten-foot enclosure, the room must have looked enormous to him. His parents hugged him and kissed him to reassure him, but he wasn't used to physical contact, and he arched backward to escape their embraces.

The closing segment of the story, filmed about a week later, showed that the child was growing more comfortable with life outside the bubble. But on the day of his emancipation, it was clear that his fear of confronting the unfamiliar was stronger than his desire to embrace his parents and join the rest of the world.

That little boy lived for five years inside his bubble. The couples that we see have been living for two, ten, twenty—as many as fifty—years inside a restrictive, growth-inhibiting relationship. With so many years invested in habituated behaviors, it's only natural that they would be reluctant to change.

THE PROMISED LAND

TO GIVE YOU more insight into our reluctance to change, we want to recount our modified version of the story of Moses and the Promised Land, which we view as a parable of the human psyche.

Many centuries ago, the Israelites were a great tribe of people living in a country near the Mediterranean Sea. Years of punishing drought came to their land. In order to survive, the Israelites migrated south to Egypt, where the bins were full of grain. But in exchange for the grain, they were forced to become slaves to the Egyptians and were subjected to cruel treatment and the dreary labor of making bricks without straw. After more than four hundred years of this meager existence, along came a man named Moses, who said to the Israelites, "Good grief. You're going through painful, repetitive behavior that is getting you nowhere. You've forgotten your heritage. You're not slaves of the house of Egypt, you are the favored children of the great God Yahweh!"

Moses's words stirred a sense of recognition in the Israelites, and they became aware of their mental imprisonment. This made them restless and unhappy—not unlike many of the people who come to us for counseling. Lured by a vision of the Promised Land, the Israelites followed Moses into the wilderness. The Israelites were not prepared for the hardships of the journey, however, and they had little faith in God's protection. When they came to the first obstacle, the Red Sea, they complained bitterly to Moses, "You got us out of our comfortable huts with a promise of a better way of life. Now our way is blocked by an enormous sea! Was it because there were no graves in Egypt that you brought us to the desert to die? What is going to happen to us?"

Moses himself wasn't sure what to do, but he believed that if he had enough faith, a way would appear. While he was pondering their fate, a huge cloud appeared behind them. To the Israelites' horror, they realized it was a dust cloud kicked up by thousands of rapidly approaching Egyptian soldiers, who were coming to capture them and put them back in chains. At this moment, Moses lifted his hand, and miraculously, a strong east wind parted the Red Sea. Awed by this great wonder, the Israelites summoned their courage, took one last look back at Egypt—the only home they had known—and followed Moses fearfully into the watery chasm. They saw immense walls of water to their right and to their left. When they were safely across the seabed, Moses raised his hand once more and the great sea walls collapsed, drowning all the pursuing Egyptians in a torrent of water.

The Israelites had only moments to celebrate their safe passage. As they looked ahead at the new land, they saw that they had arrived on the edge of a barren, trackless desert. Once again, they cried out to Moses, "You disrupted our secure lives. You urged us to follow you on a long journey. We were almost captured by the Egyptians. We were nearly drowned in the Red Sea. And now we are lost in a barren land with no food or water!"

Despite their fears, the Israelites had no choice but to continue. They wandered for many months in the foreign land, guided by a pillar of cloud by day and a pillar of fire by night. They encountered great hardships, but God was merciful and made their burden lighter by performing more miracles.

Finally, the Israelites arrived at the end of the desert. "Just over the ridge," said Moses, "is the Promised Land." Scouts were sent ahead to survey the territory. But when the scouts returned, they brought more bad news. "The Promised Land really does flow with milk and honey, but it is already occupied! This is the home of the Canaanites, gigantic creatures seven feet tall!" The listening crowd cried out in terror and once again yearned for the safety and security of their life in Egypt.

At this point, God spoke to them. "Because you have no faith and because you keep remembering Egypt, you have to wander in the desert for forty years until a new generation arises that does not remember the old ways. Only then can you go into the Promised Land." So for forty more years, the Israelites camped out in the desert. Children were born, and older generations died. Finally, a new leader arose to take them into Israel to begin the hard work of wresting the land from the Canaanites.

How can this familiar story help us in our exploration of love relationships? One of the first truths is that most of us go through our love relationships as if we are asleep, engaging in routine interactions that give us little pleasure. Like the Israelites in their four hundred years of servitude to the Egyptians, we have forgotten who we are. In the words of Wordsworth, we come into the world "trailing clouds of glory," but the light is soon extinguished, and we lose sight of the fact that we are spiritual beings connecting in a tapestry of being. Instead, we live impoverished, repetitious, unrewarding lives and blame our partners for our unhappiness.

The story also teaches us that we are prisoners of the fear of change. When we ask couples to practice new behaviors, they become angry with us. There is a part of them that would rather divorce, break up the family, and divide up all their possessions than acquire a new style of relating. Like the Israelites, they tremble in front of the Red Sea, even though the way lies open to them. Later, when they are in a difficult stretch of the journey, their emotional difficulties seem like hordes of pursuing Egyptians and seven-foot-tall monsters. But unlike the case of the Israelites, the enemy is within; it's the denied and repressed parts of their being threatening to come to awareness.

The final truth in the story of Moses is that we expect life's rewards to come to us easily and without sacrifice. Just as the Israelites wanted the Promised Land to be the Garden of Eden, God's ready-made gift to Adam and Eve, we want the simple act of falling in love to cure all our ills. We want to live in a fairy tale where the beautiful princess meets the handsome prince and they live happily ever after. But it was only when the Israelites saw the Promised Land as an opportunity, as a chance to create a new reality, that they were allowed to enter. And it is only when we see love relationships as a vehicle for change and self-growth that we can begin to satisfy our unconscious yearnings.

What Lies Ahead

THIS CHAPTER MARKS a turning point in the book. Until now, we've been describing the unconscious partnership, a relationship characterized by old-brain reactivity. In the rest of the book, we will explain how to transform your partnership into a safe and joyful union.

Here's an overview of what lies ahead. Chapter 7 explores an old-fashioned idea—commitment—and explains why it is a necessary precondition for emotional growth. Chapter 8 introduces you to our most fundamental process, which helps you discover your partner for the first time. Having this knowledge will help you see your partner as another struggling human being who is seeking joy and fulfillment. Chapter 9 shows you how to rekindle romantic love by bringing back the caring behaviors and loving attention that were characteristic of the early days of your relationship. Chapter 10 helps you identify the unspoken wishes that underlie your criticisms of your partner and then communicate them in ways that are most likely to elicit a positive response. Chapter 11 explains how to create a zone of safety by eliminating negativity from your relationship to the greatest extent possible. When you banish negativity, you are creating the safe and secure environment that is necessary for emotional growth. Chapter 12 introduces two couples who are well on the way to creating a conscious partnership.

Part 3 features a series of exercises that will help you translate the insights you have gained in earlier chapters into logical, practical steps that will help give you the love you want.

COMMITMENT

A life allied with mine, for the rest of our lives—
that is the miracle of marriage.
— DENIS DE ROUGEMONT

YEARS AGO, WHEN we met a couple for the first time, we knew little or nothing about them. All we knew was that they had lost the vital connection between them and were mired somewhere in the power struggle. They might have been anywhere along that path. They might have been newlyweds reeling from the shock that they had married the wrong person. They might have been a middle-aged couple trying to cope with the stress of having two careers, teenage children, and a relationship that was filled with strife. They might have been an older couple who had lost their love and affection for each other and were contemplating a "friendly" divorce. But whatever their circumstances, we assumed that they had journeyed past the romantic stage of their relationship and become unhappy with each other. They had lost something; they wanted it back; but they didn't know how to get it. This is still true today when couples come to our workshops, although we are now seeing more couples take a preventative approach: proactively seeking the tools and knowledge to buffer their relationship from becoming another divorce statistic.

Years ago, the therapists' approach while working with

couples was to wade into the details of their power struggle. In the first few sessions, we would determine whether a couple's main problems centered on communication, sex, money, parenting issues, role expectations, alcohol or drug dependency, and so on. Over the course of the next few months, we would help them gain more insight into their difficulties.

An important part of the therapeutic process was teaching them to communicate their feelings more directly: "Tell Mary how you felt when she said that." Or "Turn to George and explain why you hung up the phone on him." At the end of each session, we would help them negotiate a contract that would specify an agreed-upon course of action. George, for example, would agree to give Mary one compliment a day, and Mary would agree to express her anger in words instead of withdrawing into silence. This was standard problem-oriented, conflict-resolving, contractual relationship counseling. Many therapists still employ these techniques.

The couples learned a lot about each other in the time that we spent together, and they gained valuable communication skills. But to our dismay, few of them were able to transcend the power struggle. Instead of arguing about the issues that brought them into therapy, they began to argue about who had violated the contract first. At times, it seemed as though our function as therapists was to quantify and formalize their conflicts. My (Harville's) work was being supervised in those early days, and I would share my frustration with my adviser. What was I doing wrong? Why were my couples making such slow progress? All I seemed to be doing was giving people something new to fight over. My adviser would smile knowingly and then chide me for having a vested interest in whether or not my clients were able to change. If they wanted to change, he assured me, they would. Perhaps I was confusing my agenda with theirs. My role, he reminded me, was to teach people communication skills, help them gain insight into their problems, and let them go on their way.

Years later, we (Harville and Helen) discovered that relationship therapy cannot dwell on surface issues like money and roles and sexual incompatibility. Underneath these problems is a much larger issue. As one woman once said, "My husband and I had a bigger fight going on that other therapists couldn't help us with. We couldn't put the problem into words, and they couldn't see it. But it was the fuel that ignited all our other conflicts."

This "larger problem" she was referring to is common to most couples who seek help for their relationships. As we talked about earlier, many children experience a rupture in their connection with their caregivers. For one reason or another, their caregivers failed to satisfy their basic needs for safety, affection, and stability. Years later, when they have an intimate partner, a similar rupture can split apart their adult love relationship. The two individuals no longer feel a sense of connection with each other, and they begin to criticize each other or withhold their affection. Learning new communication skills and making behavioral contracts were not going to build the bridge back to intimacy.

We realized that we had to look at relationship therapy in a new way. While mulling it over, we recalled the words of Harry Stack Sullivan, a psychiatrist who wrote *The Interpersonal Theory of Psychiatry* in the 1950s. Sullivan wrote, "It does not matter so much what happens inside an individual. What matters is what happens between them." That brought to mind Martin Buber and his well-known book *I and Thou*. Buber made it clear that his interest was not so much on the "I" and the "Thou"— in other words, on the two individuals—but on the relationship between them, represented by the hyphen between "I" and "Thou," which he called sacred.

As we reflected on Sullivan and Buber, a lightbulb went on in our heads. When we worked with couples, we decided to shift our attention away from the individual partners and their specific concerns to the quality of their interactions. Focusing on the relationship itself would help create a safe and stable connection between them. Significantly, as they became more secure in a new way of relating, they would also be repairing the ruptured connection they had experienced decades earlier with their imperfect caregivers. From a neurological point of view, the old neural pathways formed during painful episodes in their past would be neutralized by new pathways created by the caring interactions with their partners. As we developed this relationship-centered approach, couples began to make remarkable progress.

THE NEED FOR COMMITMENT

VIEWING COUPLES FROM this new relationship paradigm, we quickly learned that one of the necessary first steps was to ask both partners to commit to the process. In therapy, one of the first rules is that they have to agree to come to at least twelve consecutive therapy sessions. Barring emergencies, they are to orchestrate their lives so that they could come to each and every appointment. In workshops, we ask couples to commit the entire weekend to their relationship, practicing and sharing as guided, and to "turn off" the ordinary outside disruptions such as housework, responding to emails, updating statuses on social media, and making nonurgent phone calls. At the end of the weekend, we ask for a ninety-day commitment to specific daily practices.

The reason we ask for a commitment is that we know from our own experience and from statistical surveys that a majority of couples quit therapy before their fifth appointment or give up on new habits within twenty-one to thirty days of implementation. Interestingly, this is about the time it takes for unconscious issues to begin to emerge, which can trigger anxiety. As we know, a tried-and-true method for reducing anxiety is avoidance. Some couples react to their growing anxiety by claiming that therapy is making matters worse, and they fire the therapist. Others report that they "can't find time" to focus on their relationship or keep their appointments. And others still find reasons to quit the practices ("I did all the work"; "I feel like I'm losing myself"; "We are just too different"). A commitment would help counteract this understandable avoidance. A commitment also offers a taste of what is possible when we can give our unconditional and untethered attention to our relationships. Remember, energy follows attention.

When you are working on the exercise section of this book, you may also experience a reluctance to complete the process. Some exercises will be easy for you—even fun. But others will give you new information about yourself and challenge you to grow and change. As you do the more demanding practices, the temptation will be to put the book aside or alter the instructions. It is precisely at these moments that you need to commit yourself wholeheartedly to the process. You will discover that if, before you begin, you make a strong commitment to finish all the exercises and do them exactly as prescribed, it will be easier to overcome your resistance.

Our second order of business is to help couples define their relationship vision. Before we heard all the things they *didn't* like about their relationship, we wanted them to articulate how they would like it to be. In other words, what would it be like if they had the relationship of their dreams? Defining the vision turns their energy away from their past and present disappointments toward a more hopeful future. Achieving their vision is the goal of a conscious relationship.

It is surprisingly easy for couples to create this vision—even those who are in turmoil. To get them started, we ask them to list a series of positive statements beginning with the word *we* that describe the kind of relationship they would like to have. They are to frame these statements in the present tense as if the future were already here. Here are some examples: "We enjoy each other's company," "We are financially secure," "We spend time together doing things we both enjoy," "We spend more time together as a family." Fairly quickly, they are able to define their separate visions, share their statements out loud, identify the common elements in them, and combine them into a shared goal. Once the vision is defined, we ask them to read it daily as a form of meditation. Gradually, through the process of repetition, the vision becomes embedded in their subconscious.

THE COMMITMENT AGREEMENT

AS SOON AS the work on the vision is completed, which is usually about the second or third session, Imago therapists ask couples to make a second commitment, and that is to stay in their relationship for the initial twelve weeks of therapy. For three months, they are neither to separate nor end the relationship in a more catastrophic way, such as by suicide, divorce, or insanity. (Although separation and divorce are by far the most common ways couples contemplate terminating their relationships, a significant minority have a feeling that they might go crazy, and there have been several couples who fantasized about more violent options.) We call the decision to close all these escape routes the Commitment Agreement. When you turn to part 3, you will see that this is one of the first exercises you will be asked to do.[1]

It is common for two people in a love relationship to react to the Commitment Agreement in opposite ways. Typically, one partner feels relieved that they've agreed to stay together for twelve sessions; the other feels threatened. The one who feels relieved is usually the *fuser* in the relationship, the one who grew up with an unsatisfied need for attachment with a neglectful parent. The agreement helps reduce the fuser's fear of abandonment. The one who feels threatened is the *isolator*, the one who had an unsatisfied need for autonomy with an intrusive parent. Having been frustrated in his or her quest for independence, the isolator may feel an upwelling of anxiety about the decision to close all escape hatches.

During the period of this agreement, Imago therapists work to ease the anxiety of clients who feel trapped. We remind them that the commitment is for only three months. At the end of that time, they are free to make other decisions. Because they are dealing with a finite amount of time, most people find they can cope. Furthermore, we explain that when they agree to stay together for three months, their partners may become less clingy or invasive and will not feel the same need to chase after them.

Some couples experience a startling reversal. The person who wants more closeness begins to retreat. The partner who wants more freedom discovers an unmet need for closeness. It's as if the couples collude to maintain a set distance between them. If one person starts encroaching on the other's territory, the other has to back away. If one person starts vacating the territory, the other starts to pursue. As with a pair of magnets with like charges facing each other, there's an invisible force field keeping them a critical distance apart. There is not enough safety in their relationship for them to feel comfortable being more closely connected.

NONCATASTROPHIC EXITS

ONE COUPLE HAD mastered this game of push and pull. Sylvia and Ricardo had so many ways of avoiding each other with activities we refer to as *noncatastrophic* exits that they were rarely together. One indication of their success at staying apart was that they hadn't made love in over three years. Noncatastrophic exits are often difficult to detect; nonetheless, they can drain a great deal of energy—and intimacy—from a relationship.

As an assignment, Sylvia and Ricardo were asked to spend just one day together doing something they both enjoyed. The very next day, which happened to be a Saturday, they agreed to go for a hike in the country and then go out to dinner. That morning, just as they were about to leave the house, Sylvia suggested that they invite a mutual friend along on the hike. It had been a long time since they had seen this friend, she reasoned, and, besides, the friend always liked to get out of the city. Ricardo said that sounded like a bad idea. The whole purpose of the day was to spend time together. They argued heatedly for a good hour; then Ricardo gave in. Sylvia called the friend, who was happy to come along. As they waited for him to show up, Sylvia read the paper and straightened the house, while Ricardo disappeared into the den to work his way through a stack of bills.

The friend arrived, and the three of them got in the car and drove out to the country. On the drive, the two men sat in the front seat of the car—ostensibly because they had longer legs and needed the legroom—while Sylvia sat in the back seat, reading a book. During the hike, either Sylvia or Ricardo talked with the friend, while the other partner tagged along behind.

When they got back to the city, the friend went home and the couple made plans to go out to dinner. They decided to go to a restaurant that featured live entertainment. At the restaurant, Ricardo suggested they choose a table in front of the stage so they could pay attention to the music. They had dinner and tried to carry on a conversation but gave up because the music was so loud they couldn't hear each other. They left the restaurant at precisely a quarter to nine so they could be home in time for a favorite TV show. As soon as they entered the house, they poured themselves a couple of drinks and stationed themselves in front of the television. Sylvia went to bed at eleven o'clock (after ritually urging Ricardo not to drink too much), and Ricardo stayed up until one in the morning, happily nursing his scotch and watching TV.

With consummate skill, they had managed to spend the whole day together without a moment of intimacy. Although they didn't realize it, they were living an invisible divorce.

The Invisible Divorce

TO ONE DEGREE or another, most couples who are involved in a power struggle follow a similar pattern: they structure their lives so that true intimacy is virtually impossible.

The way that they do this can be ingenious. By asking partners a simple question, "What does your spouse do to avoid you?" we have come up with a list of over three hundred different answers. Here's a fraction of that list. According to our informants, their mates were avoiding them by: "reading romance novels," "disappearing into the garage," "facebooking, tweeting, or snapchatting," "camping out on the phone," "worshiping the car," "spending too much time with the kids," "being wedded to the computer," "volunteering for every committee at church," "spending too much time with the boat," "spending time at her mom's," "having an affair," "avoiding eye contact," "spending hours reading the *New York Times,*" "falling asleep on the couch at eight o'clock at night," "being a sports junkie," "coming home late for dinner," "fantasizing while making love," "being sick and tired all the time," "not wanting to be touched," "four scotches a night," "spending too many evenings at the Rotary," "lying," "refusing to make love," "having sex but not making love," "living on the tennis court," "jogging ten miles a day," "going on weekend fishing trips," "going shopping," "having her own apartment," "daydreaming," "refusing to talk," "smoking pot," "playing video games until two in the morning," "talking on the cell phone," "working on the house all the time," "masturbating," "playing his guitar," "keeping separate bank accounts," "picking fights," "reading magazines," "doing crossword puzzles," "refusing to get married," and "going to bars."

The fact that so many couples perforate their relationships with exits raises an obvious question: Why do men and women spend so much time avoiding intimacy? There are two good reasons: anger and fear. Why the anger? In the romantic stage of a relationship, people find it relatively easy to be intimate, because they are filled with the anticipation of wish fulfillment. Their partners seem to be Mommy and Daddy, lovers, and therapists all rolled into one. Months or years later, when they come to the realization that their partners are committed to their own salvation, not theirs, they feel betrayed. A tacit agreement has been broken. In retaliation, they erect an emotional barricade. In effect, they are saying, "I am angry at you for not meeting my needs." Then they begin to seek pleasure and satisfaction outside the relationship. Like a cow in a pen stretching its neck under a fence to graze on green grass, they look elsewhere for gratification. The husband who stays late at the office even when he has finished the day's work, the wife who spends the entire evening reading to the children while her husband watches TV— both of these individuals are trying to find substitute pleasure.

The other reason couples avoid intimacy is fear. On an unconscious level, many people react to their partners as if they were enemies. Any person—whether parent or partner or next-door neighbor—who is perceived by the old brain to be a source of need gratification and then appears to be withholding that gratification is cataloged as a source of pain, and pain raises the specter of death. If your partner does not nurture you and attend to your fundamental needs, a part of you fears that you will die, and it believes that your partner is the one who is allowing this to happen. When a basic lack of nurturing is coupled with an onslaught of verbal and in some cases physical abuse, the partner becomes an even more potent enemy. The unconscious reason some people avoid their partners, therefore, is not that they're looking for greener pastures but that they are fleeing death. The appropriate image in this case is not the bucolic scene of a cow foraging for food but that of a terrified lamb running away from a lion.

In most cases, the fear of the partner is unconscious. All that couples are aware of is a mild feeling of anxiety around each other and a desire to be with other people or to be involved in other activities. Occasionally, the fear is closer to the surface.

One woman told us that the only time she felt truly safe around her husband was when the two of them were in the therapy office. He had never physically abused her, but their relationship was so filled with conflict that a part of her felt that her life was in danger.

NARROWING YOUR EXITS

WHAT DO WE mean by "exits," and why is it important to limit them? Basically, exits are a way to act out our feelings rather than put them into words. As an example, it's easier to stay late at work than to tell your partner that you feel unhappy every time you walk in the front door. You have an understandable reason for staying away—you don't want to feel depressed. Also, it would take a tremendous amount of courage to tell your partner how you really feel about being together. It is far simpler to spend more time with your grandchildren, for example, and avoid the pain and the drama.

But to rebuild their partnership, both partners need to draw their energy back into the relationship. Two people cannot reconnect with each other until they are physically and emotionally available.

To help couples overcome their resistance to narrowing their exits, we rely on the principle known as *graduated change*.[2] You've probably discovered this principle in your own life. It is easier to tackle a difficult project if you divide it into small, manageable tasks. You can then rank the tasks in order of difficulty and attend to the easy ones first. Graduated change makes the entire project seem more manageable.

In part 3, you will find complete instructions for narrowing and then closing or modifying your exits. We want to emphasize that this is an ongoing process and not a onetime event. Basically, it involves talking with each other about your feelings rather than avoiding each other.

Here is an overview of how it works. Imagine two people who are trapped in an unsatisfying relationship. To make up for their emptiness, they have filled their lives with substitute pleasures. The woman is engaged in her career and has two children. In addition, she has an active social life, a position on the community board, a passion for physical fitness, and an addiction to science fiction novels. These activities help reduce her underlying feelings of despair, but they drain vital energy away from her marriage.

If this woman were to decide to cut back on some of her activities, she would first have to determine which of her numerous involvements could properly be termed an exit. Like many people, she would probably find a degree of validity in virtually everything she did. When you do the commitment exercise in part 3, you may have this same confusion: What is an exit, and what is an essential activity or a valid form of recreation? The way to find out is to ask yourself the following question: "Is one of the main reasons I'm doing this activity to avoid spending time with my partner?" Most people know whether or not this is the case. If the answer is yes, that makes the activity an exit and a potential topic of conversation with your partner.

Let's suppose that this woman has asked herself this question and identified activities that she would be willing to curtail or eliminate. Next, she could rank them according to difficulty and choose the ones that would be easiest for her to give up. For example, she might decide to jog three days a week instead of five and to read her novels on her lunch hour, not in the evenings when she could be spending time with her husband. She might also decide that it would be difficult but not impossible for her to find someone to take over her position on the community board. Other changes would be even more difficult. If she were to go ahead and make the two easy changes, however, she would be liberating several hours a week to devote to her relationship. This would be a good place to start. Other changes, if necessary, could come later.

At the same time, her husband would be going through a similar process. He, too, would be examining his activities, identifying his exits, asking for a conversation about those exits, and beginning a systematic program of reduction. As a result of this exercise, they would be spending significantly more time together.

As we have said, and it bears repeating, the commitment to closing an exit is not a specific event that occurs at a particular moment. It is a process that may take considerable time, sometimes several months. It requires a lot of soul-searching for people to identify their own exits and the reasons behind them. Then it takes courage to discuss the exits with their partners. But paradoxically, once the conversation has taken place, the exits become easier to narrow and eventually close. Talking openly about them creates a deeper sense of connection between the couple and reduces their need to stay isolated.

TILL DEATH DO US PART

WHEN WE LEAD couples through these series of commitments—an agreement to: (1) come to a minimum of twelve therapy sessions or to a full weekend workshop, (2) define their relationship vision, (3) stay together for a specified period of time, and (4) gradually commit to closing their exits—we let them know that all these separate agreements can lead to a larger commitment: a decision to join together in a journey that will last the rest of their lives.

Although this decision cannot be made when couples are in pain, we want them to know that they need to stay together not for three months or three years or even three decades but for all their remaining years in order to reap all the benefits of a conscious partnership. Childhood issues do not present themselves to be resolved in one tidy package. They come to the surface slowly, usually the more superficial ones first. Sometimes a problem has to present itself a number of times before it is even identified as a significant issue. And sometimes a psychological need is so deeply buried that it is only triggered by a crisis or the demands of a particular stage of life. Ultimately, it takes a lifetime together for a couple to identify and heal the majority of their childhood wounds.

In a culture where serial monogamy is a way of life, the idea of a permanent commitment to one partner has a quaint, old-fashioned ring to it. The prevalent question of the 1950s—"Can this relationship be saved?"—has become "Should this relationship be saved?" And millions of people decide that the answer is no. In fact, ironically, many people now view divorce as an opportunity for personal growth. It's not within a relationship that people grow and change, according to this increasingly popular view, it's when the relationship falls apart. People believe that separation opens their eyes to their self-defeating behaviors and gives them an opportunity to resolve those problems with a new partner. But unless they understand the unconscious desires that motivated their dysfunctional behavior in the first relationship and learn how to satisfy those desires with the new partner, the second relationship is destined to run aground on the same submerged rocks.

Ironically, the more that we have become involved in a psychological study of love relationships, the more we find ourselves siding with the more conservative proponents of love relationships. We have come to believe that couples should make every effort to honor their vows to stay together "till death do us part"—not for moral reasons but for psychological ones: fidelity and commitment create a zone of safety that allows couples to resolve their long-standing issues and become joyfully alive and connecting.

DISCOVERING YOUR PARTNER

And ye shall know the truth,
and the truth shall make you free.
—JOHN 8:32

ONCE A COUPLE has made a commitment to stay together and work on their relationship, the next logical step is to help them become allies, not enemies. It's fruitless to take two people who are angry with each other and try to lead them along a path of spiritual and psychological growth—they would spend too much time trying to knock each other off the road. In order to make the surest and fastest progress toward their relationship vision, they need to become friends and helpmates.

But how is this going to happen? How can couples put an end to their power struggle when they haven't had the opportunity to resolve their fundamental differences?

Although we all agree in principle that our partners have their own points of view and their own valid perceptions, at the emotional level, we are reluctant to accept this simple truth. We like to believe that the way we see the world is the way the world is. When our partners disagree with us, it is tempting to think that they are ill-informed or have a distorted point of view. How else could they be so wrong?

Some people are particularly entrenched in their private view of the world. This was especially true for Gene. The director of a successful corporation, he was very bright and accustomed to dominating those around him with the sheer force of his intellect. He totally eclipsed his wife, a gentle and good-hearted woman named Judy, who would sit beside him with her chin drawn in and her shoulders hunched forward, looking like a chastened child.

One of my (Harville's) objectives during their initial therapy sessions was to bolster Judy so that she would have enough courage to express her opinions in front of her imposing husband. (In psychology textbooks, this is called *implementing the therapeutic balance.*) Normally, as soon as she would utter a few sentences, Gene would pounce on her and refute whatever she had to say. "That's a lie! That's absolutely not true," he would blurt out. Then he would launch into a defense of his position. His summation was invariably the same: "This is not just my opinion. It happens to be the literal truth." And it was obvious he truly believed that his point of view was the only valid one, that he alone had a grip on reality.

It was pointless to try to convince him verbally of the narrowness of his vision; he would have turned our conversation into a forensic debate, and I had no doubt who would win. At the beginning of our eighth session together, however, I had a sudden inspiration. Judy had just ventured an opinion about a recent encounter between Gene and his father. Apparently, she and Gene and her father-in-law had gone out to dinner together, and Gene's father had said something to Gene that had wounded his pride. Judy's perception was that Gene's father had been trying to give him some constructive criticism; Gene's perception was that his father had been cruel and spiteful. "You are wrong again, Judy," Gene intoned. "How could you be so blind?"

I interrupted their conversation and told them that I wanted them to put their differences of opinion aside for a moment and spend ten minutes listening to a classical music tape that I happened to have in the office, a recording of Franck's Violin

Sonata in A Major. I slipped the tape into the cassette player and invited them to listen to the music and pay attention to any images that came to their minds. They both were a little puzzled by my request, and I sensed an impatience in Gene: How was listening to music going to help them resolve their difficulties? But by now, Gene had enough confidence in me to allow me to run the therapy sessions; he figured there must be some reason for my unusual suggestion.

The three of us sat back and listened to the music. I stopped the tape after the second movement and, knowing full well that I was walking into a minefield, casually asked Judy and Gene what they thought of the music.

Gene spoke first. "What a lovely piece," he said. "It was so lyrical. I especially enjoyed the violin part in the first movement." He hummed several bars, and I was impressed by his ability to remember the notes and to hum them on key. Among his numerous attributes, he apparently had perfect pitch. "Such a beautiful melody," he continued. "For some reason, the image that came to my mind was of the ocean. There were qualities to the music that reminded me of a Debussy sonata. Even though Franck is less impressionistic, there is the same sensuous texture. It must be the French heritage."

I turned to Judy and asked for her opinion.

"That's funny," she said in a voice that was so low I had to strain to hear her. "I had a different feeling about the music." She burrowed deeper into the leather armchair, showing no desire to elaborate. How could she measure up to her husband's learned critique?

"Tell me what you saw in it, Judy," I urged. "I'd like to know what you were thinking, too."

"Well," she said, clearing her throat, "I guess the music seemed kind of stormy to me. Especially the piano part. All those chords, I got the image of storm clouds and wind—and a darkening sky."

"Honey, what makes you think it was so dramatic?" Gene

asked in the patronizing tone of voice he reserved for his wife. "I almost fell asleep, it was so soothing. Listen to it more closely, Judy, and you'll see what I mean. It has to be one of the most lyrical pieces of music ever written. Don't you agree, Dr. Hendrix?" (Like many people, he spent a great deal of time trying to get his therapist to see his side of the story.)

"Yes, I do, Gene," I said, obliging him. "I sensed a gentleness to the music, a romantic quality that at times was very soothing." Then I turned to Judy and said, "But I also agree with you, Judy. There were parts that seemed to have a real sense of passion and drama. I guess I'm agreeing with both of you." Gene started drumming his fingers on the arm of his chair.

"I have an idea," I said. "Why don't the two of you listen to the tape again, but this time, I want you to see if you can find evidence that supports your partner's point of view. Gene, I want you to look for the dramatic tension; Judy, see if you can find the lighter, poetic touches."

I rewound the tape, and they listened to the piece for the second time. Once again, I asked for their opinions. This time both Gene and Judy heard qualities in the sonata that had previously eluded them. Gene made an interesting observation. The first time he had listened to the sonata, he said, he had been instinctively drawn to the violin. When he forced himself to pay more attention to the piano, he could see why he and Judy had had such different initial reactions. "There is a lot of tension to the music," he conceded, "especially in those piano arpeggios in the beginning of the second movement. That was a beautiful passage that slipped by me the first time through. My mind must have been on something else. I can see how someone might think the music was stormy." Judy, meanwhile, had been able to understand Gene's first impression. The music hadn't seemed so overwhelming to her the second time around. "There are some lovely, quiet parts," she said. "In fact, the whole first movement is really quite subdued."

By listening to the music from each other's point of view, they had learned that the sonata was a richer piece of music than either of them had first perceived. There were serene passages and dramatic passages; it was complex, multifaceted.

Given their new spirit of cooperation, I guided Gene and Judy back through a discussion of Gene's encounter with his father. Gene was able to entertain the idea that there had been some goodwill behind his father's criticism. Perhaps he had been screening out his father's good intentions, just as he had screened out the piano part to the Franck sonata. Judy, in turn, gained a greater appreciation for the long-term tension between father and son. When she mentally reviewed the dinner conversation in the context of the troubled history between Gene and his father, she could understand why her husband had been so upset by what had at first seemed to her to be a casual, well-intentioned remark. All of a sudden, they had binocular, not monocular, vision.

This mirrors what couples experience when they are in the power struggle and is the fundamental problem of all relationships: the inability to see the other. If we could summarize the human condition, it would look something like this:

- We live in a connecting universe.
- We experience a rupture in this fundamental reality sometime during childhood due to neglectful or intrusive parenting.
- As a result of this rupture, we experience anxiety, become self-absorbed, and develop elaborate defense systems to protect ourselves (remember: pain = danger).
- This self-absorption prevents us from seeing other "truths" if they seem different from our own and cuts off our ability to feel empathy.

This becomes the challenge: to understand that your partner has a valid point of view and that reality is larger and more complex than either of you will ever know. All you can do is form impressions of the world—take more and more snapshots, each time aiming for a closer approximation of the truth. But one thing is certain. If you respect each other's point of view and see it as a way to enrich your own, you will be able to take clearer, more accurate pictures.

To Know Is to Not Know

WHEN YOU ACCEPT the limited nature of your own perceptions and become more receptive to the truth of your partner's perceptions, a whole world opens up to you. Instead of seeing your partner's differing views as a source of conflict, you realize that they are a source of knowledge: "What are you seeing that I am not seeing?" "What have you learned that I have yet to learn?" Relationships give you the opportunity to be continually schooled in your own reality and in the reality of another person. Every one of your interactions contains a grain of truth, a sliver of insight, a glimpse into your hiddenness and your essential connectedness. As you add to your growing fund of knowledge, you are creating reality love, a love based on the emerging truth of yourself and your partner, not on romantic illusion.

In chapter 6, we discussed a number of specific areas in which you can increase your knowledge. You have the opportunity to become more aware of the hidden agenda you bring to your relationship, of your partner's inner world, and of the healing potential of your relationship. As you can see from this brief look at Judy and Gene's relationship, acquiring this information depends to a large degree on your willingness to value and learn from each other's perceptions. Once both of you demonstrate a desire to expand your individual conceptions of the world, the details of everyday life become a gold mine of information.

One of the ways to deepen each other's perceptions is to "un-know" your partner, a willingness to move from judgment to curiosity and wonder. One of the things I (Helen) was proud of in my early relationship with Harville was that I knew him so well, I would tell him (or anyone that would listen) what he thought, felt, or needed, without him having to ask. Coming out of a painful divorce from my first husband, I was determined to truly pay attention so that I could anticipate his every need. While this came from an earnest place, Harville seemed to be resentful of my assumptions. I remember one of the turning points for me. It was a day where I stopped the stories in my own head about what he needed and felt and, instead, sat with him and asked him how he was feeling overall—about his work, his life, and his goals for the future. He paused, started reflecting with me, and he ended up talking—with me just listening (and occasionally repeating back his words)—for hours. Then he said, "Helen, just sharing with you like this means so much. I don't want all your gifts and efforts. I just want you to be present for my experience of things." My being present to his experience, wondering and asking, "Is there more?" allowed Harville to feel far safer in our relationship. Harville wanted me to be curious, to wonder about how he was feeling on the deepest level. This began a whole new transformation in our relationship and an important addition to our work with couples.

The un-knowing process is an essential step in transforming your relationship. It's a paradox. The only way to discover your partner is to first not know them. You don't assume you know what your partner wants. You don't negate what they feel. You listen and invite them to share their experience. You move into the stance of curiosity. But how do you move from this abstract concept into practice? How do you stop the internal and incessant chatter in order to discover your partner? Simply, you need to discover your partner—as separate from you.

UNDERSTANDING YOUR PARTNER'S
INNER WORLD

THROUGHOUT THE COURSE of your relationship, your partner has given you thousands of hours of testimony about his or her thoughts and feelings and wishes, but you have in turn registered only a fraction of this information. In order to deepen your understanding of your partner's subjective reality, you need to train yourself to listen and communicate more effectively.

To do this, it helps to know something about semantics, the science of describing what words mean. Even though you and your partner speak the same language, each of you dwells in an idiosyncratic world of private meanings. Growing up in different families with different life experiences has given you separate lexicons. As a trivial example, let's explore what the simple words *Let's play tennis* might mean in two different families. In family A, the full, unspoken definition of this phrase is: "Let's grab any old racket that happens to be lying around, walk to the local park, and lob the ball back and forth across the net until someone wants to quit. Rules are secondary; it's the exercise that counts." In family B, however, *Let's play tennis* has quite a different meaning. It means: "Let's reserve an indoor court at the private club, get out our $200 rackets, and then play tough, competitive tennis until one player is clearly the winner." Mark, raised in family A, is going to be taken aback by the aggressiveness and determination that his wife, Susan, raised in family B, brings to the game.

A less trivial example would be the associations that Mark and Susan might bring to the phrase *Let's talk about it.* Assume that in Susan's family *Let's talk about it* means "All the adults sit around the table and calmly and rationally discuss their various points of view until they come up with an agreed-upon plan of action." In Mark's family, the same words mean "This is a topic that we will talk about briefly and then shelve until further notice."

Underlying Mark's family's more casual approach is the philosophy that even the most difficult problems work themselves out over time. When Susan proposes to Mark that they "talk about" the fact that their son is getting poor marks at school, and Mark says a few sentences and then switches on the TV, she feels irate. Mark, in turn, is going to be stunned when Susan storms out the door and does not return for several hours. What did he do wrong? What he did wrong was assume that he and his wife shared the same unspoken language.

When our partners behave in ways that deviate from our idealized view of them, we have an arsenal of weapons to help us maintain our illusions. We can condemn them: "You are a bad (ungrateful, insensitive, boorish, stupid, spiteful, uninformed, crass, unenlightened, etc.) person for feeling that way." We can "educate" them: "You don't really feel that way. What you really feel is . . ." We can threaten them: "Unless you change your mind, I'm going to . . ." We can ignore them: "Uh-huh. Very interesting. As I was saying . . ." And we can analyze them: "The reason you have such unacceptable thoughts and feelings is that years ago your mother . . ." In all these responses, we are trying to diminish our partners' sense of self and replace it with our own self-serving illusion. Unfortunately, this is exactly what happened to our partners in childhood. In dozens of ways, their caretakers told them, "Only some of your feelings are valid. Only a portion of your behaviors are permitted." Instead of helping our partners repair this emotional damage, we add further injury.

THE IMAGO DIALOGUE

TO MOVE BEYOND this tragic state of affairs, we have to learn a new way of talking, which, as you will soon see, is also a new way of knowing. Earlier, we mentioned that there was one core skill that all couples needed to learn in order to create the conscious relationship. We call this new way *Imago Dialogue.* Imago Dialogue involves three different steps—mirroring, validating, and empathizing.

The Imago Dialogue plays a number of roles in the creation of a conscious partnership. First of all, it focuses your attention on the actual words your partner is saying. If you are like most people, you do not pay full attention when your partner is talking. When you should be listening, you are instead responding to the impact of what you are hearing: "My partner just said that he wants a separate vacation. What does that mean? Does he want to spend less time around me? Is he going to meet someone else?" In a sense, you are listening to yourself react. When you focus on your inner reaction instead of on the words your partner is saying, your partner senses that disconnect. Second, when you listen carefully and then ask your partner what those words mean to him or her, you discover that you do indeed live with another person, someone whose inner experience is quite different from yours. This awareness is called *differentiation,* and it is a necessary precondition for a safe, intimate relationship. While there are many similarities in nature—leaves on the same tree, for example, are very similar to one another—no two leaves are the same. Difference is a fact of nature. When you assume that your partner is identical to you, you are negating your partner's existence. In a healthy relationship, you realize that you live with another person who is not an extension of you. Your partner is a unique individual who has an equally valid point of view. Failure to recognize each other's separate existence is the major source of conflict between partners.

Finally, the regular use of the Imago Dialogue creates a deep emotional connection between you and your partner. This is especially true when you are in conflict. Using this structured way of talking creates emotional safety, which is necessary for a lasting connection. When you feel safe, your defenses relax. You become aware of parts of yourself that have been hidden from view since childhood, and you sense enough trust in the relationship to express them: "I really am musical." "I am basically a peaceful person." When you put these experiences into words, they are rewoven into the fabric of your being, and you feel fully alive and joyfully connecting. Ultimately, this experience extends beyond your personal boundaries and helps restore your experience of original connecting. When talking together reaches this profound level, it becomes a spiritual experience. When you connect at the local level of a personal relationship, you connect at the cosmic level with the transcendent.

THE SETUP

BEFORE BEGINNING AN Imago Dialogue, when you (the Sender) want to share something with your partner (the Receiver), you first check to see if this is a good time to talk, using something like, "I would love to talk about an experience I had at work today. Is now a good time?" If now is not a good time, the Receiver can say something like, "Not now, but I can be available in an hour."

Requesting an appointment might feel awkward and formal, but it honors your partner's boundaries, allowing him or her to be fully available to listen to you. It also helps you develop the necessary muscle to be more intentional rather than reactive (especially around a difficult topic), preventing you from dumping on your partner "in the heat of the moment."

When the time mutually works, you both face each other, make eye contact, and take three deep breaths—which induces calming affects throughout the body.

When we coach couples in our workshops, before beginning an Imago Dialogue, we also guide the Sender to use Sender Responsibility:

1. Use *I* language: For example, instead of blurting out, "You made me feel so ashamed when you treated our neighbor that

way," you say, "I felt ashamed when you treated our neighbor that way."

2. Avoid all criticism: Instead of making critical remarks about your partner's character, focus instead on how you experience your partner's behavior. Instead of saying, "You are always late. You have no sense of responsibility," you say, "When you are late, I feel frustrated and scared."

Being a responsible Sender is just as important as being a good listener, and it is essential for maintaining safety in the Space Between.

THE THREE STEPS OF THE IMAGO DIALOGUE

AFTER AGREEING TO a time and reviewing the Imago Dialogue rules, now you can begin the Dialogue process. Let's take a closer look at the three steps of the Imago Dialogue.

Mirroring

THE FIRST STEP is called *mirroring*. You begin by stating that thought or feeling in a short sentence beginning with *I*. For example, "I don't enjoy cooking dinner for you when you don't seem to appreciate all the effort involved." Your partner restates the sentence, using either "word for word" or an accurate paraphrase and then asks if the message was received correctly. "Let me see if I got it. You find it hard to put the effort into cooking dinner every night when I don't show my appreciation for all that you've done. Did I get you?" You repeat this process until your partner clearly understands what you mean to say.

Mirroring, like many of the tools we use in Imago Relationship Therapy, had its origin in our relationship when we were engaged in an intense discussion, determined to get our points across. Suddenly, Helen paused the conversation and said, "Stop. We're not listening to each other. I have an idea. Why don't we take turns talking and listening? You can talk while I listen. Then I'll say back to you what I heard. Then we can switch. I'll talk, and you listen." We were not strangers to the value of listening, but, as was often the case in our early relationship, we seldom practiced what we preached. We ended up having a very good conversation. In fact, we felt unusually close to each other.

Mirroring is designed to help each of you understand what the other is saying. It involves listening to your partner's comments, restating them without altering their meaning, and then asking for confirmation that you "got it." Mirroring is elementary in the dual meaning of the word: it is both simple and basic.

Mirroring alone is a potent tool for creating an I-Thou relationship. To mirror your partner, you have to turn down the volume on your own thoughts so that you can listen attentively; you have to switch the channel from "me" to "you." With this shift in focus, you are telling your partner, in effect, "I am no longer the sole person in the universe. I am acknowledging your separate existence. Your thoughts are important to me."

Mirroring also requires us to listen accurately. You can't be like a fun house mirror and twist your partner's thoughts, leave out important details, or embellish them with your own. If you commit one of these common errors, your partner is to coach you until you get it right. "You got part of it right, but you left out what I said about my feelings." Asking for confirmation is humbling and tedious, but it's the best way to know if you truly understand what your partner is saying.

Just as important, asking for confirmation empowers your partner. They get to persist until you interpret the message correctly. Very few of us had this latitude as young children. Whether or not we were understood was dependent on the mood and presence of mind of the adults around us. They could diminish what we had to say, ignore it, counter with their own views, or shame us for even daring to express it. Sadly, many people perpetuate this pattern in their daily conversations with their partners.

Mirroring stops this destructive pattern in its tracks. When you mirror each other, you both get to experience what it is like to have someone pay close attention to you, understand exactly what you have to say, and honor your uniqueness. But mirroring goes deeper than that. Unbeknownst to you, your old brain, your unconscious mind, pays close attention as you work your way through this exercise. Having no sense of time and unable to make a clear distinction between individuals, your unconscious mind perceives the attention and respect you are receiving as coming from a caregiver, not just from your present-day intimate partner, and vice versa. As a result, a few repair stitches are made in the ruptured connections you both experienced in childhood.

After checking for accuracy, and the Receiver got the Sender's message "right," the Receiver then asks, "Is there more about that?" This gives the Sender a chance to expand on the topic. "It takes me at least an hour to cook dinner, and I do my best to make it attractive and delicious. I feel sad when you eat without comment." The Sender continues adding more information until he or she has no more to say.

We consider the "Is there more about that?" phrase truly magical. It's a wonderful feeling to have your partner's full attention and to be asked to reveal even more about what you are thinking and feeling. Very few of us had caregivers who expressed much curiosity about our inner world. We were most visible to them when we excelled or when we caused trouble. Our partners' keen interest in our thoughts helps repair those feelings of neglect from long ago. This, in turn, makes us feel much safer in our partner's presence, and we begin to discover parts of ourselves that have been hidden since childhood. We become more visible, safe, and connected.

You benefit in another way as well, because you gain enough additional information about your partner that you can more fully comprehend his or her point of view. Meanwhile, your partner discovers that being encouraged to keep on talking can bring up thoughts and feelings that he or she hasn't been able to put into words before. Saying them out loud at long last helps your partner share their story.

Although mirroring is a relatively straightforward process, it is very different from the way that couples normally talk to each other, a phenomenon that might be called a *parallel monologue*. Breaking the old habits can require a great deal of practice. Here's an example of the common problems that people have with mirroring (it's also a good example of a parallel monologue). The following conversation took place at a *Getting the Love You Want* Couples' Workshop. We asked if there was a couple that was willing to volunteer to come to the front of the group and talk about a sensitive issue, just as they would at home. Greg and Sheila, a young couple who had been living together for only a few months, volunteered. Greg started the conversation.

GREG: Sheila, I'm really bothered by your smoking, and I'd like you to be more considerate when you smoke around me.

Because I had yet to introduce Sheila and Greg to the mirroring exercise, Sheila followed her natural instincts and responded with an automatic defense.

SHEILA: You knew that I smoked when you asked me to live with you. You accepted that fact in the beginning. Why are you always so critical of me? You should accept me as I am. You know that I'm trying to cut down.

Greg, operating on automatic pilot, returned her remarks with an intensified criticism. The conversation was turning into a tennis match.

GREG: I acknowledge your efforts to smoke less. But I find it interesting that, when we come here and the sign in the dining room says No Smoking, you follow it. Yet I feel invaded at home with the smell of tobacco smoke all over the place.

SHEILA: Well, this is not my home. And I feel I have a right to smoke in my own home!

Sheila delivered this last message with some force, and there was a smattering of applause from the crowd. The score was love-fifteen. It was time for me to referee.

HENDRIX: OK. Let's start this all over again and see if we can turn it into an exercise in connection, not confrontation. Greg, would you repeat your opening statement?

GREG: I'm really glad that we're making a home together, but with regard to your smoking, when we joined together, I didn't realize how difficult it was going to be for me.

HENDRIX: OK. Now I would like you to simplify that statement so it will be easier to understand.

GREG: Let's see . . . Your smoking bothers me. I didn't think it would at first, but it does.

HENDRIX: Good. Now, Sheila, I want you to paraphrase Greg, trying to mirror his feelings and thoughts without criticizing him or defending yourself. Then I want you to ask Greg if you have heard him correctly.

SHEILA: I'm truly sorry that my smoking interferes—

HENDRIX: No, I'm not asking you to apologize. Just reflect back to Greg what he was saying and show your understanding and acceptance of his feelings.

SHEILA: Could he possibly repeat himself?

GREG: Your smoking bothers me. I didn't think it would at first, but it does.

HENDRIX: Now try to feed that back to him with receptive warmth.

SHEILA: I think I'd rather stop smoking! (*Group laughter*)

HENDRIX: Take a deep breath and be aware that he is experiencing some discomfort at one of your behaviors. Rather than hearing it as a criticism of your behavior, hear it with concern for his well-being. Whether it's justified or not, he is feeling uncomfortable, and you care about him. I know this is hard to do in front of a lot of people, and I know that this is an issue you feel strongly about.

SHEILA: What could be done—

HENDRIX: No, don't try to solve it. You just want to paraphrase his message and the emotional content behind it, so that he knows that you understand what he is feeling.

SHEILA: (*Takes a deep breath*) OK. I think I get it now. I understand that it really bothers you that I smoke. You didn't realize how much it would bother you until we actually started living together. Now you are very troubled by it. Is that what you are saying?

HENDRIX: Excellent. I could hear Greg's concern reflected in your voice. Did that check out with you, Greg? Is she hearing what you have to say?

GREG: Yes! (*I could see his facial muscles relax.*) That's just how I feel. What a relief! This is the first time she's ever really bothered to listen to me.

As Greg's reaction shows, there is a tremendous satisfaction in simply being heard, in knowing that your message has been received exactly as you sent it. This is a rare phenomenon in most relationships. After demonstrating this exercise for workshop groups, couples in the room practice sending and receiving simple statements. Invariably, they return to the group reporting that it was a novel, exhilarating experience. It is such an unexpected luxury to have your partner's full attention.

Once there is "no more," we ask the Receiver to summarize everything they have heard thus far. "Let me see if I got it all." This summary mirror is the bridge to the next step in Dialogue.

Validating

ONCE COUPLES HAVE become adept at mirroring each other, we encourage them to go on to the next step of the Imago Dialogue: *validating*. In this part of the exercise, couples learn how to affirm the internal logic of each other's remarks. In essence, they are telling each other, "What you're saying makes sense to me. I can see how you are thinking and why you would think that way."

I (Harville) had my first and most indelible experience with the power of validation when I was a young man. It was 1960, and I had been sent to Louisville, Kentucky, to be a chaplain in a mental hospital where I was assigned to a ward for schizophrenic patients. I was given very little training in the beginning. Basically I was told, "Go in there and relate the best you can." As time went on, I would be given more supervision, but in the first few weeks, it was sink or swim. One of the first patients I tried to get to know was a gaunt man in his fifties whom I will call Leonard. Leonard was a chain-smoker. I always saw him through a veil of smoke. But the reason he has stayed in my mind all these years is that he was convinced he was Jesus.

"Hello, Leonard," I said to him when we were first introduced. "My name is Harville."

"I'm Jesus," he replied calmly, drawing on his cigarette, "not Leonard."

I was taken aback, but I covered up my reaction. "Oh," I said. "I'm a theological student, so I have a different concept of Jesus. But I'm pleased to meet you."

As the days went on, I found myself drawn to Leonard, primarily because I was so fascinated by his unshakable conviction that he was Jesus. I didn't try to convince him otherwise because I could see it would have been pointless. I just studied his internal logic. Eventually, Leonard began to feel safe enough with me to share some of the voices inside his head. When I found out exactly what the voices were saying to him and that those voices were as real to him as the words coming out of my mouth, Leonard's view of himself as Jesus began to make complete sense to me. I hasten to add that I didn't think he was Jesus, but I could see why *he* thought that he was. It made all the sense in his world.

The day came when I decided to address Leonard as Jesus. This didn't seem blasphemous to me. Indeed, it seemed a form of respect. Why add yet more conflict to his life when his head was already a battleground? If he thought he was Jesus, I was going to go along with it. I walked up to him that morning and said, "Hello, Jesus." To my surprise, he said, "I'm not Jesus. I'm Leonard." I sputtered for a moment and said, "But you've been telling me for weeks that you're Jesus!"

"Yes," he said, "but my voices are now telling me that I don't have to be Jesus with you." Validation had moved him one step closer to sanity.

Once you have listened to your partner and fully understand what they have to say, you then strive to see how their thoughts make sense to them. You do not have to agree with your partner. You need to see them as they are, not as you wish them to be. Many people spend much of their time trying to get their partners to think the same way they do—this is a common obstacle to experiencing connection—but it is important that you affirm the logic of your partner's thinking—to see your partner as an "other" and no longer an extension of yourself: "You are not crazy. From all that I'm learning about you, I can see why you think that way." Many of us had parents who could not transcend their own worldviews. If we didn't agree with them or heed their advice, they ignored us or implied that we were stupid, misguided, rebellious, disrespectful, or crazy. The fact that two quite different points of view could be equally valid— especially opposing views between a parent and child—was beyond their comprehension. Validating establishes the fact that there are two realities; both are correct.

Even today, we are impressed by how aggressively each of

us defends our separate reality. It is connected to our fear of the loss of self. If I see it your way, I will have to surrender my way. If I feel your experience, I will have to invalidate mine. If what you say is true, then what I say must be false. There can be only one center of the universe, and that center is me! (Essentially, as we say in our workshops, "You and I are one, and I am the one!") But if I muster the courage to suspend my own point of view for a moment and then manage to see a fraction of your reality, something miraculous happens. First of all, you feel safer around me. Because I am no longer challenging your worldview, you can start to lower your defenses. As you do this, you become more willing to acknowledge a portion of my reality. Because I have abandoned my centrist position, you are more willing to let go of yours. To our mutual surprise, a drawbridge begins to descend on its rusty hinges, and you and I connect.

Empathizing

THE THIRD AND final step in Imago Dialogue is *empathizing*. It makes sense that empathy would follow on the heels of validation. If you listen carefully to your partner, understand the totality of what he or she is saying, and then affirm the logic behind your partner's words, you are ready to acknowledge and respond to the feelings behind those thoughts. Your first task is to try to imagine what those feelings might be. If your partner's feelings are conveyed beyond his or her words, by facial expression or tone of voice, you will have little trouble intuiting them. If your partner's feelings are not so obvious, you will have to imagine what they might be. In either case, you need to check with your partner to see if you perceived their feelings accurately. "Given the fact that you said I neglected you, I'm wondering if you feel hurt by my neglect. Is that how you feel?" Checking to confirm the accuracy respects your partner's reality and enhances your emotional "presence," an essential ingredient of healing.

Asking for confirmation also deepens your partner's experience of empathy; they will think, *My partner is being very respectful of my feelings. They care how I really feel.*

For some people, validation of their thought processes is more important to them than validation of their feelings. But for others, empathy is the key to their healing. Once someone affirms their raw emotions, they begin to feel loved and connected. Historically, women have tended to value empathy more than men. In our culture, indeed in most cultures, women are encouraged to express their feelings more freely than men. Although this is changing, many men still believe (or are taught to believe) it is unmanly to disclose their emotions, especially their tender feelings or feelings of fear and weakness, preferring instead to focus on steely logic. But regardless of the category into which either partner falls, it is still generally the case that one person in a relationship is more attuned with their emotional expressions while the other gravitates more toward their logical side.

When couples master the three-step process of mirroring, validating, and empathizing, these differences begin to diminish. A person who is emotionally repressed starts to value empathy as much as their partner. Simultaneously, a person who is emotionally volatile can become less so because they no longer need to amplify their feelings in order to have their stoic partner acknowledge them. This is especially true for anger. It is always surprising to us to see how quickly anger will dissipate once it's been received and fully acknowledged.

As you might imagine, the ease with which you can empathize with your partner depends a great deal on the situation. It's very easy to be sympathetic when the two of you share the same experience and react similarly to that event. Let's suppose we have just been through a major earthquake. We survived the quake without any injuries, and we are relieved to see that the house still stands on its foundation. But there were several frightening minutes when we both thought we were going to die. "I was so terrified!"

your partner exclaims. You respond immediately, "I can see that you were! I was, too!" Because you've had the same response to the same situation, there is no stretching involved. What you feel, I feel. We had the same reaction.

Empathy is a more challenging response. It is the ability to understand what another person is experiencing even though you have not had that identical experience. Let's assume that your partner was in the earthquake but you were gone on business five hundred miles away. Your partner reaches you on the phone, describes the horrific event, and then cries out to you, "I was so terrified!" Although you didn't experience the earthquake yourself, it's not too much of a stretch to imagine that you might have been terrified as well. "I can imagine you were," you reply with only a moment's hesitation.

Problems tend to arise when two people react quite differently to similar events. For example, your partner might be terrified of flying, but you can fall asleep during takeoff or landing. You're going to have a harder time empathizing with your partner's fear because you've never experienced it in this situation. "Just breathe deeply," you tell your partner. "Think about something else, and the feelings will go away." And quite frankly, you wish that they would disappear. They seem so irrational. You want to deflect your partner's feelings, not empathize with them.

The most difficult situation of all, however, may be those times when your partner has strong, negative emotions, and you, poor soul, seem to have triggered them. "I am so angry at you that you told Janice she could go to the movies when you know I already told her she has to stay home and clean her room! You always do this!" Or "I felt so humiliated when I saw you flirting with Paul in front of all our friends. You know how jealous that makes me!" Your instinctual response is to defend yourself and then counterattack. Being empathetic is the furthest thing from your mind. To do so requires tremendous discipline, practice, and emotional maturity.

The word *empathy* comes from the German term *Einfuhlung*,

which means "to feel as one with." When you and your partner are empathic with each other, you are as emotionally close as two people can be. As the poet Rumi said, "Out beyond ideas of wrong doing and right doing, there is a field. I will meet you there."

THE POWER OF IMAGO DIALOGUE

"LOVE HEALS ALL" is a well-known sentiment. And it can. It can even heal the deepest emotional wound of all—the ruptured connection between you and your parents. But it needs to be a specific kind of love. It needs to be a mature, patient love that is free of manipulation and distortion, and it needs to take place within the context of an intimate relationship. Receiving empathy from a friend may be very moving, but it does not reach all the way down into your psyche. In order to heal the painful experiences of the past, you need to receive love from a person whom your unconscious mind has merged with your childhood caregivers.

We now regard the Imago Dialogue as being the single most effective tool for creating a conscious relationship. Its power goes far beyond communication. The results, when practiced and integrated, are what all couples yearn for: feeling safe and being joyfully connected.

BUT! ISN'T DIALOGUING WITH YOUR PARTNER TEDIOUS?

AS HELPFUL AS the Imago Dialogue may be, people initially have an almost universal response to it: "Do we really have to go through all those steps in order to communicate something meaningful?" The answer to this specific question is no. If all you're seeking is effective communication, then mirroring alone may be sufficient. But if you want to move beyond communication to communion, then you need to include all three steps. That said, we don't want to diminish how time-consuming and artificial the Imago Dialogue can seem. There are times when you will rebel at the structure and want to revert to old habits. We are reminded of the seventeen-year-old son of a friend of ours, who is a superb baseball player. He is so good, in fact, that he's been singled out by a ball club for special instruction even before leaving high school. To the boy's dismay, however, his new coach wants him to change virtually everything about the way that he pitches and hits the ball. He's been given a series of exercises to help him build up certain muscles and stretch out others, and he is required to hit a hundred balls a day using an alien-feeling stance and grip. At times, he has been close to tears because he feels as though he's had to abandon everything he knows about baseball.

So it is with the Imago Dialogue. It requires you to abandon some deeply ingrained habits and adopt a formulaic way of relating. Much of the time, it's going to feel forced. But as you begin to experience some of its benefits, you will become less resistant. Eventually—and it may take years—you will have transformed your relationship to the point that you will be able to abandon the exercise altogether. When that day arrives, you will be communing, not just conversing.

Throughout the rest of this book, there are variations of Imago Dialogue for specific goals: understanding how your partner's past is influencing the present, gathering information about what caring behaviors touch their hearts, working through conflict with specific requests. But when we first introduce Imago Dialogue to couples, we encourage them to start with baby steps. Start with sharing an appreciation. Go through your day mirroring everything your partner says. "If I heard you correctly, you said, 'Pass the salt.' Did I get that? . . . Is there more about that?" Make it fun to master the skill. As you become more adept at the mechanics, you can brave more complicated and conflictual subjects using the full Dialogue process.

CREATING A ZONE OF AFFIRMATIONS

Perfect love means to love the one through
whom one became unhappy.
— SØREN KIERKEGAARD

OFTEN, WHEN COUPLES begin therapy (and according to
our colleague John Gottman, they begin five to seven years after
problems start to emerge), they are unable to see anything beyond what their partner is doing wrong. They are consumed
with negativity and arrive with the goal of having the therapist
"fix their partner."

Immediately, in therapy and at our workshops, we introduce
couples to mirroring an appreciation. "One thing I appreciate
about you is . . ." This helps slow down the reactivity and defensive posture by engaging the prefrontal cortex, the part of
your brain that regulates anxiety. But sharing appreciations,
while effective in turning the relationship, is not enough.
Couples need a repertoire of tools to bathe their relationship in
affirmations—behaviors that create sustained safety and restore loving feelings in the relationship.

From our earlier studies in behavioral sciences, we learned
that we could influence the way a couple feels about each other
by helping them artificially reconstruct the conditions of romantic love. When two people treat each other the way they

did in happier times, they begin to identify each other as a source of pleasure once again, restoring safety in the relationship, the necessary ingredient for change.

INSIGHT AND BEHAVIORAL CHANGE

IN PSYCHOANALYSIS, WE were taught that the goal of a therapist was to help clients remove their emotional blocks. Once they had correctly linked feelings they had about their partners with needs and desires left over from childhood, they were automatically supposed to evolve a more rational, adult style of relating.

This assumption was based on the medical model that once a physician cures a disease, the patient automatically returns to full health. Since most forms of psychotherapy come from psychoanalysis, which, in turn, has its roots in nineteenth-century medicine, the fact that they rest on a common biological assumption is not surprising. But years of experience with couples convinced us that a medical model is not a useful one for relationship therapy. When a physician cures a disease, the body recovers spontaneously because it relies on genetic programming. Each cell of the body, unless it is damaged or diseased, contains all the information it needs to function normally. But there is no genetic code that governs relationships. Long-term love relationships are a cultural creation imposed on biology. Because people lack a built-in set of social instructions, they can be trapped in unhappy relationships after months or even years of productive therapy. Their emotional blocks may be removed, and they may have insight into the cause of their difficulties, but they have a tendency to still cling to habituated behaviors.

Like many couples' therapists, we came to the conclusion that we would have to play an active role in helping couples redesign their relationships. Insight into childhood wounds is an element in therapy, but it isn't enough, nor is it the critical element. Above all, people need to learn how to let go of counterproductive behaviors and replace them with more effective ones.

CARING BEHAVIORS

A BEHAVIORAL APPROACH proved especially useful in restoring a couple's sense of love and goodwill. In his book *Helping Couples Change: A Social Learning Approach to Marital Therapy*, psychologist Richard Stuart presents an exercise for couples that helps them feel more loving toward each other simply by engaging in more loving behaviors. Called Caring Days, the exercise instructs husbands and wives to write down a list of positive, specific ways their partners can please them. For example, a man might write down: "I would like you to massage my shoulders for fifteen minutes while we watch television." Or "I would like you to bring me breakfast in bed on Sunday morning." The partners are to grant each other a certain number of these caring behaviors a day, no matter how they feel about each other. Stuart discovered that the exercise generated "significant changes in the details of the couple's daily interaction during the first seven days of therapy, a very firm foundation upon which to build subsequent suggestions for change."[1]

To see whether or not this behavioral approach actually worked, I (Harville) decided to try it out on Harriet and Dennis Johnson. I chose the Johnsons because they were as unhappy with each other as any couple in my practice. One of Harriet's main anxieties was that Dennis was going to leave her. In a desperate effort to hold his interest, she flirted conspicuously with other men. To her dismay, Dennis responded to her flirtatious behavior the same way he responded to just about everything else she did—with stoic reserve. During one session, he mentioned that he was even trying to adjust to the fact that Harriet might one day have an affair. His quiet heroics exasperated his wife, who was trying everything within her power to penetrate his defenses and get him to be more interested in her. Those rare times when she managed to get him riled up, he would behave in a typically reactive way and flee the house. Most of their fights ended with Dennis's zooming off to safety in his Audi sedan.

To lay the groundwork for the exercise, I asked Dennis and Harriet to tell me how they had treated each other when they were first in love. As I listened to them, I had the strange feeling that they were talking about an entirely different couple. I couldn't imagine Dennis and Harriet going on long Sunday bike rides together, leaving work to meet each other at the movies, and calling each other on the phone two or three times a day.

"What would happen," I asked them when I recovered from my amazement, "if you were to go home today and start doing all those things again? What if you were to treat each other the same way you did when you were courting?" They looked at me with puzzled expressions.

"I think I would feel very uncomfortable," Dennis said after a moment's reflection. "I don't like the idea of acting differently from the way I feel. I would feel . . . dishonest. I don't have the same feelings toward Harriet that I used to, so why should I treat her as if I did?"

Harriet agreed. "It would feel like we were playacting," she said. "We may not be happy, but at least we try to be honest with each other."

When I explained that taking part in the experiment might help them over their impasse, they agreed to give it a try, despite their initial objections. I carefully explained the exercise to them. They were to go home, make their lists, and volunteer to give each other three to five of those behaviors a day. The behaviors were to be gifts. They were to view them as an opportunity to please each other, not as a bartering tool. And most important of all, they weren't to keep score. They were to focus only on the giving end of the equation. They left the office promising to give the exercise an honest effort.

At the beginning of their next appointment, Dennis reported on the results of the experiment. "I think you're really onto something, " he said. "We did what you asked us to do, and today I feel a lot more hopeful about our relationship."

He continued, "Well, the day after our appointment, I found myself driving around town in a black mood; I can't even remember what made me feel so down. Anyway, I decided that it was as good a time as any to do what you asked, so I stopped off at a variety store and bought Harriet some flowers. That was one of the requests on her list. So I gritted my teeth and picked out some daisies, because I remembered she always liked daisies. The clerk asked me if I wanted a note card, and I said, 'Why not?' I remember saying to myself, *We're paying a therapist a lot of money to make things better, so I'd better do this all the way.* When I came home, I signed the card 'I love you.'" He paused for a moment. "The thing that surprised me was that, as I handed Harriet the flowers, I really did care for her."

"And when I read the card," Harriet added, "tears came to my eyes. It's been so long since he's told me he loved me." They went on to describe all the other things that they had done to please each other. She had cooked him pot roast and potato pancakes, his favorite dinner. He had agreed to curl up with her in bed as they fell asleep instead of turning his back to her. As they were recounting these events, there seemed to be remarkably little tension between them. When they left the office, I noticed that as Dennis helped Harriet on with her coat, she smiled and said, "Thank you, honey." It was a little thing, but it was the kind of pleasurable give-and-take that had been so absent in their relationship.

Dennis and Harriet continued to give each other caring behaviors, and at each session, they reported a gradual improvement in their relationship. They not only were treating each other more kindly but were also more willing to explore the issues underlying their discontent. They spent less of their time in my office complaining about each other and more time exploring the childhood issues that were the reasons for their unhappiness in the first place.

Because Stuart's exercise proved so helpful for Dennis and Harriet, we began using it in our workshops as a model for an expanded exercise that we labeled Caring Behaviors (similar to Stuart's Caring Days) because it effectively restored the conflict-free interactions of romantic love.[2] We introduced the Caring Behaviors exercise to other couples and had them share behaviors they currently receive from their partner (current behaviors), behaviors they received in their earlier romantic days together (past behaviors), and behaviors that their partner does not do but, if they did, would make them feel loved or cared about (future behaviors). Almost without exception, when couples began artificially to increase the number of times a day that they acted lovingly toward each other, they began to feel safer and more loving. This intensified the emotional bond between them, and as a result, they made more rapid progress in their relationship.

We will explain the details of the Caring Behaviors exercise more fully in part 3. When you carefully follow the directions, you, too, will experience an immediate improvement in the climate of your relationship. The exercise is not designed to resolve your deep-seated conflicts, but it will reestablish feelings of safety and pleasure and set the stage for increased intimacy.

WHY DOES IT WORK?

WHY IS THIS simple exercise so effective? The obvious reason is that, through daily repetitions of positive behaviors, your old brain begins to perceive your partner as "someone who nurtures me." Painful memories are overlaid with positive affirmations, and your partner is no longer categorized as a bringer of death but as a wellspring of life. This opens the way for intimacy, which is only possible in a context of safety and pleasure. The same way negativity springs forth anxiety and activates defenses, positivity creates safety and relaxes defenses. The original rupture begins to heal. Daily connecting interactions that are affirming, on a chemical level, replace cortisol (the stress chemical) with endorphins (the pleasure chemical).

But there are other, subtler reasons the exercise works so well. One is that it helps people erode the infantile belief that their partners can read their minds. During romantic love, people operate out of the erroneous belief that their partners know exactly what it is that they want. When their partners fail to satisfy their secret desires, they assume that they are deliberately depriving them of pleasure. This makes them want to deprive their partners of pleasure. The Caring Behaviors exercise prevents this downward spiral by requiring couples to tell each other exactly what pleases them, decreasing their reliance on mental telepathy.

The exercise also defeats the tit-for-tat mentality of the power struggle. When couples take part in giving Caring Behaviors, they are instructed to pleasure each other on an independent schedule; they mete out a prescribed number of loving behaviors a day, regardless of the behavior of their partners. This replaces the natural tendency to hand out favors on a quid pro quo basis: you do this nice thing for me, and I'll do that nice thing for you. Most relationships are run like a commodities market, with loving behaviors the coin in trade. But this kind of "love" does not sit well with the old brain. If John rubs Martha's shoulders in the hope that she will let him spend the day going fishing, a built-in sensor in Martha's head goes: "Look out! Price tag attached. There is no reason to feel good about this gift, because I'll have to pay for it later." Unconsciously, she rejects John's attentions, because she knows that they were designed for his benefit, not hers. The only kind of love that her old brain will accept is the kind with no strings attached: "I will rub your shoulders because I know that you would like it." The back rub has to come as a "gift."

This need to be unconditionally "gifted" comes straight out of our childhood. When we were infants, love came without price tags. At least for the first few months of our lives, we didn't have to reciprocate when we were patted or rocked or held or fed. And now, in adulthood, a time-locked part of us still craves this form of love. We want to be loved and cared for without having to do anything in return. When our partners grant us caring behaviors independent of our actions, our need for unconditional love appears to be satisfied.

A third benefit of the exercise is that it helps people see that what pleases them is the product of their unique makeup and life experience and can be very different from what pleases their partners. This reinforces the fact that they are separate people. Often, partners in a relationship cater to their own needs and preferences, not to each other's. For example, Sheryl went to a great deal of trouble to give her husband, Bobby, a surprise fortieth birthday party. She invited all his friends, cooked his favorite foods, borrowed a stack of his favorite 1960s rock-and-roll records, and organized lively party games. During the party, her husband acted as if he were enjoying himself, but a few weeks later, in the middle of a counseling session, he got up the courage to tell his wife that he had been secretly miserable. "I've never liked having a fuss made about my birthday," he told her. "You know that. And especially not my fortieth birthday. What I really wanted to do was spend a quiet evening at home with you and the kids. Maybe have a homemade cake and a few presents. You're the one who likes big, noisy parties!"

His wife had taken the Golden Rule, "Do unto others as you would have others do unto you," a little too literally. She had unwittingly given her husband a party that suited her tastes, not his. The Caring Behaviors exercise circumvents this problem by training couples to "Do unto others as they would have you do unto them." This turns their random caring behaviors into *target* behaviors, behaviors that are designed to satisfy their partners' unique desires.

When couples regularly give each other these target behaviors, they not only improve the superficial climate of their relationship, they also begin to heal their earlier childhood experiences. For example, one of the things that I (Harville) asked Helen to do for me is to turn down the covers before we go to bed. This request comes from an experience I had over forty years ago. After my mother died, I was taken in by my sister Maize Lee. She was only eighteen at the time and recently married, but she did a wonderful job of caring for me. One of the things that touched me most was that she would always find time to go into my room before bedtime, turn down my covers, and put out a glass of orange juice or milk for me to drink. Today, when Helen turns down the covers for me before I climb into bed, I remember Maize Lee and all that she did for me (to protect me from the deep loss), and I feel very loved indeed. On a deep level, this simple action is re-creating the vital parent-child bond. I feel secure again, and the injury of my childhood (the loss of my parent) is repaired in an adult relationship that has become a zone of love and safety. Caring Behaviors became the first exercise to what we later called *re-romanticizing* the relationship.

The Surprise List

AFTER INTRODUCING THE Caring Behaviors exercise to scores of couples, we began to notice a curious phenomenon: the positive value of doing this exercise seemed to flatten out after a few months. The couples were faithfully following the instructions, but they were no longer experiencing the deep pleasure they had when they began doing the exercise. It occurred to us that we needed to build the concept of *random reinforcement* into the exercise. Random reinforcement, one of the principles of behavioral science, is the idea that a pleasurable action loses its effectiveness if it's repeated with predictable regularity. For example, if your partner brings you coffee in bed every morning, it no longer feels as special as it did when it was an occasional act, or "treat." Random rewards, on the other hand, create an air of uncertainty and expectancy that increases their impact on the receiver. This concept was discovered accidentally by a group of scientists who were training laboratory animals by rewarding them with treats. One day, the apparatus that dispensed the treats malfunctioned, and the animals were not rewarded for their efforts. The next day, the machine was repaired, and the regular reward schedule was resumed. To the trainers' surprise, the animals were even more highly motivated to perform than before. The fact that the reward had become unpredictable improved their performance.

The phenomenon of random reinforcement can easily be observed in daily life. Most husbands and wives give each other presents on special occasions like birthdays and Christmas and anniversaries. These gifts are so customary that they are almost taken for granted. Although the presents may be enjoyed, they don't carry the same emotional impact as a present that is given as a total surprise. A behaviorist would say that the reason routine gifts aren't as exciting is that the "psychoneurological system has become desensitized to predictable, repetitive pleasure." The same principle applies to the Caring Behaviors exercise. When couples become locked into a particular kind of caring behavior—for example, when they give each other back rubs every night before bed or a bouquet of flowers every Saturday—they begin to derive less pleasure from them. A curveball needs to be thrown in now and then to rekindle their interest.

To add this element of suspense, we created the idea of the Surprise List exercise. These were caring behaviors above and beyond those requested by either partner. Each would generate a list by paying close attention to their partner's wishes and dreams. A woman who casually mentioned to her husband that she liked a dress she saw in a store window might be delighted to find that very dress—in the correct size—hanging in her closet. A man who expressed his interest in Gilbert and Sullivan might open the mail and find a love note from his partner and two tickets to a Gilbert and Sullivan opera. We playfully call these cues *random droppings.* When couples added unanticipated pleasures like these to their regular caring behaviors, the beneficial effect of the exercise continued on a gentle rise. Surprises can also trigger dopamine, which boosts joy and safety in the Space Between.

THE FUN LIST

AS TIME WENT on, we asked couples to engage in several high-energy, fun activities a week. These were to be spontaneous, one-on-one activities like wrestling, tickling, massaging, showering together, jumping up and down, or dancing. Competitive sports like tennis qualified only if a couple could play the game without stirring up tension.

The reason we added more exuberant activities to the list was that most people seem to have forgotten how to have fun together. In our case, neither Harville nor I (Helen) had ever been allowed to have fun in our homes. Harville had constantly worked on the farm or held other jobs. And around my dad, we kids had to be serious. We were both raised to be "critical thinkers," in the best sense of the words. As a result, we were badly "fun-impaired." We were both great at critiquing theory or researching footnotes. But we grew to realize that when couples have fun together, they identify each other as a source of pleasure and safety, which intensifies their emotional bond. When the old brain registers a positive flow of energy, it knows that the person associated with the energy is connected to life and safety. Wearing Groucho Marx glasses while reading jokes, singing silly songs and reading made-up limericks about each other, and baby talking to each other while cuddled up in bed are all ways a couple can intentionally add fun into the relationship.

Your neural pathways cannot experience humor and anxiety at the same time. We discovered this was a great way to transform the energy in relationships.

The Fear of Pleasure

WITH THE ADDITION of the Surprise List and the Fun List, we now had useful tools to help couples fill their Space Between with positive, affirming behaviors. But like any exercise that leads to relationship growth, these simple exercises were often met with resistance. A certain degree of resistance is to be expected. When a couple has been treating each other like enemies for five years, it's going to feel strange to start writing love notes again. The exercise is going to feel artificial and contrived, and to the old brain, anything that is not routine and habituated feels unnatural. The only way to lessen this automatic resistance is to repeat a new behavior often enough so that it begins to feel familiar and, therefore, safe.

A deeper source of resistance to the exercise, however, is a paradoxical one—the fear of pleasure. On a conscious level, we go to great lengths to seek happiness. Why, then, should we be afraid of it? To make sense of this reaction, we need to remember that the sensation of being fully alive is deeply pleasurable. When we were young children, we had boundless energy and experienced intense joy. But some of our pleasure was curtailed by our caregivers so that we could be safe and conform to social norms: "Don't yell and run." "Don't jump on the couch." "Be careful! Come down from that tree." "You're making too much noise." But our fun was also cut short because it threatened the repressed state of our caregivers. Many adults have long given up diving into the lake, rolling down the hill, skipping down the sidewalk, and jumping up and down for joy. As these limits were imposed on us, sometimes in punitive ways, we began to make an unlikely association between pleasure and pain.

If we experienced certain kinds of pleasure or perhaps a high degree of pleasure, we were ignored, reprimanded, or punished. On an unconscious level, this negative stimulus triggered the fear of death. Eventually, we limited our own pleasure so that we could reduce our anxiety. We learned that to be fully alive was dangerous.

However, applying the strange logic of children, we didn't blame our parents or society for equating pleasure with pain; it simply appeared to be our lot in life. We told ourselves, "My parents limited my pleasure, so I must not have been worthy of it." It was somehow safer to believe that we were intrinsically undeserving than to believe that our parents were incapable of meeting our needs or had deliberately diminished our happiness. Gradually, we developed a built-in prohibition against pleasure.

People who grew up experiencing a great deal of repression tend to have a particularly hard time with the re-romanticizing process. They have difficulty coming up with any requests for caring behaviors, or they sabotage their partners' efforts to carry them out. They find excuses to reject surprises. They don't find the time to engage in fun activities. For example, one man with low self-esteem wrote down on his list that he would like his partner to give him one compliment a day. This was easy for his partner to do because she thought he had a lot of admirable qualities. But when she tried to give him a daily compliment, he would immediately contradict her statement or qualify it to the point that it became meaningless. If she were to say something like, "I liked the way you were talking to our son, Robbie, last night," he would nullify it with a self-criticism: "Yeah. Well, I should do that more often. I never spend enough time with him." Hearing anything good about himself was ego-dystonic, incompatible with his self-image. His determination to maintain this negative opinion was so strong that we guided him to respond mechanically to his partner's kind remarks with a "thank you" and leave it at that.

There was one man whose resistance to the Caring Behaviors

exercise took a different form: he just couldn't seem to understand the instructions. "I just don't get the hang of this," he said after we had explained the exercise in detail. "Now, what is it that I'm supposed to do?"

We went over the instructions once again, making sure they were clearly understood. We knew, however, that his lack of comprehension was a cover-up for his inability to ask for something pleasurable. To help him over his emotional roadblock, we told him that, even though it appeared that asking his wife to do nice things for him was solely for his benefit, it was also a way for his wife to learn how to become a more loving person—which happened to be true. When it was put in this less self-serving context, he quickly understood the exercise. He was able to call a truce with the demon inside of him that told him he was not worthy of love. He took out a pencil and in a matter of minutes came up with a list of twenty-six things he would like her to do for him.

Some partners often have a difficult time with this exercise. They want to cooperate, but they just can't think of anything their partners can do for them; they don't seem to have any needs or desires. What they are really doing is hiding behind the psychic shield they erected as children to protect themselves from overbearing parents. They discovered early in life that one way to maintain a feeling of autonomy around their intrusive parents was to keep their thoughts and feelings to themselves. When they deprived their parents of this valuable information, their parents were less able to invade their space. After a while, many isolators do the ultimate disappearing act and hide their feelings from themselves. In the end, it is safest not to know.

It is often the case, as we've mentioned before, that isolators unwittingly re-create the struggle of their childhood by marrying fusers, people who have an unsatisfied need for intimacy from neglectful parenting. This way they perpetuate the conflict that consumed them as children—not as an idle replay of the past or a neurotic addiction to pain but as an unconscious act aimed at the resolution of fundamental human needs. When a fuser-isolator couple does this exercise, it results in a predictable dichotomy. The isolator painfully ekes out one or two requests, while the fuser furiously scribbles a long list of "I wants." To the casual observer, it appears that the isolator is a self-sufficient individual with few needs and the fuser has limitless desires. The fact of the matter is that both individuals have the identical need to be loved and cared for. It's just that one of them happens to be more in touch with those feelings than the other.

Whatever a person's reason for resisting this exercise, our prescription is the same: "Keep doing the exercise exactly as described. Even if it causes you anxiety, keep it up. Do it harder and more aggressively than before. Eventually, your anxiety will go away." Given enough time and enough repetition, your brain can adjust to a different reality. The person with low self-esteem can gradually carve out a more positive identity. The isolator has a chance to discover that sharing secret desires does not compromise their independence. The fear of new behaviors gives way to the pleasure they stimulate, and they begin to be associated with safety and life. The re-romanticizing exercises become comfortable, reliable tools for personal growth.

INSIGHT AND BEHAVIORAL CHANGE

THESE RE-ROMANTICIZING EXERCISES, and several other exercises that you will read about in coming chapters, have convinced us that insight and behavioral change make powerful allies. It is not enough for partners to understand the unconscious motivations that they bring to their relationship; insight alone does not heal childhood wounds. Nor is it sufficient to introduce behavioral changes into a relationship without the couples understanding the reasons behind them. In either case, the couples experience only limited growth. Experience has taught us that the most effective form of therapy is one that combines both schools of thought. As you learn more about your unconscious motivations and transform these insights into supportive behaviors, you can create a more conscious and ultimately more rewarding relationship.

DEFINING YOUR CURRICULUM

*One of the deep secrets of life is that all that is really worth
the doing is what we do for others.*

— LEWIS CARROLL

SO FAR, WE'VE described the initial steps in the creation of a
conscious partnership. We've talked about making a commitment to narrow your exits so that more of your energy is available for your relationship. We've explored Imago Dialogue as
the process for breaking your self-absorbed worldview to include
your partner's in order to create safety and establish authentic
connection. And we've talked about increasing the pleasurable interactions between the two of you to set the stage for
greater intimacy. Now it is time to discuss how we can heal our
deeper childhood wounds, as well as the challenges we experienced from either intrusive or neglectful parenting that influence your relationship. We will explore how to increase our
ability to empathize that helps pave the way for turning your
chronic frustrations about your partner into avenues for growth.

When a couple has spent several weeks practicing the re-
romanticizing exercises (described in the previous chapter),
they experience a revival of positive feelings, and they begin to
bond with each other much the way they did during the early
stages of romantic love. Just as they grow accustomed to this

more intimate, nurturing environment, however, a dishearten-
ing event occurs: conflicts begin to emerge, the very ones that
brought them into therapy in the first place. Once again, they
are plagued with the same troublesome issues, the same basic
incompatibilities. It seems as though the re-romanticizing exercises have resurrected romantic love only to let it disintegrate
once again into a power struggle.

The reason the good feelings don't last is that, through
increased pleasurable interactions, the two individuals have unconsciously identified each other as the "one who has it all," the
ideal mate who is magically going to restore their experience of
joyful fulfillment. After the anger and withdrawal of the power
struggle, they turn to each other for salvation. And once again,
they make the unpleasant discovery that neither of them has the
necessary skills or the motivation to meet the other's deeper
needs. In fact, on their own, many people make the same so-
bering discovery we made in our first marriages: what they want
most from their partners, their partners are least able to give.

What can be done to resolve this central dilemma? Given
these two facts—(1) that we enter our love relationships bear-
ing emotional scars from childhood, and (2) that we unwittingly
choose mates who resemble our caregivers, the very people who
contributed to our wounding in the first place—it seems that
intimate love relationships are destined to repeat, not repair, our
early misfortunes.

Years ago when we lectured to groups, this pessimistic view
came through loud and clear. During one talk explaining the self-
defeating nature of mate selection, a woman raised her hand to
say, "Maybe the way to avoid reinjuring old wounds is to marry
people you don't feel attracted to. That way you won't wind up
with people who have the same faults as your parents." Everyone
laughed, but at the time, we could offer no better solution. Relationships determined by signs of the zodiac, go-betweens, or
computerized dating services appeared to have a better chance of
succeeding than relationships based on an unconscious selection

process. Our tendency to select partners who share the positive and negative traits of our caregivers seemed to doom conventional love relationships from the start. Our only advice to couples was to become more aware of their hidden reasons for marrying each other and to embrace the cold, hard facts of reality. Awareness, insight, understanding, and acceptance—that was the only solace we had to offer.

At the time, I (Harville) was getting the same counsel from my own therapist. "You have to accept the fact that your mother didn't have any energy for you, Harville," he would tell me. "And your wife can't give you what you want, either. She can't make up for those early years. You just have to let go of those longings." In other words, you didn't get it then, and you're not going to get it now. Grow up and get on with life.

I tried to accept what he was telling me, but I was aware that in the core of my being, I was unwilling to let go of my unfinished business—to get needs not met in childhood met in my relationship. A part of me felt that I had an inalienable right to a secure and loving upbringing, and I could see that couples were clinging just as tenaciously to their needs. They might repress them; they might deny them; they might project them onto others. But they couldn't let go of their childhood needs once and for all. There had to be a different and better way. And there is. By becoming the person your partner needs you to be. This is what Helen did for me and what I did for her. Through this unconditional giving, we both finally got the love we had longed for all our lives.

WHY SELF-LOVE DOESN'T WORK

I (HELEN) ONCE briefly saw a spiritual director who had a more optimistic view about the possibility of resolving childhood needs than I do. She believed that it was possible for people to make up for what they didn't get in childhood through self-love. One of her techniques to help me overcome my craving for being seen and valued was to guide me through a deep relaxation exercise, then say to me, "Helen, imagine yourself as a little girl wanting your father's attention. He is at home with you, asking you about your day. Imagine how you want his attention. Call out to him. See him come over to you and pick you up with a big smile on his face. He is praising you for being so astute and intelligent at such a young age."

It was her belief that, if I succeeded in creating a vivid picture of myself being loved by my father, I would gradually fill up my need for paternal love. Her approach seemed to work for a while; after each session, I would feel less alone, more loved. But the feeling gradually disappeared, and I was once again filled with loneliness.

This approach doesn't work because it is sabotaged by the old brain. When we were infants, unable to meet our physical and emotional needs, pain and pleasure came magically from the outside world. When the bottle or the breast appeared, our hunger was satisfied. When we were cuddled, we felt soothed. When we were left alone in our cribs to cry, we felt angry and afraid. As we grew older, our old brain remained frozen in this passive worldview: good feelings and bad feelings were created by the actions of other people. We couldn't take care of ourselves; others had to do it for us. The part of us that hurt couldn't accept love from within ourselves because we had no way to receive self-love. Nor does anyone else. Salvation is not an "inside" job; it is the outcome of being nourished by others. But at that time, we did not know this fundamental truth.

The Limits of Friendship

WE (HARVILLE AND Helen) gradually resigned ourselves to the fact that healing love has to come from outside oneself. But did it have to come from an intimate partner? Couldn't it come from a close friend? We both have had opportunities to observe and experience the healing potential of friendships. Close bonds often develop between members of therapy groups, and we encouraged this love and support. And we are often able to share more with our childhood friend than with our intimate partner. But friendships, while powerful antidotes to loneliness and sources of self-esteem, are limited in their ability to heal the profound yearning we feel.

We concluded that the love we are seeking has to come not just from another person within the context of a safe, intimate relationship but from an Imago match—someone so similar to our parents that our unconscious mind has them merged. This appears to be the only way to erase the pains of childhood. We may enjoy the hugs and attentions of other people, but the effects are transitory. It's like the difference between sugar and NutraSweet. Our taste buds may be deceived by the taste of artificial sweeteners, but our bodies derive no nourishment from them. In just such a way, we hunger for love from our original caregivers or from people who are so similar to them that on an unconscious level we cannot distinguish one from the other.

But this brought us back full circle to the original dilemma: How can our partners heal us if they have some of the same negative traits as our caregivers? Aren't they the least likely candidates to soothe our emotional injuries? If the daughter of a distant, self-absorbed father unconsciously selects a workaholic for a husband, how can her relationship satisfy her need for closeness and intimacy? If the son of a depressed, sexually repressed mother chooses to marry a depressed, frigid wife, how can he recapture his sensuality and joy? If a girl whose father died when she was young moves in with a man who refuses to marry her, how can she feel loved and secure?

An answer began to take shape in our minds. If people were going to be healed, we conjectured, their partners would have to change. It was the only logical conclusion. The workaholic husband would have to willingly redirect some of his energy back to his wife. The depressed, frigid wife would have to recover her energy and sensuality. The reluctant lover would have to lower his barriers to intimacy. Then and only then would they be able to give their partners the consistent nurturing they had been looking for all their lives.

It was at this point that we began to see the unconscious selection process in a new light: while it was often true that what one partner needed the most was what the other partner was least able to give, it also happened to be the precise area where that partner needed to grow! For example, if Mary grew up with caregivers who were sparing in their physical affection, she most likely would have a husband, George, who was uncomfortable with bodily contact; the unmet childhood need in Mary would be invariably matched by George's inability to meet that need. But if George were to overcome his resistance to being affectionate in an effort to satisfy Mary's needs, not only would Mary get the physical reassurance she craved, but George would slowly regain contact with his own sensuality. In other words, in his efforts to heal his partner, he would be recovering an essential part of himself! The unconscious selection process has brought together two people who can either hurt each other or heal each other, depending upon their willingness to grow and change.

THE IMAGO WORKUP

CHANGE IS DIFFICULT. The old brain craves homeostasis and, as we have discussed throughout this book, has an elaborate defense system to protect the self from what might be perceived as dangerous. We have learned that Imago Dialogue can help us overcome these old-brain defenses and employ new brain tactics. But we also need a motivator to call forth our willingness to change. Imago Dialogue continues to be the answer for deeper discovery that elicits empathy and the will to stretch into meeting our partners' needs. It starts at the beginning — with the childhood experiences.

Once couples have been taught the Imago Dialogue, we introduce them to an information gathering tool called the *Imago Workup.* This is a guided imagery technique that helps each partner become better acquainted with their own childhood wounds. When the exercise is completed, we have them share their observations, using the Imago Dialogue. This is an effective way for couples to begin to see each other as they really are, as wounded beings on a quest for spiritual wholeness.

Before the exercise begins, we ask the couples to close their eyes and relax. We often put on some soothing music to help them shut out distractions. When they are sufficiently relaxed, we ask them to try to remember their childhood home, the earliest one they can recall. When the vision begins to take shape, we tell them to see themselves as very young children wandering through the house searching for their caretakers. The first person they meet is their mother, or whichever female caregiver was most influential in their early years. We tell them that they are suddenly endowed with magical powers and can see these women's positive and negative character traits with crystal clarity. They are to note these characteristics and then imagine themselves telling their mothers what they always wanted from them and never got.

In a similar manner, we have them encounter their fathers, or primary male caregivers, and then any other people who had a profound influence on them in their formative years. When they have gathered all the information they can about these key people, we slowly bring them back to reality and have them open their eyes and write the information down on a piece of paper.

We are often surprised by how much information people can gain from this simple exercise. For example, a young man did the exercise and realized for the first time how lonely and isolated he felt as a child. He had blocked out this crucial piece of information because it hadn't made any sense to him. How could he feel lonely in a family with four children, a minister for a father, and a devoted homemaker for a mother? In his fantasy, however, he had searched and searched around the house for his father, never to find him. When he encountered his mother, his spontaneous question to her was "Why are you always so busy? Can't you see that I need you?" Having these insights helped him understand his chronic depression. "Until this moment," he said, "my sadness has always been a mystery to me."

Once a person has completed the guided-imagery exercise, they have the information they need to construct their Imago, the inner image that guided them in mate selection. All they need to do is group together the positive and negative traits of all the key people from their childhood, highlighting the traits that affected them the most. These are the traits that they were looking for in a romantic partner.

When this work is completed, we ask couples to share what they have learned. We ask them to listen to each other with full attention, making no effort to interpret each other's remarks, enlarge upon them, compare them with their own, or analyze them. The only allowable comments are mirroring comments that indicate the degree of their understanding. By doing this exercise, people begin to see behind their partners' neurotic, puzzling, or compulsive behavior to the wounds they are trying to heal. This creates a more compassionate, supportive emotional climate.

THE PARENT (CAREGIVER)–CHILD DIALOGUE

IN THE YEARS since the original version of this book was written, a number of other Imago workshop presenters have contributed to the workshop and to Imago Therapy. Maya Kollman, a master trainer, suggested a new exercise called the *Parent (Caregiver)–Child Dialogue.* In this exercise, couples deepen their awareness of their childhood wounds and increase their empathy for each other. Sitting face-to-face, one partner takes on the role of the caregiver (the Receiver), and the other partner imagines him or herself as a small child and talks to the caregiver from a child's point of view (the Sender). The person playing the "caregiver" asks a series of questions, beginning with: "Tell me what it is like living with me." The "child" responds. After mirroring the "child" with empathy, the "caregiver" then asks, "What is the worst part for you about all that?" Once again, the "child" talks about what was most difficult. Mirroring the "child's" response with warmth and empathy, the "caregiver" now balances with positive sharing by asking similar questions about good things and the best part of living with the "caregiver." The final question by the "caregiver" is "What do you need from me the most that I don't give you?" Typically, the "child" says something like "I need you to be there for me and listen when I talk."

After mirroring, checking for accuracy, and inviting more, the partners "de-role," the Receiver (caregiver) summarizes the Sender (child) and asks, "What do you need in our relationship that would begin to meet that need?" The Sender responds, and both partners close the exercise by sharing mutual appreciation for sharing and listening. Then they switch roles and repeat the exercise.

This exercise is powerful for both partners. The partner playing the role of the child recalls his or her childhood wounds more deeply than in other exercises. The partner in the caregiving role gains a greater understanding of the other partner's early vulnerability. Through the sharing of the good memories, the partner in the caregiving role also gains information about the positive things that felt loving to the other partner that can help generate new caring behaviors. The most exciting thing about this particular exercise is that the empathic response of the listening partner is so different from the type of wounding response one might have gotten from one's actual caregiver that it begins to heal the partner's wound. If the real-life caregiver had responded this way in the past, the emotional injury would not have occurred in the first place.

What fascinates us most about the Parent (Caregiver)–Child Dialogue is that when the partner who has regressed into childhood memories talks about his or her pain from the past, the listening partner often recognizes that he or she has frustrated the speaking partner in similar ways, unwittingly reopening childhood wounds. However, the structure of the exercise prevents any reaction. Then, in the closing statement, when the regressed child says what he or she needs from the parent, the listening partner gains new insight into what needs to be done to help the other person heal. The Parent (Caregiver)–Child Dialogue is an indirect way of learning how to be each other's healers.

THE TRUTH ABOUT CRITICISM

WHILE DIALOGUING WITH your partner helps break the self-absorbed world that each of us lives in due to anxiety, looking internally can also help mine the hidden information embedded in your spoken and unspoken criticisms of your partner: "You never come home on time." "I can never lean on you." "Why don't you think of me for a change?" "You are so selfish." At the time you are making these statements, you believe them to be accurate descriptions of your partner. But the truth of the matter is that they are often descriptions of parts of yourself.

Take a look at this example to see how much information can be gleaned from one chronic, emotional complaint. Let's suppose that a woman routinely criticizes her partner for being disorganized. "You are always disorganized! I can never depend on you!" When her partner demands some specific examples, she retorts, "You are terrible about planning for vacations. You always forget the essentials when we go camping. You never remember the kids' birthdays. And you always leave the kitchen a jumbled mess when you cook!" Not surprisingly, the man's automatic response to this barrage of accusations is a blanket denial followed by a countercriticism: "That's not true. You're exaggerating. You're more disorganized than I am!"

How can this heated argument be turned into useful information? If the woman had an open mind, she might be able to gain some valuable insight about her own childhood wounds. She could do this by following a simple procedure.

First, she could write her criticism of her partner on a piece of paper: "You are always so disorganized!" Then she could answer the following questions:

- How do I feel when my partner acts this way?
- What thoughts do I have when my partner acts this way?
- What deeper feelings might underlie these thoughts and feelings?
- Did I ever have these thoughts and feelings when I was a child?

By going through this simple analytical process, she could determine whether or not her partner's behavior brought back any strong memories from her childhood.

Let's suppose the exercise helps the woman discover that her parents were always disorganized and had little time or energy to pay attention to her needs. Not surprisingly, when her partner acts in a similar manner, she is filled with the same fears she had as a child. Buried in her criticism of her partner, therefore, is a plaintive cry from childhood: "Why can't someone take care of me?"

This leads us to the first general principle about criticism:

Principle 1: Many of your repetitious, emotional criticisms of your partner are disguised statements of your own unmet needs.

There is another piece of information that can be derived from criticism, one that usually requires a great deal of soul-searching. It is possible that the woman's criticism of her partner is a valid statement about herself. In other words, while she is berating her mate for his lack of organization, she may be just as disorganized as he is. To find out if this is true, she could ask herself a general question: "In what way is my criticism of my partner also true of me?" She should keep in mind that the way in which she is disorganized may be quite different from her partner's MO. She may keep an immaculate kitchen, for example, and be a whiz at planning vacations—the areas where he has difficulties—but have a hard time prioritizing her tasks at work or managing the family budget. With this new insight, she would be able to determine whether or not she was attempting to disown a negative part of herself by externalizing it, projecting it onto her partner, and then criticizing him for it. If she found that to be true, she would have the information she needs to allow herself to separate her own negative traits from her partner's: "I am disorganized in this specific way; my partner is disorganized in that specific way." In psychological terms, she would be *owning* and *withdrawing* her projections. Jesus said it more poetically: "Cast out the log in your own eye so that you can see the mote in your brother's eye."

This leads us to a second observation about criticism:

Principle 2: Some of your criticisms of your partner may help you identify your own lost self.

Perhaps this woman had a father who imposed his "orderly fashion" on her when she was a child, to the extent that she lost her ability to be more relaxed, flexible, and spontaneous.

From these two principles, we can see that criticism is either rewounding toward your partner or abusive to yourself. Reining in your criticisms toward your partner and exploring them internally will help shine more light on your unconscious behaviors.

In chapter 12, we will talk about how criticisms—in all forms and disguises—are detrimental to the relationship.

TURNING THE THEORY INTO PRACTICE

WE BEGAN TO focus our attention on turning the healing potential of love relationships into a workable reality. The unanswered question was: How could people be encouraged to overcome their limitations so they could meet their partners' needs? Wouldn't most people be reluctant to change for their partners' sake alone? Wouldn't they want something for themselves? Of course they would! What could be more rewarding, we thought, than for them to be able to get back parts of themselves that they had repressed in childhood? We decided that this would be the "bait" that would encourage people to become a healing resource for their partners. Once partners understand the Imago workup and the wounding experiences underneath, they look at their partners in a new light—as a fellow wounded warrior seeking the same outcome: to finally get the love they needed and searched for all their lives. Now the relationship is ripe for change.

We began to develop an exercise called the Behavior Change Request Dialogue that would help make this happen. It had some of the same features as the Caring Behaviors exercise. One partner would be asked to come up with a list of requests, which the other partner would be free to honor or not. In this exercise, however, the requests would be for changes in behavior, not for simple, pleasurable interactions; in fact, virtually every one of the requests would zero in on a point of contention. For instance, people would be asking their partners to become more assertive or more accepting or less manipulative. In essence, they would be asking them to overcome their most prominent negative traits.

As in the Caring Behaviors exercise, these general requests

would have to be converted into specific, measurable, time-limited activities. Otherwise, the partner wouldn't have enough information to be able to change, and there would be too much room for misinterpretation and evasive maneuvers. Also, like the Caring Behaviors exercise, the Behavior Change Request Dialogue would have to rely on the principle of the "gift," not the contract. Otherwise, the unconscious mind would reject the change in behaviors. This was very important. If one person made a small change and then waited for the partner to match those efforts—"I'll work on becoming less domineering if you will work on becoming more nurturing"—the whole process would quickly degenerate into a power struggle. The old animosities would flare up, and there would be no possibility of healing.

People would have to learn how to overcome their limitations and develop their capacity to love not because they expected love in return but simply because their partners deserved to be loved. The unconscious mind accepts only unconditional gifts. It is not interested in "deals."

With the general framework of the new exercise in place, we began to fill in the details. How would people determine exactly what behaviors to request of their partners? Two individuals may be quick to complain and criticize each other, but they are rarely able to state in positive, specific terms exactly what they need from each other. How could they come up with this information when it was not readily available to their consciousness? Wouldn't it take months or even years of intensive therapy?

There was an easier solution, we realized, and that was for them to examine their criticisms of their partners. Couples can get an accurate picture of what they did not get in childhood by analyzing their chronic complaints about their partners. The details aren't there—who did what when—but the raw material is sitting right on the surface, ready to be mined. The months or years that the couple have spent together have worn away their softer, more superficial annoyances and exposed the stony outcrop of their fundamental needs. "You never . . . !" "You always . . . !" "When are you ever going to . . . !" At the heart of these accusations is a disguised plea for the very things they didn't get in childhood—affection, affirmation, protection, independence, attachment. To come up with the list of requests for this exercise, therefore, the couples would simply need to isolate the desires hidden in their chronic frustrations. They needed to let go of the frustration and go straight to the wish embedded within. Then they could convert these general desires into specific behaviors that would help satisfy their needs. Other Imago therapists have labeled these SMART requests—small, measurable, achievable, relevant, and time-limited. This list of positive, specific requests would become the ongoing curriculum of the couple's relationship.

DEFINING THE CURRICULUM

HERE'S AN EXAMPLE from a couples' workshop to show how the Behavior Change Request Dialogue works. To begin the demonstration, we asked for a volunteer to state a significant gripe about his or her partner. Melanie, an attractive woman wearing a bright print dress, raised her hand. She shared what at first appeared to be a superficial frustration about her husband, Stewart. "Stewart has a terrible memory," she said. "It seems to be getting worse. I'm always nagging at him about his memory. I wish he would take a memory course."

Stewart, a mustached, scholarly looking man, was sitting next to her and, as if on cue, promptly began to defend himself in a weary tone of voice. "Melanie," he said, "I'm a lawyer. I have to remember thousands of pages of legal briefs. I have an excellent memory."

Before Melanie had a chance to restate her criticism, we asked her what bothered her most about Stewart's inability to remember. When did it make her the most upset?

She thought for a moment. "I guess when he forgets to do something that I've asked him to do. Like last week, when he forgot that we had a date to go out to lunch. Another thing that upset me was when we were at a party a few days ago, and he forgot to introduce me to his friends. I stood there feeling like a complete idiot."

We then prompted her by giving her the beginning of a sentence: "And when he did that, I felt . . ." We were trying to help her pinpoint the deeper feelings, such as sadness, anger, or fear that might underlie her frustrations. Basically, we were helping her identify the desire that was hidden in her criticism. But first, it was important that she identify her most frequent feeling and then identify the fear behind that feeling. "Well," she said, "when he does those things, I feel unloved. I feel he doesn't care for me. I feel rejected." Then we gave her another sentence stem and asked her to fill in the blank so that she could make the connection of this chronic feeling to her childhood. "And when I feel that, it reminds me of . . ." Melanie filled in the blank with, "It reminds me of my father, who was never there for me. He was always so preoccupied with other things, and he often forgot to attend my sporting events." I gave her a third sentence stem: "And what scares me about that is . . ." She replied, "I am afraid he doesn't love me. That I am not important to him."[1]

Turning to Stewart, we asked him to restate Melanie's frustration and mirror everything she had said so far—to give what we call a "summary mirror." With a little coaching, Stewart finally said, "If I got it all, your frustration is that I have a poor memory. And I forget what you ask me to do and also ignore you at parties, and this reminds you of your dad's constant preoccupation, which made you feel unloved and you were afraid that he did not love you. Did I get it all?" With tears in her eyes and astonishment that he remembered everything so well, Melanie said, "Yes."

We asked Stewart if he would validate Melanie's experience and express empathy by imagining the feelings she had as a child.

While this was difficult for him and he needed some prompting, he finally said, "I get it. Given the fact that your father was often preoccupied and forgot about your sporting events, it makes sense that when I forget things you ask me to do that it would remind you of your father's forgetfulness, and it also makes sense that you would be hurt and feel that you were not loved. I get that now."

And then he showed his empathy spontaneously. "And I can imagine that you feel angry when I forget things. Is that the feeling?" She confirmed his validation with some sobbing, saying that this was the first time ever that she had felt heard, had felt important to him.

Next, we asked Melanie to state what she wanted that would remove her frustration and the fear and hurt behind it, using global terms with words like *always* and *never.* In the unconscious mind, our wishes have no boundaries. We want "everything, all the time!" We have learned that it is important for people to state this global wish. Even though they realize they will not get it, it helps them focus on the childhood wish embedded in the frustration. After she came that far, we asked Melanie to break it up into manageable, bite-size behaviors.

"What I want most," Melanie started saying, "is to know that I am important to you all the time, that you are always thinking of me, and that I am more important than your work, always." At first, Stewart's face softened with this request. But then he looked overwhelmed.

"Now, Melanie," we continued, "write down a list of specific behaviors that would help you feel more cared for, important, and loved. Will you give Stewart some concrete information about how he could become a more positive force in your life?"

She said she would.

Next, we gave Melanie and Stewart and the rest of the group some detailed instructions. We explained that their partners would ask for behaviors that could be difficult for them to enact, because they had not been allowed in childhood.

Understandably, they would feel some resistance. Some might feel that it was impossible to respond. But, we continued, if you stretch and give your partner what they need from you, it will activate that part of you that was shut down in childhood, and you will develop new parts of yourself. Your partner's needs are an invitation and opportunity for you to grow. This became another mantra of our work: conflict is growth trying to happen.

We then sent the workshop participants back to their rooms, having asked them to identify a chronic complaint, isolate the desire that was at the heart of the complaint, connect it with a childhood experience, and come up with a list of concrete, doable behaviors that would help satisfy the unmet desire. They should then look at each other's lists and rank the behaviors according to how hard they would be to act upon. We told them that sharing this information did not obligate them to meet each other's needs but that the purpose of the exercise was to educate each other and to develop their capacity for empathy. If their partners then made the decision to stretch into new behaviors, they would now possess some specific guidelines. Any suggestion of obligation or expectation on my part would reduce the exercise to a bargain, bringing with it the likelihood that the whole experience would end in resentment and failure. We also asked them to start with a "mild" frustration—something that did not generate a lot of feelings around it.

When the group reconvened, Melanie volunteered to share her list. She had followed the SMART behaviors guideline and made her requests small, measurable, achievable, relevant, and time-limited. Here are a few of them:

> "For the next four weeks, I would like you to set aside one night a week so that we could go out for the evening. And during that evening, I want you to tell me three times that you love me."

"I would like you to introduce me to your friends when I meet you at the office for lunch next Thursday; and for the next three months, each time I come to your office, I would like you to introduce me to another friend."

"I would like you to give me a special present on my next birthday that you have bought and wrapped yourself, and during my birthday, I want you to look me in the eye three times, for one minute each, and say, 'You are the most important person in my life.'"

"For the next three weeks, I would like you to call me on the phone once a day just to chat."

"For the next two months, when we go out to dinner, I would like you to remember to pull my chair out for me, and then lean over and kiss me."

"For the next two months, I would like you to reduce your hours at the office so that you don't have to work on Saturdays and Sundays."

"For the next four weeks, I would like you to call me if you're going to be more than fifteen minutes late coming home for dinner."

"For the next three months, I would like you to give up your separate bedroom so that we can sleep together every night."

According to our instructions, Stewart had reviewed Melanie's requests, ranked them according to difficulty, and chosen a request that he could honor with relative ease. In fact, he announced to the group that he would begin the exercise that very evening by remembering to pull Melanie's chair out at dinner. There was a marked contrast between his earlier, antagonistic response to Melanie's complaint about his poor memory and his cheerful response to these specific requests. Because he understood that these behaviors addressed one of Melanie's unmet childhood needs, because he was allowed to rank them according to difficulty, and because he was free to choose whether to do any of them or not, he found it relatively easy to comply.

A sign that Melanie's list contained some growth potential for Stewart, however, was the fact that there were some requests that he found very difficult to do. For example, he thought it would be very hard for him to give up his own bedroom. "I really cherish my time alone," he said. "It would be difficult for me to give that up. I'm not willing to do that now." It came as no surprise to me that that was the thing Melanie wanted most: one partner's greatest desire is often matched by the other partner's greatest resistance. "I don't feel like we're really married unless we sleep in the same bed," she said. "I cried myself to sleep for a week after you moved into your own room. I really hate it!" I reminded Melanie that letting her husband know how much she wanted him to share a bedroom with her was an important piece of information for him, but he was not obligated to cooperate. The only legitimate power she had in the exercise was to inform Stewart of her needs and to change her own behavior to meet Stewart's needs.

COMPLEX CHANGE SET IN MOTION

WHEN WE WERE through working with Melanie's list, Stewart volunteered to share his list. He, too, had identified a chronic complaint, isolated his desire, connected it with a childhood need, and composed a list of target activities. His main criticism of Melanie was that she was too judgmental. It seemed to him that she was always criticizing him. This was painful to him, he acknowledged, because he had judgmental parents. "Which," he added with a smile and a sideways glance at me, "given all the information I've gotten at this workshop, is probably one of the reasons I was attracted to her."

One of Stewart's specific requests was that Melanie praise him once a day for the next two months. Melanie acknowledged that some days it would be hard for her to do that. "I don't think I'm being hypercritical," she said with sincerity. "I think the problem is that Stewart does a lot of irresponsible things. The basic problem is not my attitude—it's his behavior!" The main reason it was going to be difficult for her to praise Stewart, we realized, was that she was denying the validity of her husband's complaint. She saw herself as a realistic judge of his character, not as a perpetual critic. One of the benefits of the Behavior Change Request Dialogue, however, is that Melanie didn't have to agree with Stewart's assessment of her in order for the healing process to work. All she had to do was comply with his simple request for one compliment a day. When she did this, she would become more aware of her husband's positive qualities, and eventually, she would learn how immersed she had been in the role of judge and critic. Ultimately, both Stewart and Melanie would benefit from the exercise. Stewart would be able to bask in some of the approval that he deserved, and Melanie would be able to accept that it was his experience of her that was paramount, regardless of her intention. In the process of healing her husband, she would become a more loving person herself.

When couples faithfully perform this exercise for several months, they discover another hidden benefit of the exercise: the love that they are sending out to each other is touching and healing their own childhood experiences—wounds they didn't even know they had. Stewart and Melanie continued to work in private therapy sessions for over a year. About six months after the workshop, Stewart was finally able to overcome his resistance to sharing a bedroom with Melanie. He didn't like the idea, but he saw how important it was to her and decided to give it a one-month trial.

The first week, he had trouble sleeping and resented that he had agreed to the change. In his own bedroom, he had been free to open the window and get more fresh air whenever he wanted to, and turn on the light and read when he couldn't sleep. Now he felt trapped.

By the second week, he was able to sleep, but he still felt as though he were compromising himself. By the third week, he found that there was some compensation to sharing a bed. First of all, Melanie was a lot happier. And second, they were having sex more often: it was much easier to make love when they didn't have to make appointments. By the last week of the experiment, he decided that he could live with the new arrangement. "I've gotten used to having her sleep beside me now," he admitted. "I guess I'm not the hermit I thought I was."

Melanie and Stewart's relationship continued to improve, and during a session several months later, Melanie said that things had gotten so good between them that she no longer needed the reassurance of having Stewart sleep with her. "I know you love your own room," she said. "I'd rather have you stay with me, but I don't think I need it anymore." Through the Behavior Change Request Dialogue, he had been able to give her enough reassurance that he cared about her and valued her that she was able to let go of that particular request. But to her surprise, Stewart would have no part of it. "I'd be lonely in my own room," he said. "I wouldn't know what to do with myself."

What was going on here? Somehow, in the act of responding to Melanie's need for more intimacy, Stewart was discovering a hidden need of his own. In subsequent conversations, Stewart discovered that his mother and father had not been comfortable with physical or verbal expressions of love. Stewart maintained that this didn't bother him. "I knew that they loved me," he said. "They just showed it in other ways." In other words, his way of adapting to their lack of affection was to decide that he didn't need any. "I remember visiting other kids' homes," he told me, "and their parents were more affectionate to me than my own. One woman would even hug and kiss me. I was really uncomfortable around her. I was much more used to my parents' style of parenting."

When he and Melanie were first married, he was drawn to her because of her affectionate nature, but eventually, her need for intimacy seemed excessive to him, and he began to withdraw, just as he had pulled away from the adults who had been physically affectionate with him when he was a child. But now, with more insight into the nature of his problems and with a desire to be more intentional in his relationship, he had been able to overcome his resistance and respond to Melanie's needs. In the process, he had discovered his own repressed need for affection and was able to satisfy a hidden need of his own.

We have witnessed this phenomenon of two-way healing so many times in our work with couples that we can now say with confidence that most husbands and wives have identical needs, but what is openly acknowledged in one is denied in the other. When the partners with the denied need are able to overcome their resistance and satisfy the other partners' overt need, a part of the unconscious mind interprets the caring behavior as self-directed. Love of the self is achieved through the love of the other.

To understand why the psyche works in this peculiar way, we need to recall our earlier discussion about the brain. The old brain doesn't know that the outside world exists. Instead, it responds to the symbols generated by the cerebral cortex. Lacking a direct connection to the external world, the old brain assumes that all behavior is internally directed. When you are able to become more generous and loving to your spouse, therefore, your old brain assumes that this activity is intended for you.

REWARDS AND RESISTANCE

TO SUMMARIZE, MELANIE and Stewart reaped three important benefits from doing the Behavior Change Request Dialogue:

1. The partner who requested the change in behavior was able to resolve some childhood needs.

2. The partner who made the changes recovered aspects of the lost self.
3. The partner who made the changes satisfied repressed needs that were identical to the partner's.

The result of all this growth was a dramatic increase in positive feelings between them. Both Melanie and Stewart felt better about themselves because they had been able to satisfy each other's fundamental needs. Meanwhile, they felt better about their partners because their partners were helping them satisfy their needs. This made them more willing to stretch beyond their resistance into more positive, nurturing behaviors. Through this simple process of defining their needs, understanding how they are connected with the past, and then converting them into small, positive requests, they had turned their relationship into a vehicle for sustained safety, growth, and healing.

RESISTANCE

THIS BENEFICIAL CHANGE always involves some resistance. One of Freud's insights was that underneath every wish is a fear of having that wish come true. When your partner starts treating you the way you long to be treated, you experience a strange combination of pleasure and fear. You like what your partner is doing, but a part of you feels that you don't deserve it. In fact, a part of you believes that in accepting the positive behavior, you are violating a powerful taboo.

An example will help clarify the nature of this resistance. Let's suppose that you grew up with parents who were quick to point out your faults. Out of a misguided attempt to help you be more successful, they highlighted every one of your failings. They assumed that making your faults known to you would motivate you to correct them. All they managed to do, however, was erode your self-confidence. When you managed to triumph over their negative influence and act with a degree of self-assertion, you were told, "Stop being so cocky!" You were stung by their reaction, but you were a young child and had little choice but to cooperate. Anything else was dangerous to your survival. Over time, you began to identify with their negative view of you: "I am cocky!" Outside of your awareness, these negative feelings toward yourself deepened into self-hatred. When you looked for a mate, you unwittingly chose someone who perpetuated your parents' critical nature, and once again, you were under attack—but this time from both the inside and the outside.

Let's suppose that for some reason your partner begins to treat you more kindly. At first, you thrive on this turn of events. But gradually an inner voice makes itself heard: "You can't be respected," says the voice. "That's not allowed. If you continue along this path, you will not survive. Your existence is in the hands of others, and they won't let you be whole!" To appease this voice, you find ways to undermine your partner's behavior. Maybe you deliberately pick a fight or become suspicious of his or her motives. Ironically, you are looking for a way to deny yourself the very love and affirmation you so desperately want. Why do you do this? On an unconscious level, accepting love from your partner feels too dangerous because it contradicts a parent's view that you are unworthy of love. Going against a parent's edicts can trigger the fear of abandonment and death. To your old brain, it's far safer to turn away your partner's love than to trigger a parent's rage.

The defense against receiving love is more common than most people would believe. The fear can range from an inability to accept compliments to an inability to form an intimate partnership. The way to overcome this fear is to keep on with the process. We urge our clients to continue using the Behavior Change Request Dialogue until their anxiety becomes more manageable.

Given enough time, they learn that the taboos that have been impeding their growth are ghosts of the past and have no real power in their present-day lives.

One man was doing an excellent job of stretching into new behaviors. In response to his wife's requests to be more available to her and their children, he was slowly rearranging his priorities at work. He had stopped bringing work home on weekends, and he was home by six o'clock in the evening most days of the week. But when his wife asked him to become a more active parent, he ran headlong into his resistance. One day, he exploded, "If I have to change one more thing, I'm going to cease to exist! I'm no longer going to be me! It's going to be the death of my personality!"

To change in the way his partner wanted him to change meant that the "me" that he was familiar with had to go away. The rushed, successful executive was going to have to become more of a relaxed, nurturing parent. On an unconscious level, this change was equated with death. If you experience similar anxiety during this process, be assured that you will feel anxious from time to time, but you will neither die nor disappear, because you are not your behaviors, your values, or your beliefs. You are much bigger than all those things combined. In fact, if you were to change some of your more limiting behaviors and beliefs, you would become more fully the person you are—the connected, loving, spiritual being you were as a child.

Continue stretching into new behaviors that your partner requests. Stretch beyond your comfort level in ways that you can sustain. Small change produces sustainable change. At first, you might hear a voice from deep inside you saying, "Stop! This is too much! I'm going to die!" Or, "I'm always doing too much for her! What about me?" But if you continue to change, eventually your old brain will relax, and the voice will quiet down. Ultimately, the fear of death will no longer be an inhibiting factor in your mutual campaign for joyful connecting.

AGAPE

WHEN THE BEHAVIOR Change Request Dialogue is integrated into your relationship, the healing power of love relationships is not just an unconscious expectation, it is a daily fact of life. A love relationship can fulfill your hidden drive to be safe and deeply connected with another human being. But it can't happen the way you want it to happen—easily, automatically, without defining what it is that you want, without asking, and without reciprocating. You have to moderate your old-brain reactivity with a more intentional, conscious style of interaction. You have to stop expecting the outside world to take care of you and begin to accept responsibility for your own interactions. And the way you do this, paradoxically, is by focusing your energy on meeting the needs of your partner. It is when you direct your energy away from yourself and toward your partner that deep psychological and spiritual healing begins to take place.

When making a request—rather than reacting—becomes your standard method for dealing with criticism and conflict, you will have reached a new stage in your journey toward a conscious partnership. You will have moved beyond the power struggle and the stage of awakening to the stage of transformation. Your relationship will now be based on mutual caring and love, the kind of love that can best be described by the Greek word *agape*.[2] Agape is a self-transcending love that redirects eros, the life force, away from yourself and toward your partner. Agape is not dependent upon the worth or value of the other, and when it is expressed, it carries no obligation. It is an unconditional gift. As one transaction follows another, the pain of the past is slowly erased, and both of you will experience the reality of your essential connectedness.

CREATING A SACRED SPACE

Before you speak, ask yourself: Is it kind?
Is it necessary? Is it true? Does it
improve on the silence?
— SHIRDI SAI BABA

THROUGHOUT THIS BOOK, we have been talking about the vital role that safety plays in creating lasting love. Two people cannot be passionate friends unless they feel safe in each other's company. Couples need to feel physically safe, to be sure, but they also need to feel emotionally safe. Without safety, they cannot say what's on their minds, express their full range of feelings, or be who they really are. They cannot lay down their armor and connect, even if they truly want to. We are all built that way. Danger activates our defenses.

During our early work, we designed five processes, discussed in earlier chapters, to help couples create a climate of safety in the Space Between. To refresh your memory, the exercises are: (1) closing down the exits that prevent intimacy, (2) practicing the Imago Dialogue to deepen understanding and compassion, (3) injecting re-romanticizing techniques such as caring behaviors and surprises, (4) reimaging your partner by sharing information about your childhood such as in the Parent (Caregiver)–Child Dialogue, and (5) restructuring frustrations by transforming criticisms into respectful requests through the Behavior Change

Request process. These exercises help couples develop trust and goodwill and experience more joy in their daily lives.

In addition to developing these basic exercises, we have also spent many years searching for ways to help couples manage their intense feelings of anger and sorrow, those outbursts that are typically fueled by childhood pain and disappointment. When people spew these archaic emotions at their partners, the relationship can become a war zone. But on the other hand, when they repress their feelings, they can also jeopardize the relationship. When people deny this critical part of their being, they dampen their enthusiasm for life and their capacity to love. To make the relationship a safe haven, couples need to find a way to manage their intense feelings, which brings them closer together and sustains a feeling of connection.

HARVILLE'S STORY

I (HARVILLE) KNOW firsthand the destructive power of repressed feelings. I endured subclinical depression for the first thirty-three years of my life, and my emotional numbness was one of the main reasons for the failure of my first marriage. I was depressed because I was not in touch with my sorrow and anger over the deaths of my parents. When I look back, it is astonishing to me that I could lose both of my parents by the age of six and not experience any emotional pain. My father died when I was eighteen months old, and I have no memory of that event. My mother died from a sudden stroke five years later. I am told that I showed little reaction. I didn't even cry. In fact, I remember my adult siblings taking me aside and praising me for being such a "brave boy." Operating on naive childhood logic, I converted their compliment into a blanket assumption: "I am loved when I deny my pain."

I learned the lesson well. In young adulthood, I was able to look back on my early life and tell myself I was fortunate that both my parents had died: it gave me the opportunity to leave the farm and live in town with my sisters, where I got a better education. This myth had its uses. I went through my childhood numb to the pain of abandonment. I pictured myself as a "lucky" person, not a poor orphan boy, and I wasted little time bemoaning my fate. I took on challenges well beyond my years and succeeded at most of them. I was on my way.

But decades later, my repressed sorrow wreaked havoc on my first marriage. Cut off from my pain, I was not fully alive. To survive, I had anesthetized an essential part of my being. Unconsciously, I looked to my first wife for what I was missing. I hungered for emotional and physical contact, but she was unable to give me enough—partly because of deficiencies in her own childhood and partly because she experienced me as withholding, cold, demanding, and needy. It was a vicious cycle. The more I wanted, the more she withheld.

One of the most telling moments in our relationship took place the day after her father died. We were alone in our bedroom, and her grief over his death was just hitting her. She cried and cried. I circled my arms around her, but my body was stiff and unyielding. There was no warmth in my embrace. Inside, I felt deeply conflicted. Intellectually, I knew that it was reasonable for her to cry over her father's death, and I wanted to comfort her. But a larger part of me was cold and unsympathetic. That part was thinking, *What's the problem? I lost both of my parents when I was a little boy, and I didn't cry. Why is she so emotional?* Lessons learned early in life persist.

A few years later, when I was thirty-three, I saw a therapist for the first time—not because I thought I needed any help but because personal therapy was a recommended part of my training. In one of the first sessions, the therapist asked me to tell him about my parents. I told him that they had both died when I was very young but that a lot of good luck had come my way as a result. Because they both died, I got to live with my sisters, get out of southern Georgia, get a better education, and so on.

"Tell me about your mother's death," he said to me, cutting short my highly edited autobiography.

I started to tell him how she died, but for some reason, my throat felt constricted.

"Tell me about her funeral," he said.

Once again, I tried to talk. Once again, my throat seized up. Then, to my great astonishment, I burst into tears. I began to sob. There was no stopping me. I was an adult man, and there I was sobbing like a six-year-old boy. After a few minutes, my therapist looked at me kindly and said, "Harville, you are just beginning to grieve over your mother's death."

After that momentous day, I began to feel my own pain and anger—not just from the past but from the present as well. I became less anxious. I had more compassion for other people. If my needs or wishes were disregarded, I experienced the normal feelings of sadness or anger—but not rage or depression. Because I was being reunited with my full range of feelings, I was beginning to feel fully alive. I was more in touch with who I was and where I had been, and I became open to the rhythm of my own heart.

AN EXERCISE THAT FAILED

IN THE ORIGINAL edition of this book, published in 1988, we included an exercise to help couples release their repressed anger. We called it the Full Container exercise. It was based on the psychodynamic model of psychology that views the self as a container that is filled with pent-up emotions. According to this school of thought, purging those emotions helps people relieve their anxiety and depression and go on to live more satisfying lives.

Based on this theory, we adapted a new technique for couples that started with a frustration, linked it to a childhood experience, and amplified the annoyance until it turned into outright anger. We would guide the Receiver with ways to protect the psyche, such as creating an imaginary shield to deflect the anger and to keep from feeling under attack. "The anger is not just about you," we would advise the Receiver. "Its roots are deep in your partner's childhood." Once the catharsis was complete, we would help the couple deal with the original frustration by using the stretching principle described in chapter 10 to stretch into new behaviors to help alleviate the frustration.

As time went on, we saw that the Full Container exercise produced mixed results. The final portion of the exercise, the stretching and gifting of new behaviors, always worked. But sometimes the catharsis that accompanied the emotional purge had the opposite effect of the one we intended. Couples would become more conflicted than they were before. Eventually, from newer clinical research and from the ambivalent responses, we stopped using the Full Container exercise. Having two people in a love relationship vent their anger at each other—even within the confines of a structured exercise and under the watchful eye of a therapist—could cause more harm than good. This was a clear example of reality not supporting the theory.

Why Anger Breeds Anger

WHAT WAS WRONG with the Full Container exercise? First of all, some partners on the receiving end of the anger still felt threatened by the outburst, no matter how much they tried to deflect the torrent. Their old brains couldn't comprehend that their partner's anger was part of a clinical exercise. When the Receiver felt threatened, they had a hard time feeling empathic. They might mirror their partner's experience and mouth the right words—"I'm sorry you're in so much pain," but their primal instinct was to batten down the hatches (fight) or abandon ship (flight).

There was another, more puzzling problem with the exercise.

After the exercise, the partner who had vented the anger could feel angrier than usual in coming days. The exercise that had been designed to release stored-up anger seemed equally capable of generating it.

About this time, I (Helen) started reading books about neuroscience. I was fascinated by this field, partly because it shed new light on relationship dynamics. As mentioned earlier, the brain is more "plastic" than we first thought. Neuroscientists have known for decades that a young person's brain is greatly influenced by experience. If nerve connections are not stimulated, they are "pruned" away. When a child has new experiences, however, new pathways are formed. This plasticity gives the child a highly efficient, adaptable brain, ready for all that life has to offer.

Once upon a time, scientists believed that the adult brain was hardwired, thus immune to experience. The only way the brain changed beyond adolescence, according to early thinking, was to lose neurons with advancing age. This bleak view of the adult brain has now been revised, thanks to sophisticated imaging devices that can show physical changes in brain activity. These images have made it very clear that what adults do, think, and feel alters the physical structure of their brains. The adult brain remains a highly responsive organ that is frequently shaped by the interactions with others. Broadly speaking, people are wired for connection. Thus, feeling disconnected has a negative impact on their physical and emotional health. Focusing more on positive concepts and problem solving and asking certain questions from time to time can result in growing both the relationship and the brain in a healthier way.

A number of studies have shown that the more time adults engage in a particular activity, the more nerve cells are marshaled to the task. The brain acts like a military commander summoning new troops as they are needed. In one such study, Harvard medical researchers instructed a group of volunteers to practice a simple piano exercise for two hours a day for a week. After each practice session, the neuroscientists took images of the volunteers' brains so they could measure the size of the area devoted to finger activity. By the fifth day, they observed a significant increase in the size and activity of that area. Apparently, one of the reasons that "practice makes perfect" is that repeating an activity commandeers more neurons to the job.

Remarkably, researchers discovered that the same brain expansion takes place when people merely imagine doing a specific activity. As an extension of the piano experiment, the Harvard team asked another group of volunteers to imagine that they were playing a simple piece of music. They had no pianos in front of them. In fact, they were asked to keep their hands and fingers perfectly still. When the volunteers' brains were scanned at the end of a week, the scientists were amazed to see that the virtual piano players had the same expanded neural pathways as the people who actually played the piano. They had discovered that both mental and imaginary training can literally rewire the brain.

For the purposes of our work with couples, we were keenly interested in the fact that changing your thoughts can change your brain. Both the concepts of the brain being "experience dependent" and "social" can be helpful as we learn to care better for our relationships. A century ago, psychology fatalistically believed that "biology was destiny." Today, we see that people have the potential to rewire their brains with new experiences and in relationship with others.

THE HOLDING EXERCISE

NEW RESEARCH SHOWS that dwelling on anger has the potential to enhance the anger, not defuse it. We used to think that venting anger was like blowing the foam off a glass of beer: a few puffs, and you're done with it. Instead, it's like blowing on a fire—the more you blow, the hotter the flame. On a physiological level, expressing anger on a regular basis enlarges the part of the brain devoted to negative emotions. What you do is what you get. With so much cerebral real estate devoted to anger, an angry response can become a conditioned response.

Another fact about the brain is that the unconscious mind experiences all anger as dangerous to the self. It cannot determine whether the anger is directed at itself or at someone else. Indeed, new studies in the neurosciences of a phenomenon called *mirror neurons* tell us that in face-to-face situations, when neurons fire in someone else's brain, identical neurons fire in our own brain. When others are angry, we become angry. In other words, what you see is what you feel.

So now we encourage couples to share emotions—other than anger—that they experienced in childhood, such as grief, fear, and sadness. These less volatile emotions underlie the anger, and we have found that expressing them to a receptive partner helps relieve the hostility without reinforcing it. When couples share their childhood wounds with one another, they deepen their understanding of each other's past. They also experience renewed empathy for each other's suffering. Ultimately, they begin to see one another as "wounded" people, not "bad" people. Through this more accurate lens, they can see that most of their conflicts originate from childhood pain, not from any present-day malicious intentions. But we also encourage couples not to dwell on the past. The main purpose is to shed light on yesterday's pain and how it relates to today's conflict.

In addition to the Parent (Caregiver)–Child Dialogue, another exercise we use to facilitate the sharing of childhood experiences is called the Holding exercise. Unlike the Full Container exercise, this one helps relieve repressed feelings without generating more negative emotions. Using an earlier model of therapy in which the therapist holds and comforts a client— essentially "reparenting" them—we developed a similar Holding exercise. But instead of having the therapist hold the client, we asked the partners to hold each other so that the bonding experience would take place between the partners rather than with us. We asked one partner to sit in a comfortable position and hold the other partner with his or her head across the heart. From this position, they would recount painful childhood experiences while the holding partner gently and warmly mirrored their comments.

When we decided to experiment with the Holding exercise at our couples' workshop, an older couple, Gus and Vivian, volunteered to be the first guinea pigs. Gus was instructed to sit against a wall and hold Vivian in his arms as though she were a young child, with her head next to his heart. Being guided, Gus asked his partner to recall memories from her childhood. To facilitate the flow of memories, we suggested that he make encouraging sounds and mirror back to her what she was saying. When she was through expressing a thought or feeling, he might ask, "Is there more about that?"

After the momentary embarrassment of publicly taking part in such an intimate exercise, Gus and Vivian began to follow the instructions. Vivian spoke in a very quiet voice, keeping most of what she had to say between the two of them. Gus bent over her, listening intently. Their murmured expressions went on for several minutes. Then suddenly, Vivian began to sob. Gus held her more tightly and began to rock her. Tears filled his eyes as well.

The experience was very powerful for the couple. Gus's compassion for Vivian's pain was evident to everyone in the room. Later in the session, we had them switch roles, with Vivian holding Gus, and he was able to experience what it was like to feel safe and nurtured as he told his own story. When the two of them talked about their experience in front of the group, they said they had learned a lot about each other's inner worlds and felt deep empathy for one another. Like many couples, they discovered that they had endured many of the same insults in childhood but had adapted to them in different ways. The unconscious agenda that each had brought into the marriage was beginning to be revealed, and their earlier childhood experiences were healing in the process.

When couples take part in the Holding exercise, they get the response they have been longing for all their lives. Their old brains perceive their partners as surrogate parents. Only this time around, those parents have become attuned parents: accepting, nurturing, calm, attentive, and nonjudgmental. Pain from the past can be healed in the present when you receive attention and empathy from a loving partner.

REMOVING ALL NEGATIVITY

ONCE WE REMOVED the Full Container exercise from Imago Therapy and added the Holding exercise, couples began to make more rapid progress. Their conflicts became more subdued, and their mutual admiration grew. But there was yet more ground to gain.

We discovered that couples had an even more joyful relationship when they abolished all forms of negativity. This involved getting rid of blatant forms such as anger, shame, and criticism, but also eliminating more subtle forms as well, including such well-known ploys as "helpful" criticism, inattention, condescension, "the silent treatment," and using a bored or weary tone of voice. Ideally, this ban would extend all the way to eliminating even negative thoughts. Because we all have internal radar that makes us astute at picking up nonverbal cues from our partners, we can detect the subtle changes in posture and expression that accompany their negative thoughts, which means that a complete transformation cannot be made until that aspect of negativity is addressed.

Keep in mind that the goal is not to repress the feelings behind our negative thoughts and behaviors—that would only add to our store of pent-up emotions—but rather to bring them out into the open and see them for what they really are: a warning sign that some aspect of the relationship needs work. And as we have discussed in earlier chapters, the best way to start solving a relationship problem is to look at your own contribution: "Here I am, having critical thoughts about my partner again. What does this say about me? What am I doing or not doing right now that is feeding my negative attitude?"

The task may seem daunting, but the rewards are great. As negativity recedes, goodwill rushes in to fill the void. Without conscious effort, you find yourself focusing on your partner's admirable qualities, much as you did during courtship. Only this time, you will have the insights and tools you need to sustain your regard. Meanwhile, your partner will also be seeing you in a much more positive light, and you will both thrive in its warm glow. Eventually, a sacred space will well up between you, one that both of you want to nurture and protect. With conflict removed, connection will deepen and passion will flow.

WHAT IS NEGATIVITY?

WE WANT TO stop for a moment and clarify what we mean by negativity. Negativity is any thought, word, or deed that tells your partner, "You're not OK when you think what you think or act the way that you act." In essence, you are rejecting your partner's "otherness." We sometimes feel the need to negate our partners when they do or say something that makes us uncomfortable. Usually, they are just being themselves. But from our point of view, they are threatening an image that we have of them, or they are failing to meet an unspoken need of our own.

Typically, negativity makes its first appearance in a love relationship as denial: "I can't believe you did that!" "You never said anything like that before!" "You can't really mean that." "You're not that kind of person." The fact that your partner is a separate individual with wishes and needs different from yours is starting to dawn on you, and you feel threatened. Your denial is a desperate ploy to hold on to your illusions: "Say it ain't so!"

When your partner continues to depart from your projected image, the tendency is to bring out the big guns, one by one. Your arsenal includes shame, blame, criticism, invasiveness, avoidance, and finally, blanket condemnation. First you shame. "How do you think that feels?!" "You ought to be ashamed by the way you treated my friend." In essence, you are trying to make your partner feel guilty for being who he or she is.

Then you blame. "You were late, and that made me really upset. That's why I haven't been talking to you." "If you hadn't been so angry, we would have been able to settle the matter in very little time." When you blame, you put all the burden of your frustrations on your partner.

Next, you begin to criticize your partner's character traits in addition to his or her unacceptable behaviors: "You are so insensitive." "You are untrustworthy." "You always think about yourself first." You are attempting to paint your partner not only as the source of all your frustration but also as a "bad" person.

A subtler ploy is to invade your partner's psyche and act as if you had x-ray vision: "That is not what you really think." "The reason you're so crabby is that you are obsessing too much about work." "If you'll just listen to me, I'll tell you what you need to do."

The final weapon is absolutism: "You never listen to me!" "You always leave the hard work for me." "That's just the way you are." "Every time I make a simple suggestion, you have a big fit."

It's no wonder that our partners feel depressed, stay late at work, drink too much, don't want to make love, or stay up late by themselves. Being with us is not a safe place to be. They experience being chopped up into little pieces, dissected, and rejected. This is a form of emotional annihilation. At the base level, it expresses contempt. No one can be healed or grow in such a toxic environment. To get the love we want, we need to eliminate negativity in all its forms.

There's another good reason to stop negativity: the negativity that we express toward our partners comes back like a boomerang and affects us as well. That's because the old brain does not know whether the negativity is being directed outward or inward. This theory has been backed up by studies showing that when one person yells at another, the person being yelled at produces more of the stress hormone cortisol. That's to be expected. But perhaps more interestingly, the same increase in cortisol is seen in the angry person as well. One could say that any negativity that we direct toward others is a form of self-abuse.

THE HOME STRETCH

REMOVING ALL NEGATIVITY from our love relationship was the final turning point for us. When we succeeded, we finally achieved the relationship we had wanted all our adult lives—one that was safe, intimate, and passionate. For us, eliminating negativity was a two-stage process. The first stage was to work gradually through the power struggle. One would think that two therapists would be able to avoid the power struggle altogether, but this was not so. Like many readers of this book, we had difficult childhoods. We are also intense, highly motivated people, each burdened with a heavy dose of perfectionism. On top of that, we have strong opinions about nearly everything, and we both tend to think that we are "right." It took us a long time to realize that we had to choose between whether we wanted to be "right" or whether we wanted to be in a relationship! During the worst of times, our conflicts were on a par with many of the couples we counseled.

Over a period of many years, we overcame most of our problems by using the exercises in this book. We practiced the Imago

Dialogue and used it with some success within our own relationship and with our children. We still marvel at its power to defuse conflict and forge understanding. We became more thoughtful lovers and made frequent expressions of love and gratitude through words, notes, gifts, and thoughtful gestures. Over time, we also learned how to work together harmoniously as business partners. There were moments when we felt deep love and empathy for each other. But it was not enough. We still felt a lingering tension lurking in the relationship.

The underlying problem, we eventually discovered, was that we were allowing negativity to rupture the connection between us. It didn't take much. A critical comment. Impatience. A raised tone of voice. Sometimes, we would degenerate into loud arguments. Whenever we descended into negativity, our pain was acute. Negativity never got us what we wanted. It always made matters worse. When we cooled off, we realized that it would take us hours or even days of repair work to feel connected again. Eventually, it became clear as day that being negative with each other was irrational, abusive, and counterproductive. We agreed that the only solution was to eliminate all forms of negativity once and for all. We took a Zero Negativity Pledge and decided to go cold turkey.

To enforce our decision, we purchased a calendar, put it on our bedroom wall, and spent a few minutes every evening evaluating whether either of us experienced negativity from the other. If one did, we would draw a frowny face on the calendar. If we were successful in getting through the day without experiencing negativity, the day would receive a smiley face. For a while, our calendar had more frowny faces than smiley ones, but the calendar challenged us to be more positive and trained us to be more intentional and affirming. We also developed the reconnecting process to help quickly repair a rupture. You can find the Zero Negativity Pledge and Reconnecting Process in part 3. Eliminating negativity is the most powerful way to transform your relationship. Indeed, it is the foundation for lasting love.

We also instituted another rule: whoever initiated a negative comment or behavior would have to counter it with three positive statements about the other person. "I appreciate the fact that you were an attentive listener to me last night, even though you were very tired." "You gave me such great feedback on the letter I was writing to the board members." "I loved it when you took the time to go for a walk with me, even though you were busy." Each positive statement had to be unique and specific, and we couldn't repeat anything we had said before. A hidden benefit of this rule was that we discovered many wonderful things about each other that we had been overlooking when we were upset.

Our statements of appreciation increased the flow of love between us. Every time we told each other something we genuinely admired about the other, we were deeply moved—each and every time. Our admiration gradually evolved into a state of "chronic adoration."

Finally, we were giving each other the respect we both wanted on a continual basis. What's more, we found it easier and easier to do. Our relationship had become such a sacred place for us that we had no desire to violate it. To slip back into old behaviors became unthinkable.

We felt so blessed by what we had achieved that we held two recommitment ceremonies, the first of which was at our annual conference with our colleagues in the Imago community. We wrote new vows of commitment that were in keeping with all we had learned and recited them before the group. Afterward, our colleagues lifted us high in the air and paraded us around the room while everyone sang and danced. Two months later, we held a New Year's Eve ceremony in the majestic Riverside Church in New York City, where we were members. Our pastor led us through our vows in front of 250 family members and friends, after which we retired to a grand hall on the Hudson River, where we ate and danced and were roasted and toasted until midnight. When the fireworks exploded, we felt like they were just for us. We included all the celebrants of the new year as witnesses to our love and our future.

SAM AND AMELIA

IT WASN'T LONG before we were integrating all we had learned about negativity into our therapy sessions and workshops. Since then, we have been pleased to discover how rapidly some couples can weed out negativity, even those who have at times been in grave distress. We witnessed a particularly amazing and rapid transformation at a weeklong Imago workshop. Sam and Amelia's story is a poignant illustration of the healing power of "owning" and then subsequently withdrawing the negativity that you bring to a love relationship.

Sam and Amelia stood out from the other couples from the very first day. During group sessions, all the couples sat side by side in a semicircle. Most of them talked easily with each other during the breaks. Several couples who were there to enrich, not salvage, their relationships would give each other affectionate looks and touches on a regular basis. But not Sam and Amelia. They talked to each other only when taking part in an exercise. They kept their chairs more than a foot apart, preventing even casual contact. We could see that Amelia's face and body were heavy with grief. Sam had a blank look on his face, and he seemed withered and wan. The two of them came to the dining room at different times or sat down at separate tables. They seemed to be a couple barreling toward divorce.

On the third day of the workshop, however, after I (Helen) had spent some time counseling them individually, Amelia had a profound breakthrough. She and Sam were working on an exercise designed to help them identify their exits—the tactics they used to distance themselves from one another. At one point, Amelia put down her notebook and walked over to me. "Is criticism an exit?" she asked in a quiet voice. "Is it possible to exit a relationship by constantly criticizing your partner?" I replied that criticism was a tried-and-true exit and that intimacy was not possible when either or both partners were under attack. Amelia nodded and went back to her chair. When the exercise was completed, we asked the couples to spend thirty minutes talking privately about their exits using the Imago Dialogue.

The group reassembled in the early afternoon, and I asked if anyone wanted to talk about what they had learned. Amelia was the first to raise her hand. "I feel utterly devastated," she whispered, her voice low and tremulous. The other couples leaned closer so they could hear. "I'm at a total loss. I've just realized that I criticize Sam all the time. I've been in therapy before, several times, and we've been to two marital therapists, but I've never seen this about myself. I feel so horrible about what I've done to this relationship. And I have no idea where to go with it. I don't know what to do. If I take away the criticism, there's nothing left. I'd have nothing to say to him. I feel like I've just stepped off a ledge and I don't know how long I'm going to fall or where I'm going to land." We were all transfixed. People rarely make such a candid confession in front of others.

I asked Amelia and Sam if they were willing to come up to the front and continue their story. They both nodded. We took two chairs and turned them so they were facing each other. As Amelia and Sam sat down in the chairs, Amelia drew in a ragged breath. Sam reached out and took her hands, and they looked into each other's eyes. All exits were closed.

I knelt down so that I was at their eye level. "Would you be willing to talk about what it feels like to be in your relationship?"

Amelia began, "My criticisms aren't subtle. They are overt. Right in your face. If Sam does anything that threatens me, I won't let him get away with it. If he does something I don't like, like flirting with a woman at a party, I give him the third degree on the way home. I tell him exactly what I saw him do. And he will say, 'No, I didn't do that.' I'll tell him, 'For an hour, this is exactly what you did. You looked at her this way. You said this. You touched her there.' The blaming has been so intense, and I was 100 percent sure I was right. I thought that if I could just beat him into believing how bad he was, he would change. I did that for twenty years. More, maybe."

"Did it work?" I asked.

"No. Never!" She laughed at the absurdity.

Sam took his turn. "We almost didn't come to this workshop because we were going to get a divorce anyway. During most of the first day, I was mentally planning where I was going to live. I wasn't even thinking about resolving anything. I couldn't listen to what you and Harville were saying. There was nothing I had to learn. Nothing I had to resolve. I just kept thinking, *What am I doing here with this person? I have to get away.*"

I asked Sam how he defended himself against Amelia's criticism. Amelia jumped in and answered for him.

"Sam didn't counter-blame," she said. "He'd just retreat. He'd disappear emotionally or go to another room. And I chased him so I could blame him some more."

Amelia continued with the same remarkable candor. "During these last two days, I have had no place to go but to accept the fact that I am a blamer. To deny it, I would have felt even more pain than I was in already. It was the bottom. I was so overwhelmed by my insight into myself, I couldn't listen to anyone. I couldn't talk. I realized, *This is what I do. I blame all the time. I try to control everything. I want to keep Sam in a little box so that I can know what he's doing. I want to keep him in a box so that I can try to survive over here.* But all of a sudden, this afternoon, I realized I couldn't control him or blame him anymore. I have to stop. I have no choice. Now that my eyes are opened, I have to stop the constant criticism. It's insane. Criticism doesn't work. It gives you the opposite of what you want. It makes you feel very bad."

Later that day and the next, Amelia and Sam sought me out for more private counseling and support. During breaks, the two of them would sit off by themselves, talking intently, looking dazed and earnest. Their body language was the opposite of what it had been when they arrived at the retreat. They leaned toward each other, looked into each other's eyes, and touched each other constantly. The connection between them was palpable.

On Friday, the final day of the workshop, Amelia asked if she and Sam could talk to the group once again. Something remarkable had happened to them the night before that they wanted to share. They came up to the front of the semicircle holding hands.

Sam began, "We haven't slept in the same bed for years. We didn't want to be that close to each other. So last night, I was lying in my bed unable to sleep, and Amelia was over in her bed. I could hear her sighing."

Amelia said, "I was wide awake, and I was having negative thoughts about Sam. I tried to stop them, but I couldn't. Suddenly, I knew that if I stayed in my own bed and remained in my critical state of mind that it was going to be the end of our marriage. There would be no hope for us if I didn't act on what I was learning. I knew I should go over and talk with him. But I was frightened—if I broke out of our mold, everything would be different. I had no idea what was going to happen. Then I heard Harville and Helen say in my mind, *Just keep on pedaling. Keep on working the exercises.* So I got up and lay down next to Sam and said that I wanted to have an Imago Dialogue with him. He agreed. I began telling him what I was thinking and feeling. He was present. He listened to me. He supported what I was saying. He mirrored me back. He validated me. He was absolutely incredible. The next thing I knew, all my fear had turned into peace and calm, and I felt this amazing love for him. I've treated him so badly, yet he still was willing to listen to me and understand me."

"It was easy for me to do," Sam said. "I just followed the steps of the Imago Dialogue exercise. Because I knew how to respond to her, what would work, I felt much more self-confident. I could handle her. I didn't need to retreat or run away. I could just hold her in my mind and see her as a wounded child."

"This was my very first glimpse of real power in this relationship," said Amelia. "The real way to be safe. Before, I thought that safety depended on being on guard. I found that being honest and vulnerable in front of him—instead of being critical and controlling—was the only way to connect. For the first time in decades, we both feel safe enough to reach out to each other. We found the bridge to connection."

In just one week's time, Sam and Amelia had gathered most of the insights and skills they needed to transform their relationship. They have a great deal of work ahead of them, and they've wisely decided to continue the work with a therapist. But in our mind, they've made the most important transformation already. They've realized on a gut level that their reliance on the complementary defenses of criticism and avoidance was destroying their love for each other. Once Amelia found the courage to acknowledge the extent of her negativity, Sam was able to open his arms, forgive her, and comfort her. For the first time, Amelia felt safe enough to lay down her weapons.

CORE SCENE REVISION

CORE SCENE REVISION is another exercise that we rely on to help couples eliminate negativity. It is designed for couples who go beyond criticism and avoidance and engage in yelling matches and long, drawn-out fights. We call these recurring battles *core scenes* because they replay the central childhood traumas of both individuals. Basically, the childhood adaptations of one partner are pitted against the childhood adaptations of the other, making the encounter doubly wounding. Typically, core scenes end in an impasse, with both individuals in deep emotional pain. These futile, hurtful exchanges must end before love can begin.

One couple, Jack and Deborah, had recurring fights that

would last until the early hours of the morning. They named them "three o'clockers" because, typically, that's when the fights would end. These were not explosive fights, but wearing, exhausting, and repetitive confrontations that ended without resolution. Following a three o'clocker, the two of them would be tired and depressed for days.

During one therapy session, they recounted several of their recent fights to see if they could identify what the fights had in common. Jack was quick to see their repetitive nature, and once they had reduced their fights to their lowest common denominators, they both laughed. But then Jack said with a note of sadness, "This isn't something that I feel very proud of. Why do we fall into the same trap over and over again? I'm sick of it."

According to their description, their core scene goes something like this:

Act I: It is five o'clock in the evening. Jack comes home from work and is confronted by Deborah, who wants him to do a chore. It could be anything—help plan a vacation, do some yard work, sort through the mail. Jack says he would be happy to do it—later. After he has had a chance to take his evening run.

Act II: Jack goes jogging. He comes home. As he enters the door, Deborah approaches him again and asks if he will now do X. Jack says, "Sure. After I take a shower."

Act III: Jack takes a shower. Deborah tracks him down and insists that now is the time to do X. Jack says, "Just let me have a drink."

Act IV (the climax of the drama): Jack has several drinks. He begins to relax and enjoy himself. Deborah enters the room, irate. "Why don't you either do it now or tell me you aren't going to do it?" Deborah yells. "You are driving me crazy!"

"But I do want to do it," counters Jack. "Just give me time. I'm tired. I want to relax. Back off."

Jack works on a crossword puzzle or watches TV and ignores his wife. She gets hysterical. "I hate you!" she cries out. "You never do what you say. You never listen to me! I feel like I'm living with a robot! I have no feelings for you!" Jack tries to block out her anger by concentrating more intently on what he is doing. Then, finding no peace, he gets up and leaves the house.

Act V: Jack comes home hours later. He's had several more drinks. Deborah launches into her attack once more. The fight continues, with Deborah delivering devastating criticisms and Jack trying either to placate her or ignore her. Eventually, they both get tired of the melodrama and turn away from each other in despair.

Let's analyze this drama for a moment. If one were to search for Jack and Deborah in the psychology textbooks, Jack would be described as *passive-aggressive*. He is angry at Deborah for organizing his life and intruding on his space, but is afraid to express it directly. Instead, he stalls—jogs, showers, drinks, works on the crossword puzzle—in other words, he takes full advantage of the numerous exits he has built into the relationship. Deborah would be labeled as *aggressive-aggressive*. "She's a bulldog," says Jack, not without admiration. She is up front with her demands and her anger. The irreducible element in their core scene is that the more Deborah attacks, the more Jack retreats, and the more Jack retreats, the more Deborah feels abandoned. Deborah's anger at Jack's passivity is, in reality, disguised panic. She is terrified of being left alone, and Jack's inertness makes her feel as if she were dealing with a nonentity, a ghost partner.

In order for Deborah and Jack to end the impasse, they need to rewrite their play—not metaphorically but literally. Their homework assignment was to go home, take out paper and pencils, and rewrite the drama to give it a happier ending. It might help to read their new script several times so that the new options would be just as instructive to them as their habituated ones. They were assured that any change at all would be beneficial. Indeed, just being able to recognize a given fight as a core scene would be a positive step. Then, even if they managed to change just one of the acts, they would be creating the possibility of a new resolution.

Here are a few ways Jack and Deborah's core scene might be revised: Deborah could become less aggressive, essentially honoring Jack's request to "back off." After asking him once to do a particular chore and getting no response, she could stop making the request. Jack's need to withdraw might become less intense. He might gain the psychic space he needs to be able to do the chore before taking a shower or doing the crosswords.

Or the script might be rewritten so that Jack states his position more openly. "No. I don't want to do X. It's not all that important to me. I'd rather do Y." Deborah would be startled by his assertiveness, but if he persisted in affirming his own priorities, she would eventually become relieved. After all, what she really wants is a partner who is an independent, confident human being, not an automaton.

In both revised scenarios, there would only be one act: the Request and the Response. But if the frustration continues, they could move into act II: Deborah could ask for an appointment for a Behavior Change Request Dialogue and transform her frustration into SMART requests.

This practice of defining a core scene and then writing alternative versions can be an effective tool. When couples are able to objectify their arguments, identify the key elements in the drama, and then create different options, they are using the rational new brain to defeat the old brain's fight-or-flight response. They are creating new neural pathways that channel their feelings into a more calm and positive direction.

POSITIVE FLOODING

THERE IS ONE more Imago exercise that helps couples leave their negativity behind them and look toward a future free of emotional toxins. This final exercise is the grand finale, the ultimate expression of love and regard between couples. We call it Positive Flooding.

In its basic form, two people in a love relationship write down all the things they appreciate about one another. The list can include what they love about each other's bodies and character traits, appreciation for favors or activities they've done in the past, and overall statements of love and adoration. Then the partners take turns "flooding" each other with these specific expressions of love.

In the second part of the exercise, each person gets out a piece of paper and makes a list of all the qualities he or she would like to have praised. "Tell me that you appreciate how hard I work to support us." "Tell me that you like how intently I listen to you." "Tell me that you like my long, shapely legs." Then the partners exchange lists and take turns flooding each other with their specific requests. It's like making a list of all the things you want for Christmas, only in this case, you get to receive them all.

We (Harville and Helen) practice the flooding exercise for our own relationship regularly. Even though we designed the exercise and have watched it performed over and over again, we still feel moved by the intensity of the love and affirmation we receive from each other. It makes us feel deeply, thoroughly loved.

In the workshop version, all the couples perform the exercise simultaneously. One person in each couple sits in a chair (the Receiver) while the other partner circles around the chair (the Sender). For the first minute, the Sender describes what they like about the Receiver's physical features—a graceful curve to the lips, silky skin, a handsome nose, and so on. For the next minute, the Sender speaks a little louder and talks about the Receiver's admirable character traits—trustworthiness, honesty, kindness, bravery, intelligence, and so on. The third time around, the Sender speaks louder still and proclaims their gratitude for favors the Receiver has done for them—nursing them through a cold, putting chains on the tires in the middle of a snowstorm, going willingly to a family reunion, being a source of comfort when a family member had died. At the culmination of the exercise, the admiring partners proclaim their overall feelings of love and appreciation for each other, often while jumping up and down and shouting, *"I can't believe I am married to such a marvelous person!" "I love you, I love you, I love you!" "You are the woman of my dreams!" "You are my best friend and lover!"* The energy is contagious. There are bursts of laughter, bear hugs, and tears of joy from both the Sender and the Receiver.

Many of us have never heard someone say to us in a strong voice, "I love you." "You are wonderful." Instead, we've heard people yell, "Be quiet!" "Go away!" "Mind your own business!" "You are crazy!" This exercise opens the floodgates and inundates people with joy.

PORTRAIT OF TWO RELATIONSHIPS

> What makes a happy marriage? It is a question which all men
> and women ask one another. . . . The answer is to be found, I think,
> in the mutual discovery, by two who marry, of the deepest need
> of the other's personality, and the satisfaction of that need.
> — PEARL BUCK

I (HARVILLE) STARTED my career as a minister, not a therapist. As a young boy, I was a member of the First Baptist Church
in Statesboro, Georgia. At age fifteen, when I was a student at
Statesboro High School, I competed for a national award in
public speaking and won sixth in the nation. When my pastor
learned about that, he asked me to deliver the sermon on Youth
Sunday. Although I had just won a national award for speaking
and a trip to Washington, D.C., I remember standing behind the
pulpit dressed in a suit and tie, drenched in a cold sweat. The
church was filled with young people and their parents, and when
I started speaking, my anxiety disappeared, and I preached such
a passionate sermon that several people came up to me afterward
and said, "You should be a preacher."

Apparently my minister, George Lovell, thought so, too,
because several weeks later he called me to his office. "Harville,"
he said, "there's a little Baptist church about twenty miles out
of town. They just lost their minister. They called me and asked
if I knew anyone who could preach for them the next couple of

Sundays. Would you like to do that?" Flushed with success from my youth address, I said that I would, and I did.

From that point on, George Lovell began to think of me as his "preacher boy," and for the next few years, when other small communities needed a stand-in minister, he would send me. At seventeen, I became the permanent preacher at Pine Street Baptist Church in a little town called Guyton, Georgia. This was a full-time church position with two sermons every Sunday and all other pastoral duties. At nineteen, I was invited by a larger church to become their pastor, where I served until I finished college.

During my ministry at these two churches, between ages seventeen while in high school and twenty-one while finishing college, I baptized over fifty people, preached funeral sermons for and buried eighteen parishioners, and married four couples. While in high school, the church was only thirty miles away, but when I went to college at Mercer University in Macon, Georgia, the trip took three hours. My salary was enough to pay for a reliable car and my college tuition of $450 a semester. I studied hard during the week and drove back to the Pine Street Baptist Church each weekend to deliver the sermon. In the summers, I was a youth evangelist traveling up and down the Georgia and Carolina coast preaching youth revivals, bringing many to Christ.

Then, in my third year of college, I took an excellent course in philosophy and the critical study of the Bible. A whole new world of logical thinking opened up to me. As I became absorbed in the realm of abstract ideas, nothing seemed simple anymore, and when I went out to preach, my sermons were filled with probing theological questions.

I soon discovered that you don't win souls to Jesus by engaging in a linguistic analysis of the Bible. The summer after completing those fateful philosophy and Bible classes, I returned to the road preaching my new understanding of Jesus and the Bible, which clashed with the views of Christians in southern

Georgia. I was leading a revival at a church in a fairly good-size town where I had worked wonders the year before. The first night, all the seats in the arena were filled with more than 1,500 people eager to hear the new preacher boy. To their surprise, my opening speech was about the concept of "eternal life" and whether the word *eternal* referred to the quality of life or its duration. When I got up to speak the second night, I noticed that there were some empty seats in the balcony. By the third night, there were empty seats riddling the main floor. At the end of the weeklong revival, only a faithful few had stayed to listen. When it was all over, the minister took me aside for a heart-to-heart talk. He brought up the fact that the previous year, I had convinced 120 people to devote their lives to Christ; this year, only 8 people had ventured down the aisle. "You've started college, Harville, haven't you?" he said, the disappointment evident in his voice. I nodded. "Well, college has ruined you," he concluded.

My brief career as an evangelist rapidly drew to a close, but my intellectual curiosity about philosophy and biblical studies flourished. In my remaining year of college, I added a third interest—psychology. To me, theology, philosophy, and psychology were three portholes into one central reality, the reality of human existence, and each one offered a slightly different perspective and a consuming lifelong passion.

I (Helen) also had a religious upbringing. Raised in Dallas, Texas, my mother was a Southern Baptist and my father an oilman. Given that both my parents were busy with other things, I was not close to either one of them. I was raised to become a "Southern belle" in a culture where women deferred to men in many areas, especially with money. I went to Southern Methodist University for college, and a young man proposed to me and we married. After graduation, while it was never expected I was smart enough to get an advanced degree, I worked two years as a teacher in an all-black high school in a low-income part of Dallas until I became a mother.

My husband worked for the oil company, but after some financial challenges, we had a painful divorce. I became more focused on finding my own voice, because I knew I had a calling to help those in pain. I boldly pursued a master's in psychology, with the hopes of becoming a therapist. When I met Harville, I treasured meeting someone with whom I could discuss what was really important to me. After a prolonged courtship, I proposed to him. He accepted! I continued my studies and went halfway through a Ph.D. program in clinical psychology. Once our family oil company got to the point when I received dividends, I focused the funding on women's philanthropy to help strengthen women's equality. By empowering women, their voices and values were released into the culture to be in partnership with men's voices.

In these earlier years, I became conscious of the disparity between the haves and the have-nots, the roles assigned to men and women, the separation between God and sinner, the rupture between faith and feminism. Everywhere I looked, we were broken.

For both of us, our various "dives" into separate lenses — theology, philosophy, education, philanthropy, psychology, feminism — held this common theme of brokenness. For us, this rupture was visible in every door we opened — whether it was economic, gender, or racial disparity; our fall from God; or the Freudian repression of our inner sexual desires.

In our years of dating, we both read *The Tao of Physics* by Fritjof Capra, which led into our mutual cursory explorations into quantum physics and neuroscience to try to make sense of the separation that caused this brokenness. But we discovered that if you look deep enough in all these fields of study, a common thread emerged: relationship. All things are connected and interconnected. No matter where we look — from subatomic particles to neurons to universes — nothing is singular, nothing is separate. We may sometimes lose our awareness of connection, but that separateness is just an illusion. We cannot not be connected. And if our earlier relationships are responsible for our feelings of isolation, then our most intimate relationships are the best way to restore our experience of connecting.

As we have shared throughout this book, we (Harville and Helen) know personally what it's like to be a "difficult couple." Yes, even the top New York City therapists failed to help us. We admitted defeat and announced we were divorcing. Our wake-up call came one day when we realized that our relationship was filled with negativity. Our Space Between was filled with judgment, criticism, and shame that created anxiety, which resulted in the rupture of the connection we once had. It was committing to Zero Negativity and practicing a Zero Negativity Check each night that saved our marriage and restored our connection.

Ultimately, we learned that bringing safety to the Space Between invited the spirit of God to come and live with us in that sacred space. We both have come full circle to our roots. What leads us to believe that couples' therapy is a spiritual path? How can talking to people about mundane things such as "behavior changes" and "caring behaviors" and "childhood experiences" have anything to do with helping them experience the divine? They do because these practices guide us outside ourselves so that we can experience authentic wonder about our partners. And when we shift from judgment to curiosity often enough, our partners can truly become a wonder in our lives.

When we use the word *spiritual,* we're not giving the word its most common usage. We're not talking about going to church or following the doctrines of a particular religion or attaining a rarefied state of mind through meditation, fasting, or prayer. We're talking, instead, about a native spirituality, a spirituality that is as much a part of our being as our sexuality, a spirituality that is a gift to us the moment we are conceived, a spirituality that we lose sight of in childhood but that can be reclaimed in adulthood if we learn how to heal old wounds and experience joyful connecting. When we regain awareness of our essential inner unity, we make an amazing discovery: we were never cut off from the rest of the world. But it is only when we are in touch with the miracle of our own being that we are free to experience the beauty and complexity of the world. The universe has meaning and purpose, and we experience ourselves as part of a larger whole. Early in our relationship, Helen quoted a passage from Fyodor Dostoyevsky: "The man who desires to see the living God face-to-face does not seek God in the empty firmament of his mind, but in human love." It is in our love relationships where we have the opportunity to experience God face-to-face.

It is our conviction that one of the surest routes to this exalted state of being is the humble path of mutual selfless caring for one another. When we gather the courage to search for the truth of our being and the truth of our partners' being, we discover that the most gratifying journey a person can take is that of creating a psychological and spiritual partnership.

INTEGRATION

THE PREVIOUS CHAPTERS detail various ways in which this healing process takes place. Now let's stand back and get an overview of the entire process. The first step is to redesign our relationships to heal our wounds. To do this, we first build an atmosphere of safety and trust. By closing our exits, renewing our commitment to each other, and deliberately affirming each other, we create a safe and nurturing environment. We create this feeling of safety and validation by learning to communicate openly and effectively. As we overcome our resistance to this new way of relating, we begin to see our partners with even more clarity. We learn that they have fears and weaknesses and desires that they have never shared with us.

We then move into intentionally affirming our partners, flooding the Space Between with caring behaviors, fun, and surprises. This continues building safety and joy into the relationship. We embrace the knowledge that affirmations and negativity cannot travel the same neural pathways at the same time.

We then become more conscious of our old wounds. We look into the past for evidence of how we were denied adequate nurturing and how we repressed essential parts of our being. We do this through therapy, prayer, and reflection and by becoming more astute observers of everyday events. As we gather new insights, we share them with our partners, because we no longer assume they can read our minds. When our partners share their thoughts and feelings with us, we listen with understanding and compassion, knowing that this sharing is a sacred trust. Gradually, we start to reimage our partners, to see them as they really are—wounded children seeking salvation. We listen to and share with each other in order to illuminate our mutual darkness. Gradually, we come to accept the fullness, the dark and the light of our own being.

The next step in the healing process is perhaps the most difficult: we make a decision to act on the information we are acquiring about ourselves and our partners and become our partners' healers. We go against our instinct to focus on our own needs and make a conscious choice to focus on theirs. To do this, we must conquer our fear of change. As we respond to our partners' needs, we are surprised to discover that, in healing our partners, we are slowly reclaiming parts of our own lost selves. We are integrating parts of our being that were cut off in childhood. We find ourselves regaining our capacity to think and to feel, to be sexually and spiritually alive, and to express ourselves in creative ways.

As we reflect on all that we are learning, we see that the painful moments in life are in reality opportunities for growth. Instead of blocking the pain, we ask ourselves, "What truth is trying to emerge at this moment? What primal feelings are hiding beneath these feelings of sadness, anxiety, and frustration?" We learn that the underlying feelings are sorrow and the fear of death and that these feelings are common to us all. Finally, we find a safe and growth-producing way to transform these power-ful emotions and no longer allow them to jeopardize our rela-tionships.

One by one, the elements of our partnership that were once unconscious—the fears, the childhood needs, the archaic pain—are brought to the surface, first to find acceptance, then, ulti-mately, to be resolved. As our childhood wounds heal and as more hidden parts of ourselves come into our awareness, we have a new sense of our inherent unity and connectedness.[1]

Creating an intimate love relationship is a spiritual path, but it is not necessarily an exalted path. For the most part, it is a very practical, day-by-day sort of struggle. Eventually, you will have rewired your brain, stabilizing the changes you have been work-ing on with your partner so that your new way of relating is far more comfortable to you than your old way. You will begin liv-ing in a different reality—the reality of sustained connection. You will look for ways to spend more time together, not less. You will begin to experience your differences of opinion as creative ten-sion, as an opportunity to move beyond your isolated points of view. Your desire for sameness will disappear, and you will begin to revel in your partner's "otherness." If you happen to slip back into negativity, your reconnecting process will be quicker, easier, and less painful. One of the metaphors we give our couples is to "stay in the canoe and paddle." If you find yourselves among the rapids once again, the worst thing you can do is stop paddling. Moving forward with these new tools ensures that this, too, shall pass. To give this process greater reality, we want to share with you the story of two couples.

There are obvious differences between these two couples. When we first met them, the first couple, Anne and Greg Martin, were in their forties and had been married for only five years. Both of them had been married before and had children from their previous relationships. Both of them had full-time careers. The Martins learned about Imago Relationship Therapy early in their relationship and managed to resolve their major conflicts in just three years. Kenneth and Grace Brentano were in their midsixties and had been married for thirty-five years. They had four grown children. Kenneth provided most of their income, and Grace was primarily a homemaker. Kenneth and Grace struggled for thirty years before achieving a satisfying relationship. Much of this they did on their own before becoming acquainted with our ideas.

What these couples had in common, however, was more significant than their differences. Both the Martins and the Brentanos managed to create an intimate love relationship that satisfied each individual's need for healing—a relationship that made each individual feel safe and vital and loved and connected.

Anne and Greg

ANNE AND GREG met in Santa Fe, New Mexico, in 1981. Anne, who lived in Dallas, was spending the weekend in Santa Fe with two friends. She had been divorced for three years and had dated several men casually, and she was just getting to the stage where she wanted to remarry. "I wasn't interested in casual relationships anymore," she says. "I was looking for something permanent." That weekend, however, Anne was not thinking about meeting men; she was mainly interested in having a good time with her friends Josie and Shelley. On Friday night, the three women went out to a lounge. During dinner, Josie mentioned that she wasn't very good at meeting men. Anne jokingly agreed to be Josie's coach. "You don't have to do anything seductive," she told Josie. "If you see an interesting man, just look his way when he looks at you and smile. And if anybody asks you to dance, get up and dance. Then the guy will know that you're willing to dance and will have more courage to come over."

Anne was having a fun time giving Josie pointers on how to meet a man when she glanced up and happened to see a lone man walk into the room. He was tall and slender, and he was wearing a corduroy jacket. Anne remembers thinking that he looked "rugged yet neat." She also thought he had a presence about him, an aura of self-confidence and intelligence. Anne forgot all about her coaching job. "Now that one's mine," she said to Josie.

Greg has an equally vivid memory of the encounter. He was in town for the weekend, celebrating his imminent divorce from his third wife. In fact, he had filed the divorce papers the day before. He was interested in having a good time, but with three failed marriages behind him, he had no interest whatsoever in establishing a permanent connection. He walked into the lounge and glanced around. He noticed Anne, a tall, animated blonde in her midthirties, and was immediately attracted to her. After a while, he asked her to dance.

"We started talking right away," says Anne. "A lot of guys don't know how to talk to women, but we were going a mile a minute. I liked that about him." Another thing she liked about Greg was the fact that he wasn't daunted by her academic background. (She has a Ph.D. and is an associate professor of counseling at a Southern university.) Several of the men she had dated had been intimidated by her intelligence. To appear less threatening, she had learned to refer to herself as a "teacher." "But I knew right away that I wouldn't have to keep back anything from Greg," she says. "He told me he had a Ph.D. himself—in engineering—and that he admired bright women."

Greg and Anne talked and danced all evening, and Greg walked her back to her motel. The next morning, they met for breakfast and went for a walk. The attraction was strong on both sides, but not overpowering. That weekend might have been the beginning and end of their relationship if Anne hadn't impulsively sent Greg a card the next week. When Greg opened the card, he telephoned Anne and asked if he could come to Dallas that weekend to see her. Anne had other plans, but rearranged her schedule so that she could spend time with him.

"That was it," says Anne. "We were off and running. It was

almost as if a drug took over." When Anne reflects on those early days, she is amazed that she plunged so abruptly into the relationship. Greg had a lot of strikes against him. He had not one, not two, but three previous marriages, and he had four children from two of those relationships. Anne had written her doctoral dissertation on the difficulties of being a stepparent, so she knew exactly what she was getting into. On top of all this, she and Greg lived 250 miles apart and had well-established careers in their respective cities. "A sane person would have looked at those facts and run in the opposite direction," she says, "but the attraction between us was too strong."

What was the source of this attraction? To find out, we need to know something about their separate childhoods. Anne was an only child. Throughout her early years, her father was in the service, so she saw him only when he was on leave. Her mother joined the navy when Anne was six months old, leaving Anne in the care of her grandfather and step-grandmother. By the time her mother came back a year later, Anne had become very attached to her grandparents and once again had to sever close bonds.

This early pattern of abandonment was reinforced when Anne was seven years old and her mother and father divorced. Her father left town, and Anne didn't see him again until she was thirteen and managed to locate him by writing to the Red Cross.

Anne has clear memories of her early years with her mother. Her mother was a flighty, social woman who frequently placed her needs above Anne's. There were many times when her mother stayed out all night and didn't come home until late the next day. Anne would wake up, discover that she was alone, and stalwartly go about getting herself ready for school.

When Anne's mother did happen to be around, she was not very nurturing, according to Anne. "I don't remember being held or touched or stroked," she said. But her mother was the source of some vital approval. "She really thought I was neat and was very confident in my ability. She didn't say ugly things to me or criticize me."

Partly because of the need to care for herself and partly because her mother praised her self-reliance, Anne became a responsible, independent child. She turned to her school and to church for the nurturing she missed at home. She denied the pain that came from the lack of security and warmth in her upbringing because it was too overwhelming. To the outside observer, Anne appeared to be a self-confident, assertive young woman.

Unlike Anne, Greg was the oldest of five children and grew up on a farm in Arkansas. What he remembers most about his childhood is that there was not much affection between his mother and father. "There was a lot of yelling," he says, "mainly on my mother's side. She was a real vocal person. She had a lot of anger. But she was also very loving."

Money was always an issue in Greg's family. "My mother would bitch about money, and my father would ignore her." He describes his father as a kind, intelligent man, though without a lot of drive. "He worked hard, but he wouldn't accomplish much," says Greg. "He always seemed to be living in the future. He would say things like, 'If it rains in August, we'll get seventy bushels of corn, and everything will be all right.' Or 'If it rains, the soybeans will make it.' He was always saying, 'Next year, things will be better.' He sustained himself with a vision that things were going to be OK." One of the things that bothered him about his dad was that he had dreams that he never realized. "He always talked about wanting a plane," says Greg. "It was really important to him. But he never did anything about it. If I wanted a plane, I would make it happen. I would do whatever was necessary to realize that goal. My dad just let life slip by him."

Greg's parents were never abusive to him or his brothers and sisters, but, in his words, "it wasn't a hugging family." Greg played on his own a lot, spending time roaming around the farm creating vivid fantasies in his head. By and large, Greg remembers his childhood as being a happy period. "I was cheerful. Not much bothered me. But I was usually alone. Kind of aloof. I had friends, but I didn't let them get close. I didn't feel lonely, just apart. I had a sense that I was different from everybody else. Not worse. Not better. Just different."

Greg didn't break out of his isolation until late in life, well into his second marriage, and, surprisingly, it wasn't his second wife who managed to get close to him; it was a male friend. Greg explains how this came about. "This casual friend of mine kept wanting to get closer," he says. "I didn't like the guy at first, but he kept moving in, moving in. He kept asking me to do things with him. When that didn't work, he arranged for a foursome with our wives. I kept saying no, but he persisted. Finally I remember saying to myself, *I'd better get to know this SOB, because he's not going to go away.* He forced his way into my friendship. Kind of plowed his way in. He became my first intimate friend. It kind of broke the ice. But even though I finally learned what it was like to be close to someone, I didn't seek it out. I felt pretty self-sufficient as I was."

Greg's first marriage was to his high school sweetheart. "That one was easy," he recalls. "My first wife was more like a buddy or a friend. There never was a real strong love." The marriage lasted eleven years. Greg felt that they lived on different intellectual planes and that they had little in common, but to him, the fact that they were different kinds of people didn't justify ending the marriage. "We had two kids," he says, "and it wasn't considered proper in either of our families to divorce." Eventually, Greg got involved with another woman. "I think I was using it as an excuse to end the marriage," he says. "In everybody's eyes, an affair was a good enough reason to call it quits. You have an affair, you get divorced."

The worst mistake in his life, says Greg, was marrying the woman with whom he had been having the affair. "She wasn't a very kind person. She was smart, and I felt a strong physical attraction for her, but she wasn't the kind of person I wanted to marry. We had a lot of problems. We had sexual problems, communication problems, and she was always suspicious of me. She kept accusing me of having other affairs." Their stormy relationship lasted five years. During this time they had a child, and Greg adopted her son by another relationship. (Now he was the father of four children: two by his first marriage, two by this one.) When his second wife threatened divorce for the third or fourth time, Greg told her, "I've had it. I'm leaving and not coming back. Go ahead with the divorce."

Greg was single for four years and then married his third wife, a woman from a wealthy family in Alabama. She was five years older than he and, in contrast to his second wife, a "high-class" woman. He says that he married his third wife largely because he wanted a mother for his ten-year-old daughter, the only one of his children who was living with him. "I thought she could give my daughter a lot of things that I could not, or would not, provide for her." Greg and his third wife were good friends, and he had a lot of respect for her. There was nothing particularly bad about the relationship, according to Greg, but "there wasn't anything really wonderful about it, either. The highs weren't very high. The lows weren't very low. And there was no communication. There was no intimacy. No sharing. She was intimate with me, but my intimacy would only go so far. So that was the end of number three."

Greg's casual approach to divorce and marriage might alarm some people, but in an age where divorce is easy and genuinely helpful information on marriage is scarce, he was choosing one of the few options available to him. All he knew was that none of his three intimate love relationships worked for him. There was something missing in all of them—and in his life—that made staying married intolerable.

Anne's first marriage was similar to Greg's in that it was fairly serene, traditional, and uneventful. Her husband, Albert, was a high school math teacher in a private school. The first ten years of their marriage were smooth and serene. "Albert was busy with his teaching job, and I was busy raising our two little girls." Because of Anne's unusual childhood, she didn't have a good role model for married life. "I think I got my image of marriage from the television," says Anne, "and from books and watching other people. I didn't have any of the details. No skills. So my first one was all on the surface. But it didn't feel superficial; we were doing the best that we could."

Things went along fairly smoothly until Albert went through an emotional crisis in the tenth year of their marriage. It seemed to them that this was totally unrelated to anything that was happening in their lives. His suffering became so acute that he went to his doctor for help. The doctor told him he was suffering from anxiety and prescribed some sedatives to help him sleep. Albert dutifully listened to what the doctor had to say and went to a pharmacy to fill the prescription, but when he got home, his first words to Anne were "What does *anxiety* mean?" She couldn't explain it to him. "That's how naive we were," says Anne.

Albert went through the bottle of pills and still felt no better. Eventually, he discovered a workable solution, which was to withdraw. He spent a lot of time by himself; when he and Anne were together, he wasn't emotionally available because he was too busy trying to maintain his own internal equilibrium. Anne was deeply troubled by his withdrawal. Outside of her awareness, it brought back memories of her early abandonment. She struggled to break through to Albert, but nothing seemed to work. In desperation, she began to pull away from him. "I went back into my old childhood pattern of taking care of myself, that old coping mechanism of mine of being totally independent."

In addition to the lack of intimacy between them, Anne and Albert began to have other difficulties. "He wanted me to be a good faculty wife," Anne says. "I was friendly and outgoing and very involved, and the people at the school liked me. But there was a part of me that was not happy in this role." She, in turn, was unhappy with Albert's role as a teacher. "I wanted him to go back to school and get a degree in administration. I hoped that he would move into an administrative position at the school, which would spare him some of the pressures of teaching." When Anne reflects on the situation today, she realizes that she had hidden motives for wanting him to change careers. "Consciously, I was thinking about what the degree would do for him, but underneath it all, I think I was projecting my own unfulfilled ambitions onto him. I was the one who wanted to go back to school. I was taking my own frustrated career drive and putting it onto Albert," she says.

Albert eventually went back to school and got a Ph.D. When their children were old enough, Anne entered a master's program in counseling. She began to acquire a lot of information that helped her understand her own childhood, but she didn't learn much that she could apply to her relationship. "Most of the therapists I knew had relationships that were about the same as or worse than my own. They were getting divorced, having affairs. Why turn to them for advice?"

Meanwhile, the conflict between Albert and Anne intensified. As soon as Albert finished his degree, he decided to go back to teaching. This was devastating to Anne. "I thought all that schooling was going to be a springboard to launch him into a different career. I turned to Albert one day and said, 'What are the next twenty years of our life going to be like?' He said, 'This is it.' And I said, 'No, I don't think I want to do this.' What I was seeing in those twenty years was more of the same. I felt a void in my life. There was something very important that was missing."

By this stage of their relationship, there was little love between them. "We didn't fight much," says Anne, "but we were kind of at odds with each other. I wanted him to be different. He wanted me to be different. I was becoming more independent, and he wanted the sweet and supportive wife that he thought he had married. We were both growing individually, but we weren't integrating it back into our relationship. We didn't know where to get any help, and as I look back at it, I don't think we really wanted any. We were dead. Numb. We wanted something from each other that we weren't getting, but we didn't know what that was. We were both out of touch with our needs. On a scale of one to ten, I would say that our understanding of what was really going on in our relationship was about a three."

Anne and Albert got divorced in February of 1978. Their two children were ten and thirteen. "My older daughter took it very stoically, like her dad," says Anne. "But my younger daughter was very verbal and very clear about her pain. She acted out her anger." Anne and the two girls moved to Berkeley, California, where Anne entered a doctoral program in counseling and guidance. As part of her training, she underwent extensive therapy. Slowly, gaps in her self-knowledge started to fill in. She began to see that a lot of her discontent in her first marriage was due to the fact that underneath her confident exterior she was an anxious, fearful person. "For the first time, I realized that I was still aching from my earlier abandonment," she says. "I had all this pain and didn't know it. I was removed from it, yet it was affecting everything in my life." At one point, her therapist asked her if she had ever experienced an anxiety attack. She said, "Well, no." Later on, she realized that she had been fighting off a constant state of anxiety all her life. "It was a constant barrage. If I'd had an anxiety attack, it would have been like a pebble in the ocean. But I wasn't aware of my anxiety. It was second nature to me. That's the way the world was."

Anne eventually moved to Texas, where she became an associate professor of counseling and guidance at a large university. During this time, she learned about our views of relationship therapy. For the first time, Anne had a more comprehensive understanding of the psychology of love relationships. "And more important," she says, "I had a model of how to make it better. Once someone explains something to me and gives me a model, I can do it. Up until that time, I was really leery about remarrying. I kept asking myself, *What makes you think that the next one is going to be any different?*"

This was about the time that Anne met Greg. Let's take another look at their initial encounter to see if we can now decipher any of the unconscious sources of attraction. When Anne describes her first impression of Greg, she describes him as an intelligent, resourceful man who possessed that enviable quality of inner contentment. Now that she has a lot more self-knowledge, she can see that he was also sending her clues that he was emotionally unavailable. Like the father who was always gone in the navy and later abandoned her, and like the mother who didn't come home at night, Greg, with his extreme self-reliance and history of three divorces, was not going to let her get too close. His isolation triggered Anne's primary drive, which was to make a person who was distant and unavailable become close and dependable. Meeting Greg crystallized all her unfinished business.

Why was Greg attracted to Anne? A warm, loving, aggressive, volatile woman, Anne evoked strong memories of his mother. "I sensed that she could be just as loving as my mother," he said, "and just as aggravating. But one thing for sure, I knew she would stir things up. I may say I want peace, but the truth of the matter is, I want life to be challenging." And what he was also wanting, although he didn't know it, was to become involved with a woman who could break through his emotional barriers just as that persistent friend had done years ago. When he met Anne, he sensed that she had the willpower and the determination to do it.

Anne and Greg got married on New Year's Day 1982, only four months after they met. For the first few weeks of their marriage, intimacy came easily. "I trusted Annie more than I've trusted any other person," says Greg. But after a while, he began to feel that Anne was using intimacy as a weapon. "I felt she was asking me questions to invade my space. She always wanted to know what I was thinking and feeling." Gradually, he began to shut down. Being self-contained was a safe and familiar experience for him; being emotionally vulnerable was not. When Greg withdrew, Anne experienced it as a repetition of the withdrawal of her first husband, Albert. She became angry and demanding and was convinced that Greg was planning to leave her. "She would go really crazy," says Greg. "She would have all kinds of suspicions and want to know what I was planning. Well, I wasn't planning anything. I was just licking my wounds to get ready for the next offensive." The independence that Anne admired in Greg and the aggressiveness that Greg admired in Anne were now developing into a power struggle.

Anne remembers one significant episode. "I was really upset about something. Something had happened at work that was really painful. I was talking about it with Greg, and I started crying. He looked at me and said, 'I don't console people. I'm not good at it, so I don't do it. Don't turn to me for comfort.' And, of course, that's what I wanted from him more than anything else."

Soon there were other difficulties. Having four teenaged children between them, they had a relationship that was fraught with complexity. There were numerous times when they both wanted to call it quits. The only reason she stayed in the relationship, says Anne, is that "I was very aware of the fact that, if I broke up with Greg, I would be bringing the same issues to another relationship. And when I looked at him, I realized that he was someone I wanted to be with. He was worth the effort. The pain we caused each other was intense, but the attraction between us was very strong."

Knowing that they would not be able to deal with their problems without outside help, Anne invited Greg to one of our weekend couples' seminars. Although she was well acquainted with our theories, she had been reluctant to introduce them to Greg. "Because I was a therapist myself," she explained, "I was afraid of getting into the position of telling him what he was doing right and wrong. That had gotten me into trouble with earlier relationships. I wanted to have the ideas presented to him by a third person."

Greg had two important insights at the seminar. First of all, he was very moved by the exercise that helped him envision Anne as a hurting child. "I had never understood her pain before," he said. "All of a sudden, I understood what she was going through. She used to tell me that, when I wouldn't talk to her, she felt abandoned, but I didn't know what she meant. How can a grown woman feel abandoned? I had never experienced that kind of insecurity before. Suddenly, during this guided-imagery exercise, I began to see her as a hurting four-year-old child. As an eight-year-old waking up to find no one home. Here was this child being formed and I could see that and feel that—get in touch with Annie as a child. It was real touching to me, and it made me more willing to listen to her complaints and to try to change my tendency to withdraw."

The other insight Greg had at the workshop had to do with communication skills. When he saw the mirroring exercise demonstrated in front of the group, he realized that it would help him cope with his wife's intense emotions. Greg remembers the first time he tried it out. "Annie and I were driving in the car," he says, "and she was really angry. I think it was about my relationship with one of the kids. I remember that she was all fists and fury. I felt that she was throwing these lightning bolts in all directions, and all I could do was dodge them. My instinct was to throw some lightning bolts in her direction or just close down—that's what I would have done in the past—but instead, I made a conscious choice to mirror her. I didn't react. I didn't accuse. I just listened and repeated back to her what she was saying. As I listened to her, it was as if I absorbed some of her fury. She got smaller and smaller, until finally she was in a contained package. Then we were able to talk calmly and rationally. By not hooking into her anger, I was able to contain her." This experience made Greg feel good about himself and gave him renewed hope for the future of their relationship. "I was able to defend myself without attacking her or crawling inside my shell."

Eventually, Greg got so good at the mirroring technique that it became second nature to him. Whenever he felt threatened by Anne's intensity, he would put on his armor, listen, and stay in touch. "The result of all this," says Greg, "is that Anne has stopped getting so angry. She simply won't do it. It doesn't work anymore. We've progressed way beyond that. We can communicate now."

Another tool that Anne and Greg brought home from the workshop was the Behavior Change Request Dialogue. "Instead of fighting, we started asking for what we wanted," says Anne. "It's made all the difference." Initially, this exercise was difficult for both of them, though for different reasons. Greg's problem was that he prided himself on being self-sufficient. It was very difficult for him to admit that he needed anything from anybody, but especially from Anne. However, one need that Greg couldn't deny was that he wanted to have more frequent and more spontaneous sex. "I had this fantasy of coming home and finding Anne in a negligee, eager for sex. But it rarely happened." He finally learned that, if he wanted more sex, he would have to ask for it. "I had to be more direct about my needs. She wasn't going to read my mind."

Anne's problem with the exercise was of a different nature. She had no problem asking for what she wanted. Because of revelations that had come out of her individual therapy, she was well acquainted with her unmet childhood needs, and she didn't hesitate to ask Greg to change his behavior to help meet those needs. What she had a hard time doing was accepting his attentions once he responded to one of her requests. Anne gave the following example. Greg is the owner of an engineering firm and has to leave town frequently on business trips. This separation fuels Anne's fear of abandonment. To ease her anxiety, she asked him to call her up every single day, especially when he was out of town. Greg readily agreed to do this. After a few weeks of receiving these daily calls, however, Anne began to feel anxious. She began to think up reasons why Greg should stop calling her. "It's too expensive," she would say. Or "It takes up too much of your time." Greg was persistent, however, and called every day, despite Anne's unconscious attempts to sabotage his efforts. Eventually, she was able to relax and accept the gift.

Since doing the workshop, Anne and Greg have gotten better at expressing their needs and asking for what they want. One of the payoffs for Greg is that he spends less time trying to guess what Anne wants. "I used to always be trying to anticipate her needs," says Greg. "I would do all these things that I hoped would make her happy. But she rarely noticed, and I would be exhausted from trying to figure her out. Now I can relax, knowing that, if she wants something, she will ask for it. I like it much better this way. I take care of my own needs. She takes care of hers. We both will go out of our way to meet each other's needs, but we don't do so much mind reading."

One need that Anne has made abundantly clear to Greg is her need for security and affirmation. "I need and want massive doses of reassurance," Anne says. To help meet this need, she informed Greg one day that, whenever she was being overly emotional—whether angry or withdrawn or tearful—what she really wanted was to hear how much he loved her. She wrote down on a card the exact words that she wanted him to say. She handed him the card and said, "Here are your lines." The card read: "I love you. You're the person I want to be with. I want to live with you for the rest of my life." Greg, the man who had once proclaimed that he was not able to console anyone, has been able to deliver his lines with utter sincerity.

Anne and Greg have also learned a new way to fight. "We're real honest and direct," said Anne and offered an example. "I looked at Greg's hand the other day and noticed that he wasn't wearing his wedding ring. I felt hurt and betrayed. But instead of stewing about it, I spoke up immediately. I said, 'I'm really hurt that you're not wearing your ring. A ring is a visible sign to other people that we're married, and it's really important to me. I'm really upset. I don't know what it means that you're not wearing it. I don't like it, and I want you to wear it.' Instead of getting defensive or abusive, Greg listened to me and said, 'It makes sense that you feel that way. I understand that you're angry.' Later, he explained to me why he wasn't wearing it. It had to do with the fact that I had reverted to using my maiden name, and he was hurt about that. In his mind, not wearing the ring was kind of tit for tat. We didn't resolve the problem immediately, because the issues were complex. But the important thing is that we both got our feelings out. We listened to each other. We defused all the bad energy. And we're not angry anymore. Before, we would have gotten obsessed about it and gone on and on."

Through these efforts, Anne and Greg have been able to meet enough of their needs to attain a new level of acceptance. "I am secure enough in our relationship that I can now accept the fact that Greg is basically a self-contained person," says Anne. "It no longer threatens me. I can wait for him to reveal his feelings. I don't have to press him. When he's upset, my instinct is to make him tell me right now what is bothering him. I just want to get it over with. But that always puts me in the facilitator role. The other thing I found is that, if I wait before I make demands, he usually resolves things himself in his own way. And even when he doesn't, I can live with things the way they are. I've learned that I don't have to fix everything."

Anne and Greg are the first to admit that working to achieve a conscious partnership is not easy. In fact, Anne wants to go on record as saying, "Working things out with Greg is the hardest thing I've ever done." Greg voices a similar opinion. "Marriage is like growing flowers," he says. "You always have to work on it. If you don't, the weeds start to grow and choke out the flowers." He makes another comparison. "When you garden, it's important to have good tools. You can carry water by hand and dig in the dirt with your hands, but it's much, much easier to use a hose and a shovel. That's how I feel about living with Annie. We have the right tools and skills to make the kind of marriage we want."

The reason Anne and Greg are willing to put so much effort into their relationship is that they reap daily rewards. Greg thinks that one of the most obvious changes has been in their emotional states. "Early on in our relationship," says Greg, "we were both volatile people, only I kept a lid on my feelings and Anne was too free with hers. Now she's become less crazy, and I'm more emotional. Not that we're trying to become what the other person was—we've just reached a balance. We tend to oscillate around a mean. Sometimes she's more emotional than I am. Sometimes I'm more emotional than she is. But it's like we've established middle ground. Which is very reassuring."

Greg finds that what he's learning in this relationship has helped him become a more effective manager. "I've gotten quite adept at spotting hidden agendas," he says. "I know that the issue that people are talking about is not always the real issue. I look for the underlying problems." He also is better at putting himself in others' shoes. "I say to myself, *If I were that person, what would I be wanting or needing at this moment?* Being able to empathize with Anne has given me that skill. My marriage has also made me a better communicator and able to withstand more pressure. If someone at work has a problem or becomes angry, I am able to keep from getting defensive. I am able to get things done."

Anne finds that her relationship with Greg has made her a more spiritual being. "The strongest force in the universe is what I would call 'Christ in us' or the Holy Spirit," says Anne. "And to me, that's the same thing as the drive to completion. In my mind, our purpose on earth is to be the best that we can be in terms of loving and living and being kind to other people and developing our talents and our skills. I think the best way I can do this is to have full access to who I am. And that means being honest about who I am, the negative part of me as well as the positive. Being free to be complete. That has happened in this relationship. It's a great paradox. Because before I thought I was feeling self-confident, but in reality it was grandiosity. Now I just feel good about myself. All of me. I like being who I am. I can be alone and be happy. I'm more comfortable in my own skin than I have ever been. I'm walking around better on a moment-to-moment basis. My anxiety level is so low. That's a real difference. I feel truly happy and secure for the first time in my life."

We asked Anne if she had any advice for people who would be reading this book and perhaps confronting some of these ideas for the first time. "My advice would be to focus on yourself," she said. "And when I say that, I mean you should realize that what you are doing for your partner is what you're doing for yourself. I finally learned that, when I was stretching to meet one of Greg's needs, I was reclaiming a part of myself. So any time your partner asks you to do something, say to yourself, *Does this make sense? Does it behoove me as an individual to do this?* And if it makes good sense and if it behooves you to do it, then do it, regardless of how you feel about it, because in meeting the needs of your partner, you will be recapturing a part of yourself."

KENNETH AND GRACE

KENNETH AND GRACE met in the 1940s, when they were both in college. Kenneth was a premed student, and Grace was studying art history. They became friends when they happened to sit next to each other on the bus going home for spring vacation. Kenneth has a clue to what attracted him to Grace. "A woman in the seat in front of us had a screaming baby and was having a tough time comforting her. Grace asked the woman if she could hold the baby. Soon after Grace got the baby, it started to settle down. I remember thinking to myself, *That's the kind of woman that I would like to have as the mother of my children.* Deeper down—although I certainly didn't know it at the time—I was wanting some of that tenderness for myself."

Grace had a positive first impression of Kenneth. "He seemed like such a gentle, kind man." She was also pleased that during the long bus ride he expressed genuine interest in a paper she had written at school. "I liked the fact that he respected my intellect, something that other men hadn't done." She remembers telling her parents as soon as she got home that she had met a young man who was "as good as gold."

Underlying these conscious impressions were more powerful, hidden sources of attraction. What childhood need did Grace unwittingly bring to their romance? Grace was the oldest in a family of three children, two girls and a boy. She described her family as "a mixture of love and tumult." They prided themselves on being offbeat and doing unusual things. "We were all artists or musicians," said Grace. "There was a lot of spontaneity. Dad would say, 'Let's take a drive after supper. Leave the dishes!' Mother would say, 'Let me do the dishes first.' And Dad would say, 'If we don't leave now, we'll miss the sunset.' So we would all pile in the car and go off for a drive. We sang in the car, in harmony. We sang in church as a family, so we traditionally ended our family singing with the song 'Blessed Be the Tie That Binds.'"

Grace has fond memories of her early childhood. She remembers being her father's "little darling." When she was five years old, her younger sister, Sharon, was born, and she had a rude awakening. "All of a sudden, I wasn't the center of attention anymore. I felt cast out. I remember thinking, *What in the world has happened? Aren't I as cute as I used to be? Why am I not loved?* I just couldn't accept the fact that I was no longer the favorite."

Grace described her mother as a confusing mixture of warmth and petulance. She and Grace rarely got along. "She was so strong that I felt that I had to fight her to maintain my own identity," she recalls. "I think this is why I became a rebel." Her father was warm and caring and a good listener. She remembers having a very close relationship with him. "Some would say too close," says Grace. "I remember coming home from high school and lying down on the couch and having my dad rub my back. It felt perfectly comfortable and normal to me, but I know that it made Mother jealous." In later years, she would look back on her relationship with her father with some anxiety. "In a way, it was scary to be that close to him. When I got married, I remember that it was very hard on him. Right before my wedding, he told me, 'I always thought you would stay home and never get married.' He was partly kidding, but I think there was some truth to that." Besides experiencing some discomfort over the closeness of their relationship, Grace wished that her dad had a more forceful personality. "He was not very strong," she said. "He would disappear when things got rough. When Mother and I got into an argument, he would go polish the car or tend to his flowers. He would never defend me."

When Grace was about twelve or thirteen, she experienced a religious awakening. She went to a special youth service and was overwhelmed by the presence of God. She remembers feeling a confusing mixture of elation and guilt. Elation at "having God on my side, but guilt for being a wicked girl, for sassing my mother." Around that time, she remembers a day when her family was scheduled to go on a trip and she stubbornly refused to go with them. "I remember going to my room and praying and crying and carrying on. I have no idea what it was really about, but I remember an awful feeling. Some kind of emotional crisis. I remember feeling 'bad' or 'wicked.'" This negative view of herself was to be a refrain in later years.

Grace often worried about being "dumb." She got this idea from her parents, who would criticize her for doing "stupid" things. "It wasn't that I was really dumb," she says in self-defense. "I would just be thinking about something else and do dumb things." Perhaps another reason Grace developed this idea about herself is that she is by nature a "doer rather than a thinker." As a young girl, she had an assertive, take-charge personality and could be counted on to get things done with little wasted effort. After a minimum amount of planning and organizing, she would plunge right in. Sometimes Grace would pride herself on her ability to get the job done, but at other times she would agonize about not being as deliberate and contemplative as others.

One of Grace's strengths is that she is very artistic, something that was important to her as a young adult. When she was in high school, she was an assistant to the art teacher at summer camp and enjoyed helping children express themselves through art. In the following years, she won prizes for her free-form designs and surrealistic paintings, and art gradually became a primary focus in her life.

Knowing these facts about Grace, let's take a look at Kenneth's early years. Kenneth has had extensive counseling throughout his life. During our initial interview, he confessed he could "tell my life story with one hand tied behind my back." True to his word, in just a few minutes, he was able to give a comprehensive synopsis of his upbringing. "My mother was an intense, energetic, passionate woman," he began, "who wanted a lot from life and wanted a lot from my father, who was a passive, quiet, gentle man. My father was a model for me. I learned to be passive and quiet from him. My mother also wanted a lot from me. I experienced her as being hungry with me. Now as an adult looking back on my childhood, I can see it was because she wasn't being nourished by my father. She had a sharp tongue that could cut, and she was often critical and angry at me. I didn't understand why and often thought she was being unfair. I can remember as a kid wishing that I had a different mother. We would have some warm times, but I couldn't trust myself to get too close to her; I was afraid she would eat me for breakfast. I didn't even want to share my achievements with her, because I thought she would take them as a feather in her cap. And I wasn't going to let her do that."

There appears to be a basic similarity between Grace's and Kenneth's upbringings. Both had fathers who were passive and withdrawn and mothers who were aggressive and dominant. Kenneth, however, was not close to either parent. Though he greatly admired his father, his father remained at a distance. "We had some nice times together, but he was shy about talking about feelings. I wanted him to like me and be proud of me, but he never told me that he loved me. I learned from other people that he respected me, not from him." His father was especially wary of anger. "If I was ever angry, he would back away. He used the same technique with my mother. When she was angry at him, he would just withdraw. When my mother was angry at me, I tried to copy his evasive maneuver, but I could never back away far enough." Because of this early indoctrination, Kenneth learned to be afraid of his own anger; anger got him in trouble with his mother and alienated him from his father. "I decided at a young age to be nice," he says. But this persona was covering a desperate longing for, in his words, "some tender mothering and some firm and affirming fathering." And underneath this longing was a reservoir of anger at being denied those needs.

Kenneth and Grace exemplify a principle that we talked about earlier, which is that husbands and wives are often injured in the same way but develop opposite defenses. Kenneth and Grace both felt that they had to carve out a separate identity from an overbearing parent. This suggests that their key developmental struggle was in the stage that child psychologists would label "the stage of individuation and autonomy." Kenneth created his psychic space by being passive and "nice," hoping to sidestep his mother's anger; Grace established her identity by being rebellious and angry, trying to counter her mother's invasiveness. Because of their opposite solutions, it makes sense that they would be attracted to each other. Grace admired Kenneth's gentleness and goodness; Kenneth admired Grace's strength and aggressiveness. They saw in each other parts of their own essential nature that were poorly developed. What they didn't realize was that these opposite character traits were an effort to heal the very same wound.

Kenneth and Grace have some astute observations on why they were initially attracted to each other. "I made arrangements to take care of myself," says Kenneth. "I picked up Grace to re-mother me. She was full of warmth and vitality and tenderness." Grace has an equally succinct explanation for marrying Kenneth. "I was a 'bad,' 'dumb' girl looking for a 'good,' 'bright' boy. Kenneth was exactly what I needed." While these undoubtedly were some of their positive reasons for marrying each other, there were some negative ones as well. The most obvious one is that they had each chosen a mate who would perpetuate their struggle with the opposite-sex parent. Grace was dominant and aggressive—like Kenneth's mother—and Kenneth was passive and gentle—like Grace's father. They had chosen partners who had character traits that had caused them a great deal of anguish in childhood.

It was a full year, however, before these negative factors became evident. "The first year was pretty idyllic," says Grace. Problems developed in the second year of their marriage, shortly after the birth of their daughter. Kenneth was a physician at a struggling family-practice clinic. Grace was concerned that he wasn't aggressive enough about attracting new patients. "I kept seeing all these ways that he could help the clinic," recalls Grace, "but he was content with things the way they were. I kept seeing all these possibilities that he was not seeing."

They had their first real fight when Grace realized that the clinic was losing patients. "For two years, Kenneth had ignored all the signs that the clinic was going downhill. Now it was getting too late to do anything about it. Two of his colleagues left to find more lucrative employment. One night, I finally blew up." Kenneth remembers the fight and recalls that he appreciated

Grace's concern for the clinic but resented her intrusion. "On the one hand, I kind of looked to her for leadership," he says. "But on the other hand, I was furious with her for being so demanding. She seemed to think that she knew what I should be doing and that she had a right to tell me. I felt like she was my mother, making heavy demands on me."

Looking back on the episode, Grace, too, recalls having mixed emotions. "I was concerned about being too strong, too willful. I wondered whether downplaying my personality would make him more dominant. But I couldn't let things lie." The very factors that had been the key to their mutual attraction — Grace's assertive, outgoing nature and Kenneth's passive, gentle nature — were becoming the basis for a thirty-year power struggle.

Kenneth began to have some additional misgivings about Grace. "I was becoming aware of some things that I wished were different in Grace. For one thing, she didn't have the same intellectual interests that I did. I wanted her to read more and be able to discuss issues." Once again, Grace was getting the message that she wasn't "smart" enough. The young man who had once seemed so interested in her academic work was now criticizing her for not being intellectual.

When their daughter was in the first grade, Grace began teaching art part-time at a local high school. In the winter of that year, Kenneth's mother came to visit, and Kenneth and Grace had another significant confrontation. At the time, Grace was very involved in the school and was putting out a newsletter at their church as well. She was pleasant with her mother-in-law but went about her business as usual. "I was too busy to be a good hostess," she recalls. Furthermore, she refused to live up to her mother-in-law's expectation that she be a traditional homemaker and spend all her hours after work "cooking, cleaning, and mending." Kenneth's mother had to entertain herself during most of her visit and was so irate at this treatment that she left two days early, complaining bitterly to Kenneth as he drove her to the train. Being trapped in the car with his angry mother made Kenneth extremely anxious. "There I was, listening to my mother attack Grace and not daring to defend her. I didn't have the nerve to stand up for my own wife."

For Grace, this visit was an unpleasant replay of her childhood. Once again, she was relying on an ineffective, passive male to defend her against a critical, hostile mother figure. "I wanted Kenneth to stand up for me," she says, "to explain to his mother how busy I was. But he was afraid to ruffle her feathers, and then he had the nerve to be angry at me for failing to placate her!"

As Grace was recounting this episode, she remarked on the resemblance between Kenneth and her father. "My dad was a very kind, loving man, but he was not strong. I wanted him to be protective of me, to take leadership—the very same things I wanted from Kenneth." Interestingly, when she was angry with Kenneth, she treated him the same way her mother treated her father. "I would rant and rave, cry and yell, generally terrorize him with my anger. Kenneth would do his best to placate me. But the 'nicer' he got, the angrier I got. It all became quite poisonous." Unknowingly, Grace had introjected her mother's negative traits, the very ones that had plagued her as a child.

On the surface, Kenneth and Grace, like many couples, appeared to be polar opposites: Grace was the outgoing, angry one; Kenneth was the passive, pleasant one. However, underneath his superficial "goodness," Kenneth was just as angry as Grace. The way his anger revealed itself was through criticism. This tendency showed up early in their marriage. "From the word *go*, Kenneth never gave me the feeling that he admired me," says Grace. "Other fellows that I had dated treated me much more kindly. Kenneth was critical of my housekeeping, my parenting, my moods, my lack of intellect. And he was always playing teacher. He would ask me, 'Do you know such and such?'—some obscure fact that had no relevance to me. When I admitted that I did not, he would proceed to lecture me as if I were a high school student. I was able to put a stop to that particular behavior in the first few years. But he never gave me the feeling that he cherished me. He never loved me the way I wanted to be loved. Gradually, I think I lost much of the self-esteem that I had brought into the marriage."

Today, Kenneth can be quite candid about the way he used to criticize his wife. "I wanted a lot from her, and I was getting a lot. But I seemed determined to bite the hand that fed me. I needed to keep her unsettled, even though I knew how much this hurt her."

Why was Kenneth so critical of Grace? If you will recall, Kenneth's goal in life was to get tender nurturing from a dominant mother figure, but at the same time, he had to stay far enough away so that he would not be absorbed. Unconsciously, he accomplished this delicate maneuver by giving Grace enough love and affection to keep her interested, but maintaining a crucial distance through the use of constant criticism.

Because Grace was getting so little affirmation from Kenneth, she was understandably insecure about the relationship. She felt jealous and suspicious of his outside activities, especially his contacts with women. "There are so many women who fall in love with their doctors," she says, "I was sure he was having an affair." Kenneth admits that for a very long time he had "one foot in the marriage and one foot out. Like maybe somebody better would come along. Like maybe I hadn't picked the best one. It hurts me to say this, but I had only a partial commitment to Grace."

It's no wonder that Grace often felt angry. "The one thing I can't deny," Grace says, "is that there was a constant surge of anger in me." But at the time, Grace didn't know where it was coming from. The time that she was most aware of her anger was when she went to bed at night. She would say to herself, *Why am I so angry? Why is this?* But she didn't have any answers. Now when she looks back on this period of their relationship, it is plain to her that Kenneth was the source of her anger. She remembers that he often had to put in late nights delivering babies or responding to medical emergencies. When she heard the sound of his car coming down the gravel driveway, she would have a rush of what she calls "romantic feelings." She would be eager to see him, and she would greet him with an air of expectancy. But within a very few minutes, she would be angry. The romance would crumble. "I felt disappointed," says Grace. "Yet I wasn't even sure what it was that I wanted from him."

Kenneth and Grace's relationship went through many changes in those first twenty or so years. They raised four children, lived in three different cities, and had good years and bad years. But the emotional undercurrents were the same. Grace kept wanting more love, strength, and commitment from Kenneth. Kenneth kept wanting more love, softness, and, at the same time, more distance from Grace. The underlying tension was so great that had they been born in a more permissive era, they probably would have gotten a divorce. "I was always threatening divorce," says Grace. "After the first year of marriage, divorce was a frequently occurring issue. We were very different people, and we weren't willing to accommodate each other." One of Grace's deepest regrets is that she shared her anger at Kenneth with her oldest daughter. "From the time she was old enough to listen, I would complain to her about her father," she says. "To this day, I'm afraid she thinks less of him because of this."

The lowest ebb of their relationship took place when they were in their forties and Kenneth was going through a midlife crisis. Until this point in his life, he had always thought of himself as a "promising young man." Life was an adventure, and there were many avenues open to him. Now he looked around and saw that he was in a lackluster marriage, that he was a "mediocre" doctor, and that he didn't have much enthusiasm for his profession. "I was just delivering babies. I could no longer maintain the fantasy of a promising future," he says. This realization led to a long depression.

Meanwhile, Grace was going through a religious crisis. The

church had always been very important to her; suddenly, the beliefs that she grew up with no longer made any sense to her. She began to search for new meaning, but the more she searched, the less she found to hold on to. She turned to Kenneth in desperation. "I would say to him, 'Tell me what you believe and I'll believe it!' But he would only give me books to read. He gave me Paul Tillich, and I would sit and read and cry. I couldn't understand it. I finally decided that I was going crazy. I was going insane. I was too smart to be taken in by the conservative evangelists, and I was too dumb to understand the liberal theologians. I was in a religious vacuum."

Kenneth remembers Grace's tumult. "She wanted me to sort out her moral and religious confusion," he says. "I would try and fail, and there would be a storm of pain and rage from her. She was in anguish for her soul. I felt as if she had her hands around my throat, begging me for answers. I was supposed to provide something for her, and I was failing." He was distressed that he couldn't help Grace, but he was also aware that he was deliberately holding back from her something that she wanted. "She wanted me to be strong, to be decisive. And it wasn't just about religion. It was everything. She wanted to be a little girl and have me be the daddy. But that felt like an unfair position to me. I didn't want to be too strong. Then I would have to give up forever my wish to get what I needed. I wanted to be the child, too."

Gradually, the crisis began to diminish. Grace joined a church that was willing to accept her confusion and questioning, and she was deeply relieved to discover that her husband, a very religious man, stuck by her, "even though I was next thing to an atheist." At the same time, Kenneth sought help for his depression by joining a therapy group. In the course of his therapy, he made some important discoveries about himself. One of the most important ones was that he was making Grace carry all the anger in the relationship. "I was projecting all my anger onto her. I was the good, gentle one. She was the bad, angry one.

Meanwhile, I had a lot of unexpressed anger of my own, and keeping it inside of me was one of the things that kept me remote and made Grace so angry."

Slowly, Kenneth began to test out his capacity for anger. "It was while he was in therapy," recalls Grace, "that Kenneth dared to get mad at me for the first time. I don't even remember what it was about. But I distinctly remember that he actually raised his voice at me. He was dumbstruck that I didn't turn around and kill him. He didn't think he was going to survive his own anger." This was a crucial experience for Kenneth. He had challenged his internal prohibition against anger and lived to tell about it. He began to test his newfound ability. "I got mad at Grace four or five times in one week, just to prove that I could do it. Then I got so that any time she started yelling at me, I began to yell back. Only I made sure that I yelled louder." Even though she had always wanted Kenneth to be more assertive, once he started standing up for himself, Grace found it hard to get used to. At times, she yearned for the old, passive Kenneth.

Despite his wife's apprehensions, Kenneth continued to become more self-confident and aggressive, growth that was supported and encouraged by his therapy group. One of the messages that Kenneth was getting from the members of the group was that he wasn't asking enough for himself. "You act as if you're not entitled to much in life," they told him. Kenneth felt there was some truth to this observation, and he began searching for ways to feel more fulfilled. It was during this time that he had an affair. "I don't blame the group for what I did," he says. "They did nurture in me the notion that I was too self-effacing, but it was my idea to have this affair. I saw it as an opportunity to go for something for me. To spread my wings and fly. It wasn't that Grace and I were at odds with each other. We were actually doing OK at the time—not great, but OK. It's just that I wanted an exciting adventure. This was a way to prove myself."

The affair lasted only a couple of weeks. Grace found out about it when she discovered a motel receipt that had fallen from his pocket. She knew right away what had happened. "I had been suspicious of him for years. Now it had really happened." Grace reacted to the affair in a typical fashion. "I was furious. I yelled and screamed." Two days after her discovery of the receipt, she arranged for an appointment with a relationship counselor. "I wanted help dealing with this," she says. "I felt like I was going to explode. Also, I suppose, I saw therapy as a way to take him to court, make him acknowledge the pain he had caused me."

Through the therapy, Kenneth and Grace were able to come to a resolution. Kenneth agreed to stop seeing the other woman, and Grace agreed to try to rebuild her trust. In the process, Kenneth gained some important insights about Grace. "Her anger over the affair was threatening to me, but it was also very affirming. It showed me how much she cared about our marriage and that she was willing to pick up the pieces and continue to work on our relationship. We had talked about divorce for so long that I was gratified that she was still willing to see if anything good could come of a bad situation."

Understandably, it took Grace a long time to rebuild her trust. When Kenneth came home at night, she would ask him about his comings and goings in great detail. Kenneth patiently put up with her cross-examination for months, accepting full responsibility for betraying her trust. It was during this critical period of their relationship that the final crisis occurred: Kenneth had to have quadruple-bypass surgery. Even though he responded well to the surgery, Grace was more shaken by his heart condition than by the affair. "One evening," says Kenneth, "we were lying in bed and Grace told me that, if getting out of my life would make my recovery easier for me, she would be willing to leave. She knew that our marriage had not been very satisfying to either of us and thought maybe my heart problem was a sign of my 'disease.' If living apart would be a benefit to me, she would agree to a divorce. She made it clear that she didn't want to leave me, but she was afraid that living together was only making matters worse."

Grace's willingness to make this sacrifice was the turning point for Kenneth. "It was then that I decided to put both of my feet into the marriage," he says. "I knew I wasn't going to find a better woman than Grace. She was a remarkable woman. She had been hard to live with at times. But, then, aren't we all? I finally made a full commitment to our marriage."

It was suggested to Kenneth that maybe his decision to commit himself to Grace had something to do with her offering him an accepting, nonpossessive love, something that he had always wanted from his mother. He thought about it for a minute. "Yes. Yes. I believe that's exactly what it was. My mother's love always had strings attached. Grace was offering me a selfless love."

Kenneth and Grace didn't have an official ceremony to celebrate their remarriage, although there was one conversation in a restaurant that felt very significant to them. A pianist was playing the song "Someone to Watch Over Me," and Kenneth took hold of Grace's hand and said to her, "Let's make a deal. I'll watch over you, and you'll watch over me." It was a simple declaration of love: let's agree to be each other's protectors, each other's best friends.

Finally, after thirty years of an intimate love relationship, Grace was getting Kenneth's full attention and commitment. Spontaneously, along with his commitment, Kenneth gained new appreciation for Grace's good qualities. "I think he began to realize that I was intelligent. I wasn't an academic, but I was a gifted artist. I began to feel for the first time that Kenneth truly admired me." The anger that had consumed her for so many years became less intense—because, as Grace put it, "He truly loved me, and I knew it."

It was at this advanced stage of love and acceptance that Kenneth and Grace first came to one of our workshops. On their own, they had managed to work through their major impasse, but they still were able to acquire some new insights and skills. For Grace, the most significant part of the couples' workshop was watching a demonstration of the Parent (Caregiver)–Child Dialogue. She was deeply moved to see the couple learn how to connect their childhood needs to their current relationship. Grace realized the ways she continued to injure Kenneth through her subtle criticism. "I was still holding on to the global desire of him changing rather than looking at me on how I can change to heal him. It was a marvelous revelation to me!"

Since the workshop, Kenneth and Grace, like Anne and Greg, have also adopted the Zero Negativity Pledge. They both still slip into old and unintentional behaviors that land negatively on the other, but they have practiced using a signal to gently acknowledge the experience and quickly move into reconnecting. They are very conscious of what they are doing and are careful not to hurt each other in the process. "We never call each other names," says Kenneth. "We just express our frustration in a contained way. Sometimes it moves into Behavior Change Requests, but most of the time, because we learn to not reinjure each other, it is easy to move into repair and reconnect. We don't harbor grudges."

Grace believes that Kenneth's increased acceptance of her emotional nature has been the determining factor in her own acceptance of herself. "I think the fact that Kenneth accepts my energy and determination helps me accept what I call 'my mother' in me, the part of me that is like my mother, which I have always tried to deny. Because he likes who I am, I don't have to wage that battle anymore. I don't have to deny who I am."

For Kenneth, the biggest improvement in their relationship has been an increased sense of caring and safety. "We're friends now," he said. "Not antagonists. The key is that I feel safe. She's on my side, committed to my well-being. She is valuing me. Liking me. And I'm committed to liking her. Supporting her and affirming her. It just feels a lot different. The struggle with my mother is over. A woman is on my side, and it happens to be Grace. I can relax with her and feel safe with her."

Grace echoed this last sentiment. "That's important to me, too. I can relax and feel safe with Kenneth." For both of them, the primitive need of the old brain to be in a safe, secure, and nurturing environment has finally been met.

Kenneth and Grace attended two more couples' workshops, during which they noticed that we described the conscious partnership as a journey, not a destination, explaining that even in the best love relationships, there would always be struggle and the need to adapt and change. To some degree, their experience confirms this observation. "We still have problems," says Grace. "For example, Ken wants me to be more cautious in the things I tell him. To rehearse what I'm going to say, so that I don't risk hurting his feelings. But that's difficult for me to do. I'm an impulsive person. It would feel very strange to filter all my thoughts before I revealed them. And I want the opposite of him. I want him to be more spontaneous, less calculated. But that feels risky for him." They both express ambivalence about the challenge to keep growing. "Perhaps it has something to do with our age," says Kenneth. "Part of me wants life not to be a struggle anymore. Grace and I have arrived at a place that feels very comfortable. It's not that we've stopped growing and changing altogether, but this just feels like a nice place to be." In a way, they were questioning our description of love as a journey without end. It may be an endless journey, they are telling us, but it is a journey that becomes more and more effortless as time goes on.

These two relationships offer an excellent description of what we call "the conscious partnership." Anne and Greg, along with Kenneth and Grace, reveal it to be a state of mind and a way of being based on acceptance, a willingness to grow and change, the courage to encounter one's own fear, and a conscious decision to treat each other as separate, unique individuals who are worthy of the greatest level of respect. They are relationships built on a solid foundation, no longer just the infatuation of romantic love, but the feelings are just as joyful and intense.

When we look at love relationships in more detail, it is clear that the simple word *love* cannot adequately describe the wide variety of feelings two individuals can have for each other. In the first two stages of a love relationship, romantic love and the power struggle, love is reactive; it is an unconscious response to the expectation of need fulfillment. Love is best described as *eros,* life energy seeking union with a gratifying object. When both partners in an intimate relationship make a decision to create a more satisfying relationship, they enter a stage of transformation, and love becomes infused with consciousness and will; love is best defined as *agape,* the life energy directed toward the partner in an intentional act of healing. Now, in the final stage of a conscious partnership, reality love, love takes on the quality of *spontaneous oscillation,* words that come from quantum physics and describe the way energy moves back and forth between particles. When partners learn to see each other without distortion, to value each other as highly as they value themselves, to give without expecting anything in return, to commit themselves fully to each other's welfare, love moves freely between them without apparent effort. The word that best describes this mature kind of love is not *eros,* not *agape,* but yet another Greek word, *philia,*[2] which means "love between friends." The partner is no longer perceived as a surrogate parent or as an enemy but as a passionate friend. It is where we experience the original connecting, when the initial rupture is repaired, and we feel fully safe, relaxed, loved, joyful, and profoundly connected.

When couples are able to love in this selfless manner, they experience a release of energy. They cease to be consumed by the details of their relationship or to need to operate within the artificial structure of exercises; they spontaneously treat each other with love and respect. What feels unnatural to them is not their new way of relating but the self-centered, wounding interactions of the past. Love becomes automatic, much as it was in the earliest stage of the relationship, but now it is based on the truth of the partner, not on illusion.

One characteristic of couples who have reached this advanced stage of consciousness is that they begin to turn their energy away from each other toward the woundedness of the world. They develop a greater concern for the environment, for people in need, for important causes. The capacity to love and heal that they have created within the relationship is now available for others.

We have found no better description of this rare kind of love than in 1 Corinthians 13:

> Love is patient, love is kind. It does not envy, it does not boast, it is not proud. It is not rude, it is not self-seeking, it is not easily angered, it keeps no record of wrongs. Love does not delight in evil but rejoices with the truth. It always protects. It always trusts, always hopes, always perseveres. Love never fails.

THE EXERCISES

TEN STEPS TOWARD A CONSCIOUS PARTNERSHIP

THIS PART OF the book describes a ten-step process based on Imago Relationship Therapy that will help you achieve a conscious, loving, and deeply connected relationship. It contains eighteen exercises that will assist you in translating the insights you have gained about marriage into effective skills.

We have some general comments to make before we describe them. All the exercises have been thoroughly tested. With a few exceptions, they are the same exercises we have been assigning to couples for the past thirty years. These exercises have been shown to be very effective. Most of the exercises follow the principle of graduated change, which means that you will begin with an easy task first and move on to progressively more difficult ones. You will be in control of how fast you go and how much you learn. Keep in mind that the more difficult a particular exercise seems to you, the more potential it contains for growth.

You will discover that doing the exercises requires a significant amount of time and commitment. To complete them all, you will need to set aside an hour or two of uninterrupted time each week for several months. You may even have to hire a babysitter or give up some other activity to find the necessary time—just as you would if you were going to a weekly appointment with a therapist. This degree of commitment requires a clear understanding of how important a good marriage is to you and a continual affirmation of your priorities.

You may want to do these exercises but don't have the support of your partner. If you are the only one interested at present, do as many of the exercises as you can by yourself. A relationship is like a balloon filled with water: push on one part of it and you change the shape of the entire balloon. When you practice the exercises by yourself, you will begin to listen to your partner more objectively, share your feelings with more candor, block your defensive and aggressive reactions, and make more of an effort to please your partner. As a result, your relationship will improve. Eventually, your partner's resistance to change might diminish, and you will be able to go through the rest of the process together.

You can do these exercises as a couple or in a group setting where you have the support of other couples with similar goals. For more information about other resource materials, visit the website, www.ImagoRelationships.org.

As you work your way through the exercises, you will discover that the journey toward a conscious partnership is never a straight line. There will be moments of great joy and intimacy, and there will be detours, long periods of stagnation, and unexpected regressions. During the periods of regression, you may feel despondent or criticize yourself for backsliding. Couples often tell us, "We've fallen back into the same old patterns. We thought this phase of our lives was over and done with! What is wrong with us?" We respond that there is nothing linear about love and marriage. Relationships tend to move in circles and vortices; there are cycles, periods of calm, and periods of turbulence. Even when you feel as if you are going through the very same struggles over and over again, there is always some degree of change. What is happening is that you are deepening your experience or participating in a particular phenomenon in a different way or on a different level. Perhaps you are integrating more unconscious elements into your relationship or enlarging your consciousness of a change that has already taken place. Perhaps you are reacting more intensely to a familiar situation because you have opened up new feelings. Or, conversely, you may be reacting less intensely because you have managed to work through some of your feelings. These changes may seem imperceptible, but there is movement all the same. By continually affirming your decision to grow and change, and by diligently practicing the techniques described in the following pages, you will be able to make sure and steady progress on your journey to a conscious partnership.

DOING THE EXERCISES

AS WE DISCUSSED in chapter 7, making a firm commitment to work on your relationship before you begin the process will help you overcome any potential resistance to change. Take the time now to examine your priorities. How important to you is creating a more loving, supportive relationship? Are you willing to take part in a sometimes difficult process of growth and healing? If you are, take out a separate sheet of paper and write a statement indicating your willingness to participate. You may wish to use words like the following:

> Because our relationship is very important to us, we are making a commitment to increase our awareness of ourselves and each other and to acquire and practice new relationship skills. Toward this end, we agree to do all the exercises in this book in a careful, conscientious manner.

As you work on the exercises, keep in mind these two cardinal rules:

1. The information you gather in the process of doing the exercises is designed to educate you and your partner about each other's needs. Sharing this information does not obligate you to meet those needs.

2. When you share your thoughts and feelings with each other, you become emotionally vulnerable. It is important that you use the information you gain about each other in a loving and helpful manner.

Suggested Ten-Session Timeline

First session: Exercise 1

Second session: Read or recite Relationship Vision
       (Exercise 1)
       New material: Exercises 2–5

Third session: Read or recite Relationship Vision
       Do another Parent (Caregiver)–Child
       Dialogue (Exercise 5)
       New material: Exercises 6–7

Fourth session: Read or recite Relationship Vision
       New material: Exercise 8

Fifth session: Read or recite Relationship Vision
       Review the need to close additional exits
       New material: Exercise 9

Sixth session: Read or recite Relationship Vision
       Review the need to close additional exits
       Continue with 2–3 caring behaviors a day
       New material: Exercises 10–13

Seventh session: Read or recite Relationship Vision
Review the need to close additional exits
Continue with 2–3 caring behaviors a day
Continue to give surprises and engage in
high-energy, pleasurable activities and do
the positive flooding exercise again
New material: Exercise 14

Eighth session: Read or recite Relationship Vision
Review the need to close additional exits
Continue with 2–3 caring behaviors a day
Continue to give surprises and engage in
high-energy, pleasurable activities
Start daily short positive flooding
Continue with 3–4 behavior changes a week
New material: Exercise 15

Ninth session: Read or recite Relationship Vision
Review the need to close additional exits
Continue with 2–3 caring behaviors a day
Continue to give surprises and engage in
high-energy, pleasurable activities
Continue daily positive flooding
Continue with 3–4 behavior changes a week
New material: Exercise 16

Tenth session: Read or recite Relationship Vision
Review the need to close additional exits
Continue with 2–3 caring behaviors a day
Continue to give surprises and engage in
high-energy, pleasurable activities
Continue daily positive flooding
Continue with 3–4 behavior changes a week
New material: Exercises 17–18

Subsequent
sessions: Read or recite Relationship Vision
Review the need to close additional exits

Continue with 2–3 caring behaviors a day
Continue to give surprises and engage in
high-energy, pleasurable activities
Do positive flooding daily from now on
Do a Zero Negativity calendar check
Continue with 3–4 behavior changes
a week
Review Exercise 16
*New material: Add additional caring
behaviors and behavior changes as they
occur to you*

Note: You will need to save your responses to the exercises so you can refer to them later on in the process. We suggest that before you begin work, you prepare two loose-leaf note-books, one for each of you, each containing thirty or forty sheets of lined notebook paper. Do all your work in these notebooks.

Exercise 1: Your Relationship Vision

Time: Approximately 60 minutes.

Purpose: This exercise will help you see the potential in your relationship.

Comments: Do this exercise together.

Directions:

1. Take out two sheets of paper, one for each of you. Working separately, write a series of short sentences that describe your personal vision of a deeply satisfying love relationship. Include qualities you already have that you want to keep and qualities

you wish you had. Write each sentence in the present tense, as if it were already happening. For example: "We have fun together." "We have great sex." "We are loving parents." "We are affectionate with each other." Make all your items positive statements. Write: "We settle our differences peacefully" rather than "We don't fight."

2. Share your sentences. Note the items that you have in common and underline them. (It doesn't matter if you have used different words, as long as the general idea is the same.) If your partner has written sentences that you agree with but did not think of yourself, add them to your list. For the moment, ignore items that are not shared.

3. Now turn to your own expanded list and rank each sentence (including the ones that are not shared) with a number from 1 to 5 according to its importance to you, with 1 indicating "very important," and 5 indicating "not so important."

4. Circle the two items that are most important to you.

5. Put a check mark beside those items that you think would be most difficult for the two of you to achieve.

6. Now work together to design a mutual relationship vision similar to the following example. Start with the items that you both agree are most important. Put a check mark by those items that you both agree would be difficult to achieve. At the bottom of the list, write items that are relatively important. If you have items that are a source of conflict between you, see if you can come up with a compromise statement that satisfies both of you. If not, leave the item off your combined list.

Our Relationship Vision

Bill		Jenny
1	We have fun together.	1
1	We settle our differences peacefully.	1
1	We have satisfying and beautiful sex.	1
1	We are healthy and physically active.	1
1	We communicate easily and openly.	1√
1	We worship together.	1
1	We are each other's best friends.	1
1	We have secure and happy children.	1
2	We trust each other.	1
1	We are sexually faithful.	1
2	We both have satisfying careers.	2√
2	We work well together as parents.	1
2	We share important decisions.	2
2	We meet each other's deepest needs.	2
3	We have daily private time.	4
3	We feel safe with each other.	2
3	We are financially secure.	4√
4	We live close to our parents.	5√
5	We have similar political views.	3

7. Post this list where you can see it easily. Once a week, at the beginning of your work sessions, read it aloud to each other.

Exercise 2: Childhood Wounds

(*review chapter 2*)

Time: Approximately 30 minutes.

Purpose: Now that you have a vision of the future, this exercise will take you back into the past. It is designed to refresh your memory of your caregivers and other influential people so that you can construct your Imago.

Comments: You may do this exercise together or at separate times. It is important that you be free from distractions for a period of thirty minutes. Read all these instructions before carrying them out.

Directions:

1. First, do some slow stretching exercises to help you relax. Then settle into a comfortable chair. Breathe deeply ten times, becoming more relaxed with each breath.

2. When you are feeling peaceful, close your eyes and imagine your childhood home, the earliest one you can recall. Imagine yourself as a young boy or girl. Try to see the rooms from the perspective of a small child. Now wander around the house and find the people who influenced you most deeply as a child. As you encounter these people, you will be able to see them with new clarity. Stop and visit with each one. Note their positive and negative traits. Tell them what you enjoyed about being with them. Tell them what you didn't like about being with them. Finally, tell them what you wanted from them but never got. Don't hesitate to share your angry, hurt, or sad feelings. In your fantasy, your caregivers will be grateful for your insights.

3. When you have gathered this information, open your eyes and record it according to the instructions in exercise 3.

EXERCISE 3: IMAGO WORKUP

(*review chapter 3*)

Time: Approximately 30–45 minutes.

Purpose: This exercise will help you record and summarize the information you acquired in exercise 2.

Comments: You can do this exercise individually.

Directions:

1. Take out a blank piece of paper and draw a large circle, leaving about three inches below the circle. Divide the circle in half with a horizontal line. Put a capital letter *B* above the line on the left side of the circle, and a capital letter *A* below the line on the left side of the circle. (See illustration below.)

$$\frac{B}{A}$$

2. On the top half, next to the *B,* list all the positive character traits of your mother, father, and any other people who influenced you strongly when you were young. Lump all the positive traits of all these people together. (Don't bother to group them according to individuals.) List these traits as you recall them from childhood. Do not describe your caretakers as they are today. Describe them with simple adjectives or phrases like the following: kind, warm, intelligent, religious, patient, creative, always there, enthusiastic, reliable, and so on.

3. On the bottom half, next to the *A,* list the negative traits of these key people. Once again, lump all the traits together.

This list of positive and negative traits is your Imago.

4. Circle the positive and negative traits that seem to affect you most.

5. In the blank space below your circle, write down a capital letter *C* and complete this sentence: "What I needed most as a child and didn't get was . . ."

6. Now write down a capital letter *D* and complete this sentence: "As a child, I had these negative feelings over and over again: . . ."

(For the moment, ignore the capital letters. They will be referred to in exercise 5.)

Exercise 4: Childhood Frustrations

(*review chapter 2*)

Time: Approximately 30–45 minutes.

Purpose: This exercise will help you clarify your major childhood frustrations and describe the way you reacted to them.

Comments: You can do this exercise individually.

Directions.

1. On a separate sheet of paper, list the recurring frustrations you had as a child (see example below).

2. Next to the frustrations, briefly describe the way you reacted to the frustrations. (You may have responded in more than one way. List all your common responses.) Put the capital letter *E* above your reactions as in the example.

Matt's Chart

Ⓔ

Frustration	Response
Didn't get enough attention from my older brother.	Was a pest. Kept trying to get his attention.
Father often gone.	Sometimes I was angry. Usually tried to please him.
Felt inferior to older brother.	Resigned myself to my inferiority. Tried not to compete directly.

| My father drank too much. | Tried to ignore it. Sometimes I would get stomachaches. |
| My mother was overly protective. | I kept things to myself. Sometimes I was defiant. |

EXERCISE 5: PARENT (CAREGIVER)– CHILD DIALOGUE

(*review chapter 10*)

Time: Approximately 30 minutes.

Purpose: The Parent (Caregiver)–Child Dialogue is designed to help you deepen your memory of your childhood and increase your empathy for each other.

Comments: Decide who will be the Child and who will be the Parent/Caregiver. The partner playing the Child role acts as if he or she were a young child of a specific age and talks in the present tense. The Child selects which parent he or she wants to talk to. The Child may select either parent or any other significant caregiver. The partner playing the Parent takes the role assigned but responds with more compassion than the real-life parent.

Directions:
   1. Sit face-to-face. The Parent says, "I am your parent. What is it like living with me?" (If the parent was dead or was not present say, "What is it like living without me?" Or "What is it like to be my child?") The Child then describes painful childhood experiences with the parent by saying, "Living with you is . . ." or "Living without you is . . ." The Parent mirrors those memories in an empathic tone, "Let me see if I've got you. If I did, you said . . ." and checks for accuracy, adding, "Did I get you?" If accurate, the Parent asks, "Is there more about that?"

2. The Parent asks, "What is the worst part of all of that for you?" The Child replies, "The worst part of all of that for me is . . ." The Parent mirrors the Child. The Child continues the conversation by filling in the following sentence stems in order. "When that happens, I feel . . . And when I feel that, I think . . ."

3. Next, the Parent asks, "What are the good things you experience living with me?" The Child replies, "The good things I experience living with you are . . ." The Parent mirrors the Child. The Child continues with, "When I experience that, I feel . . . And when I feel that, I think . . ." The Parent mirrors, checks for accuracy, and invites more.

4. Now the Parent asks, "What is the best part of living with me?" The Child responds using the sentence stems. "The best part of living with you is . . . When I experience that, I feel . . . Then I think . . ." The Parent mirrors, checks for accuracy, and invites more.

5. Next, the Parent asks, "What do you need from me the most that I don't give you, and what would it look like if you got it?" The Child says, "What I need from you the most is . . . And what that would look like is that you would . . . (describes a behavior that would meet your deepest need)." The Parent mirrors, checks for accuracy, and invites more.

6. When there is "no more about that," the Parent summarizes the deepest hurt and need, validates, empathizes, and checks for accuracy. "Given your experience of living with me, and your deepest hurt, it makes sense that what you need from me the most is . . . and if I did that, you would experience . . . I can imagine if I did that, you would feel . . . and think . . . Did I get that?"

7. Now, step out of your roles. The Parent says, "I am no longer your parent. I am your partner. Thank you for sharing

that with me." The partner responds, "I am no longer your child. I am your partner. Thanks for listening to me."

8. Switch roles and go through the exercise again.

9. Now, on a sheet of paper, write a summary of what you learned about your partner's pain and childhood need. Review each other's summary statements for accuracy. Do not criticize your partner for any inaccuracy. Just correct the text until it fully reflects your experience.

10. When you are through, share what it was like to do the exercise.

EXERCISE 6: PARTNER PROFILE

(review chapter 3)

Time: Approximately 30–45 minutes.

Purpose: This exercise will help you define the things you like and don't like about your partner and compare your partner's traits with the traits of your Imago.

Comments: Do this exercise individually. Do not share this information at this time. The Behavior Change Request Dialogue exercise on pages 272–76 will help you make constructive use of this information.

Directions:
1. On a separate sheet of paper, draw a large circle, leaving three inches of blank space below the circle. Divide the circle in half with a horizontal line, as you did in exercise 3. Put the capital letter *F* above the line on the left side of the circle. Put the capital letter *G* below the line on the left side of the circle.

$$\frac{F}{G}$$

2. On the top half of the circle (beside the *F*) list your partner's positive traits. Include traits that first attracted you to your partner.

3. List your partner's negative traits beside the *G* on the lower half of the circle.

4. Circle the positive and negative traits that seem to affect you the most.

5. Now turn back to exercise 2 and compare your Imago traits with your partner's traits. Star the traits that are similar.

6. On the bottom of the page, complete this sentence: "What I enjoy most about my partner is . . ."

7. Now complete this sentence: "What I want from my partner and don't get is . . ."

Note: Your comments will make sense to you when you complete the next exercise.

Exercise 7: Unfinished Business

(*review chapter 2*)

Time: Approximately 15–20 minutes.

Purpose: This exercise organizes the information from exercises 2–6 into a description of your unfinished business, the hidden agenda that you brought to your love relationship.

Comments: Do this exercise separately.

Directions:
On a separate piece of paper, write down the words below that are written in boldface. Complete the sentences by filling in what you wrote beside the appropriate letters in the exercises cited in brackets.

> **I have spent my life searching for a person with these character traits** [the traits that you circled in B from exercise 3, page 254]:
>
> **When I am with such a person, I am troubled by these traits** [the traits that you circled in A in exercise 3, step 3, page 254]:
>
> **And I wish that person would give me** [C from exercise 3, step 5, page 254]:
>
> **When my needs aren't met, I have these feelings:** [D from exercise 3, step 6, page 254]:
>
> **And I often respond this way** [E from exercise 4, page 255]:

Exercise 7 completes the first portion of the exercises. You now have a relationship vision, a description of your Imago, a record of your early frustrations and coping patterns, a chart listing the things you like and don't like about your partner, and a sheet that describes the hidden agenda you brought to your relationship.

EXERCISE 8: THE IMAGO DIALOGUE

(review chapter 8)

Time: Approximately 45–60 minutes.

Purpose: This three-step exercise will train you to: (1) listen accurately to what your partner is saying, (2) understand and validate your partner's point of view, and (3) express your empathy for your partner's feelings.

Comments: Do this exercise together and often. The Imago Dialogue is a very effective tool for communication, mutual healing, and deep connection. It is the central therapeutic process in Imago Relationship Therapy. At first, it will feel like an unnatural, cumbersome way of talking, but it is an excellent way to assure accurate communication. With practice, the exercise will seem less mechanical. When you have the exercise down pat, you will discover that you do not need to use the structured process all the time. The three steps will be necessary only when you are discussing highly charged subjects or when communication breaks down. Eventually, through months of practice, you will feel safer, become less reactive to your partner's comments, and experience a deeper sense of connection and communication.

Directions:

1. Choose who will be the Sender and the Receiver. The one who decides to be the Sender starts the Dialogue by saying, "I would like to have a Dialogue. Is now an OK time?" (When using this process in your relationship, it is important that the Receiver responds as soon as possible. If that is not possible, set a time in the near future when you will be available so your partner will know when he or she will be heard.) The Sender signals his or her readiness by saying, "I am available now."

2. Both the Sender and the Receiver face each other, make eye contact, and take three deep breaths in sync.

3. The Sender now talks very briefly, sending the simple message he or she wants the Receiver to hear. The message should start with "I" and describe what the Sender is thinking or feeling. The first time you do this exercise, choose a message that is neutral and very simple. Example: "I woke up this morning with a sore throat and didn't feel like going to work. I decided to stay home."

Note: A good way to begin practicing Imago Dialogue for appreciations is by using the sentence stem, "One thing I appreciate about you is . . ."

4. The Receiver then mirrors (paraphrases) those words, starting with the words, "If I got it . . ." or "If I heard you accurately . . ." Example: "If I got it, you awoke with a sore throat, and since you don't feel well, you decided to stay home from work. Did I get it?" The Sender indicates whether or not the message was correctly received. If the answer is yes, go on to step 5. If the answer is no, the Sender explains what was missing or added without a hint of criticism. The Receiver mirrors back again. This continues until the Sender acknowledges that the message was received as sent.

5. The Receiver then asks, "Is there more about that?" If the Sender has more to say, he or she sends an additional message. The Receiver continues to mirror back the added information and then asks, "Is there more about that?" until the Sender has completed the message. (The question "Is there more about that?" is important. It helps the Sender complete all the thoughts and feelings linked with the first statement and prevents the Receiver from responding to an incomplete message. And since it is limited to "more about that," it helps the Sender limit the message to one subject at a time.)

6. When the Sender has completed the message, the Receiver then summarizes all the Sender's message with this lead-in sentence: "Let me see if I got all of that . . ." When the Receiver finishes the summary, he or she asks, "Did I get it all?" The summary is important because it helps the Receiver understand the Sender more deeply and to see the logic in what was said. This helps with the next step, validation. When the Sender indicates that all the message has been heard accurately, go on to step 7.

7. Now the Receiver validates the Sender's message starting with words such as these: "You make sense, because . . ." or "It makes sense to me, given that you . . ." or "I can see what you are saying . . ." Example: "What you say makes sense. Given the fact that you had a sore throat and felt bad, I can understand why you didn't go to work today." This response indicates that the Receiver understands the logic of what the Sender is saying. It is the Sender's "truth." The Receiver does not have to agree with the Sender, but it is essential that the Receiver "sees" the logic or "truth" of the Sender's experience. The Receiver checks to see if the Sender feels validated. If so, then move on to step 8.

8. The Receiver expresses his or her empathy by starting with the following sentence stems: "I can imagine that you might be feeling . . ." or "I imagine that you felt . . ." Example: "I can imagine that you might be feeling frustrated that you had to miss a day of work." Feelings are best stated using one word such as *angry, upset, happy,* and so on. If you use more than one word, such as *you feel you don't want to go to work,* you are probably expressing a thought. Then the Receiver checks for accuracy by asking, "Is that what you are feeling?" or "Did I get your feeling right?" If the Receiver did not imagine the right feeling or misperceived the expressed feeling, then the Sender explains what the feeling is. Once the feeling has been identified correctly, the Receiver asks, "Is there more about that feeling?" Continue the process until the exchange is completed.

9. When the Receiver has gone through all three steps—mirroring, validating, and empathizing—the partners switch roles. The new Sender (the former Receiver) can respond to the partner's original message or may express an unrelated thought or feeling. Go through all the steps, as before.

10. Now use the three-step Imago Dialogue to share what each of you learned about yourself when doing exercise 2, Childhood Wounds. As you listen, try to visualize your partner's childhood frustrations or pain. When it's your turn to talk, divide your comments into simple, easy to remember statements.

EXERCISE 9: THE COMMITMENT DECISION

(*review chapter 7*)

Time: Approximately 60–90 minutes.

Purpose: This exercise serves two purposes: (1) it assures that you will stay together while you are working through these exercises, and (2) it creates a sense of safety that gradually increases your level of intimacy.

Comments: Do this exercise together.

Directions:

1. Imagine that your relationship is represented by a rectangle with perforated sides. The open spaces are your "exits," by which we mean all the inappropriate ways that you seek safety, gratify your needs, or drain the energy away from your relationship. In essence, you use an exit to act out your feelings rather than talking about them with your partner.

Each of the four corners of the rectangle is a catastrophic exit—suicide, divorce (or separation), murder, and insanity. Examine your thoughts and feelings to see if you are contemplating leaving the relationship through any of these corner exits. If so, we urge you to make a decision now to close them for the period of time that you are working together on these exercises. If you cannot make that decision, then we urge you to call an Imago therapist and begin therapy. (Go to www.ImagoRelationships

.org to locate a nearby therapist. If you cannot find an Imago therapist, find a couples' therapist in your area.)

2. Now take out four sheets of paper, two for each of you. On your first sheet of paper, make a comprehensive list of your noncatastrophic exits. Noncatastrophic exits are such things as overeating, staying late at work, spending too much time with the children—anything that you do primarily to avoid your partner. (See page 102 for a more comprehensive list.)

3. Using the mirroring technique described in exercise 8, the Imago Dialogue, take turns sharing the list of exits you are using. (You do not have to use all the steps in the Imago Dialogue, just the mirroring portion.) Example:

PARTNER A: I am aware that I bring work home for the weekend and that I do that because I am afraid to spend time with you and get into conflict about something.

PARTNER B: You think you bring home work from the office because you are afraid to spend time with me. Did I understand you correctly?

PARTNER A: Not completely. I said that I think that one of the reasons that I bring work home is to avoid spending time with you because we get into conflicts and that is unpleasant for me. I have other reasons, too.

PARTNER B: OK. You are saying that one of the reasons you work over the weekends is to spend less time with me because we get into conflicts and that is unpleasant for you. And you have other reasons, too. Did I get you this time?

PARTNER A: Yes, you heard me correctly.

4. Now, working with your own list, put a check mark by exits that you are willing to eliminate or use less frequently at the present time. Put an *X* by those that would be difficult for you to change.

5. Write out the following agreement and fill in the blanks: "Starting this week [insert date], rather than bringing work home, I agree to ask you for a dialogue to talk about why I work on the weekends and my fear of being in conflict with you."

Note: It is important to talk about the fear behind your exit. Talking about your fear in the safety of Imago Dialogue paradoxically closes the exit of avoidance. After you talk about your feelings, it may be important also to close an exit if it is draining energy that belongs to your relationship.

EXERCISE 10: CARING BEHAVIORS

(*review chapter 9*)

Time: Approximately 60 minutes.

Purpose: By sharing specific information about what pleases you and agreeing to pleasure your partner on a regular, consistent basis, you can turn your relationship into a zone of safety.

Comments: You can do steps 1–3 separately if you wish. Do the remaining steps together.

Directions:
   1. The first step in this process is to identify what your partner is already doing that pleases you. Get out separate sheets of paper and complete this sentence in as many ways as possible, being specific and positive and focusing on items that happen with some regularity: *I feel loved and cared about when you . . .*

Examples: fill my coffee cup when it's empty.
                  let me read the front page of the paper first.
                  kiss me before you leave the house.
                  call me from work just to chat.
                  tell me important things that happen to you.

massage my back.
tell me you love me.
ask if I want a treat from the store.
bring me surprise presents.
sit close to me when we're watching TV.
listen to me when I'm upset.
check with me first before making plans.
pray with me and for me.
make special Sunday dinners.
want to make love to me.
compliment me on the way I look.

2. Now recall the romantic stage of your relationship. Are there any caring behaviors that you used to do for each other that you are no longer doing? Once again, take out separate sheets of paper and complete this sentence: *I used to feel loved and cared about when you . . .*

Examples: wrote me love letters.
brought me flowers.
held my hand as we walked.
whispered sexy things into my ear.
called me up on the phone to say how much
  you loved me.
cooked me special dinners.
stayed up late talking and making love.
made love more than once a day.
kissed me when you went out the door and
  hugged me when you came home.

3. Now think about some caring and loving behaviors that you have always wanted but never asked for. These may come from your vision of a perfect mate or from prior experience. (They should not, however, refer to activities that are a present source of conflict.) These may be very private fantasies.

Whenever possible, quantify your request. Complete this sentence: *I would like you to ...*

Examples: massage me for thirty minutes without
              stopping.
            take a shower with me.
            buy me some silver jewelry as a surprise.
            go backpacking with me three times
              each summer.
            sleep in the nude.
            go out to brunch with me once a month.
            read a novel to me over Christmas vacation.
            eat dinner on the deck.

4. Now combine all three lists and indicate how important each caring behavior is to you by writing a number from 1 to 5 beside each one. A 1 indicates "very important"; a 5 indicates "not so important."

5. Exchange lists. Examine your partner's lists and put an *X* by any items that you are not willing to do at this time. (Make sure that you are willing to do all the ones you have not checked.) Starting tomorrow, do at least two of the caring behaviors each day for the next two months, starting with the ones that are easiest for you to do. Add more items to your list as they occur to you. When your partner does a caring behavior for you, acknowledge it with an appreciative comment. As you will recall from reading chapter 8, these caring behaviors are gifts, not obligations. Do them regardless of how you feel about your partner and regardless of the number of caring behaviors your partner gives you.

6. If either you or your partner experiences some resistance to this exercise, keep on doing the caring behaviors until the re-

sistance is overcome. (See pages 144–47 for an explanation of the fear of pleasure.)

EXERCISE 11: THE SURPRISE LIST

(*review pages 141–43*)

Time: Approximately 15–20 minutes.

Purpose: The purpose of this exercise is to augment the caring behaviors in exercise 10 with unanticipated pleasures, which adds to your feelings of safety and bonding.

Comments: This exercise is to be done separately and must be kept secret from your partner.

Directions:

1. Make a list of things you could do for your partner that would be especially pleasing. Don't guess. Draw up your list from your memory of things that have pleased your partner in the past or from hints or comments your partner has made. Become a detective and ferret out your partner's hidden wishes and desires. Keep your list hidden from your partner at all times.

2. Select one item and surprise your partner with it this week. Be sure to do this at least once a week and at random times so that your partner will have difficulty anticipating the surprise.

3. Record the date when you gave each surprise.

4. On a separate sheet of paper, record and date the surprises you receive from your partner. Thank your partner for surprising you.

Exercise 12: The Fun List

(review pages 143–44)

Time: Approximately 20–30 minutes.

Purpose: This exercise is designed to intensify your emotional bond and deepen your feelings of safety and pleasure.

Comments: Do this exercise together.

Directions:

1. Make separate lists of fun and exciting activities you would like to do with your partner. These should include face-to-face experiences and any body contact that is physically pleasurable. Examples: tennis, dancing, wrestling, showering together, sex, massage, tickling, jumping rope, bicycling.

2. Now share your lists and compile a third list that combines all your suggestions.

3. Pick one activity from the list and do it each week.

4. You may experience some resistance to taking part in such exuberant, childlike activities—especially if you have a conflicted relationship. It is important that you do this exercise nonetheless. Go against your natural inclination and experiment with this brief return to childhood.

Exercise 13: Positive Flooding

(review chapter 11)

Time: Approximately 45 minutes.

Purpose: This exercise will help you and your partner experience emotional intensity connected to specific physical features, traits, and behaviors you appreciate and love. Speaking with intensity about the positive will also reduce your sensitivity to negative comments that are spoken with intensity.

Comments: Use the first 30 minutes working alone to make your lists and then do the exercise together.

Directions:

1. Take out two sheets of paper, one for each of you. Each of you takes one piece and divides the sheet into four columns. Write in the following four headings: "Physical Traits," "Character Traits," "Behaviors," "Global Affirmations." Now under the respective columns, write down the physical traits you appreciate about your partner, the positive character traits you adore, the behaviors your partner has done that you appreciate, and global expressions of love such as "I love you," "I can't believe I married someone as wonderful as you!"

2. Now, one of you sits in a chair while the other circles around saying the words he or she has written on the paper. Use about one minute for each column, and increase the intensity of your voice as you go from column to column. When you reach the Global Affirmations column, jump up and down, your feet leaving the floor.

3. Take out two more sheets of paper and design it exactly as the one above, including the same column headings. This time, each of you lists the praises you would like to hear from your partner. Examples: "Tell me that I have long, beautiful legs." "Tell me that I am a trustworthy friend." "Tell me that I do an excellent job of managing the house." "Tell me that I am a patient, loving parent." "Tell me that you love to touch my skin." "Tell me that you love to see me undressed." "Tell me that I am the best partner you have ever had." "Tell me how lucky you are to be with me."

4. Now repeat the circling exercise and take turns flooding each other with these new lists of praise. End the exercise with an intense hug. Let yourself feel all the powerful feelings the exercise evokes.

5. Talk with your partner about what the exercise meant to you, using the Imago Dialogue.

6. Repeat this exercise once a week for four weeks. Then make a practice of flooding your partner for a few moments every day.

EXERCISE 14: THE BEHAVIOR CHANGE REQUEST DIALOGUE

(*review chapter 10*)

Time: Approximately 60–90 minutes.

Purpose: The purpose of this exercise is to learn more about each other's deepest needs and to give you the opportunity to change your behavior to meet those needs. As you stretch against your resistance to change, your partner will experience emotional healing, and you will become a more whole and loving individual.

Comments: This is a very important exercise. We recommend that you give it your highest priority.

Directions:

1. The first step in this exercise is to identify the desires that lie behind your frustrations. On a separate sheet of paper, each of you makes a comprehensive list of all the things that bother you about the other. What does your partner do that makes you feel angry, annoyed, afraid, suspicious, resentful, hurt, or bitter?

After you list the frustrating behavior and the feelings that go with it, see if you can remember feeling that way as a child. Here is an example:

Jenny's List
I don't like it when you ...

drive too fast. I feel scared.

leave the house without telling me where you are going. I feel abandoned.

criticize me in front of the children. I feel shamed.

undermine my authority with the children. I feel humiliated.

read the newspaper during dinner. I feel ignored and unimportant.

criticize me in a joking manner in front of friends. I feel shamed.

don't pay attention to what I'm saying. I feel ignored.

turn away from me when I'm upset or crying. I feel abandoned.

criticize me for being indecisive. I feel guilty.

criticize me for being a poor housekeeper. I feel shamed.

keep pointing out the fact that you earn more money than I do. I feel shamed.

2. Now get out a second sheet of paper and write down the global desire that lies hidden within each of your frustrations. Skip several lines after each desire. Do not write down the frustration, only the desire. (This is necessary, because you will be showing this second sheet to your partner.)

Example:

Global Desire (corresponds to the first frustration listed above): I would like to feel safe and relaxed when you are driving.

3. Underneath each global desire, write three specific requests, each of which would help you satisfy that desire. It is important that your requests be positive and that they describe a specific, doable behavior. Remember the acronym *SMART;* each behavior should be specific, measurable, achievable, relevant to the desire, and time-limited. Then ask your partner to give you one of your requests as a gift.

Examples:

Global Desire: I would like to feel safe and relaxed when you are driving.

Specific Request 1: For the next month, when you are driving, I would like you to obey the speed limit. If the road conditions are bad, I would like you to drive even more slowly.

Specific Request 2: For the next two weeks, before we get into the car, tell me that you will drive within the speed limit, and give me a hug.

Specific Request 3: Two times next week, have a dialogue with me for fifteen minutes and ask me how I feel when you drive beyond the speed limit and help me connect my fear to childhood.

Global Desire: I would like you to always comfort me when I'm upset.

Specific Request 1: For the next month, when I tell you that I am upset, I would like you to put your arms around me and give me your full attention for five minutes.

Specific Request 2: Twice this week, I would like you to go for a walk with me after dinner so we can talk about each other's day without interruption.

Specific Request 3: This week, whenever I tell you that I am upset, I would like you to look directly at me, listen carefully, and reflect back to me what I said.

Notice that these requests are for specific, positive behaviors. The following request is a bad example because it is not specific.

Vague Request: I would like you to be more attentive.

It should be rewritten to make it more detailed:

Specific Request: For the next two weeks, I would like you to give me a warm hug as soon as you come home from work and hold me for one full minute.

This next request is a bad example because it is negative:

Negative Request: I would like you to stop yelling at me when you're upset.

This should be rewritten so that it describes a positive behavior:

Positive Request: For the next month, when you are mad at me, I would like you to ask me for what you want in a normal tone of voice. Give me a specific, time-limited, and positive request.

4. Share your second list (the one that lists desires and requests but not frustrations) with each other. Use your communication skills to clarify each desire and request so that they are all clearly understood using SMART behaviors. Rewrite the request if necessary so that the partner knows exactly what kind of behavior you want, how often you want it, how long you want it, and when you want it.

5. Now take back your own list and rank each request on the left side of the page with a number from 1 to 5 indicating its relative importance to you, 1 indicating "very important," and 5 "not very important."

6. Exchange lists once again so that you now have your partner's requests, and assign a number from 1 to 5 on the right side of the paper indicating how difficult it would be for you to grant each request, with 1 indicating "very difficult," and 5 "not at all difficult."

7. Keep your partner's list. Starting today, you have the opportunity to grant your partner three or four of the easiest requests each week. Remember that these behaviors are gifts. Regardless of how you feel and regardless of how many changes your partner is making, keep to a reliable schedule of at least three or four behavior changes a week. (You are encouraged to add more requests to your lists as time goes on.)

8. You can also use this process by choosing a "mild frustration" (something that doesn't have a lot of emotional charge to you) and have an Imago Dialogue by sharing your frustration (using "I" language), deepening the send by recalling the frustration with a childhood memory, sharing what you need from your partner (global desire), and moving into SMART behavior change requests. The Receiver chooses one of the requests to unconditionally give to the Sender.

EXERCISE 15: THE HOLDING EXERCISE

(*review pages 182–85*)

Time: Approximately 30 minutes.

Purpose: This exercise is designed to deepen your empathy and connection with your partner. It may also allow you to reexperience and release stored pain or sadness from your childhood.

Comments: Find a place where you can sit comfortably for as long as fifteen minutes. (You may want back support.) Then, take turns holding each other and following the directions below. The person being held lies across the partner's lap with his or her head against the heart of the holding partner. Let yourself be aware of your experience of holding and being held in this way.

Note: This is not what is called a *regression exercise.* Each of you will be speaking as an adult, not as a young child.

Directions:
Decide who will be the holder and who will be held. Get into a comfortable position, with the head of the person being held close to the heart of the holder.

1. The holder begins the exercise by asking, "Tell me about the pain and frustration of your childhood." The person being held talks about early, hurtful experiences. After every few sentences, the holder mirrors back what the partner has said. (If the person being held cannot remember any pain from childhood, he or she can talk about any relationship pain outside of the current relationship.) If the person being held cries or sobs, the holding partner encourages those feelings and mirrors them. "You must have felt so sad." "You went through so much pain." "I can see how much it hurt." "Your tears make me want to cry."

2. Once the memories are over, the holder says, "What was the worst part of that . . . ?" The person being held responds, "The worst part was . . ." The holder listens empathetically and then says, "Thank you for telling me." The person being held says, "Thanks for listening."

3. Change roles and repeat the exercise.

4. Now write down your own childhood pain and injury and your partner's pain and injury. In the days to come, bring to mind your partner's early experiences and visualize your partner's hurts when he or she was a child.

EXERCISE 16: OWNING AND ELIMINATING YOUR NEGATIVITY

(review chapter 11)

Time: Approximately 45 minutes.

Purpose: This exercise will help you create more safety and passion in your relationship by helping you let go of your negative thoughts and behaviors toward your partner and replacing them with loving thoughts and behaviors.

Comments: When you focus on your partner's negative qualities, you tend to ignore the positive traits. If you go one step further and criticize your partner for having those negative traits, your partner becomes defensive and may go on the attack. This climate of negativity feeds on itself. This exercise turns the tables. It focuses your attention on your partner's positive traits and encourages you to praise your partner more often. The result? You begin to feel much more positive toward each other and to treat each other with more love and respect. This positive climate is also self-reinforcing. What you pay attention to is what you get.

Directions:
Do this exercise separately and then, using the Imago Dialogue, talk about what you learned about yourself with your partner. Work alone through step 5. Then invite your partner into an Imago Dialogue for step 6. Do the remaining steps on your own at a later date. It is important that you follow the instructions exactly as stated.

1. Take out several sheets of lined paper. Think about all the negative words you use to describe your partner. Include words that you have spoken in a heated situation, when name-calling, and negative words you have thought about your partner but

not spoken out loud. Write down these words in a column on the left side of your paper, one word or phrase on every second line. (This leaves room to write a sentence or two by each trait.)

2. Now recall a behavior your partner has exhibited that illustrates each negative word or phrase. Write it beside the word. Here is an example:

Negative Trait	Related Behavior
Always late	Last night, she was late coming home for dinner.
Neglectful	She forgot to get me anything for my birthday.
Controlling	She always wants things her way. We always watch the movies that she wants to see.

3. Look through your list and circle the trait that bothers you the most.

4. Now write a second list of your partner's positive traits and behaviors. Write down as many positive traits as you wrote down negative traits. Here is an example:

Positive Trait	Related Behavior
Kind	Yesterday, she drove our elderly next-door neighbor to his doctor's appointment.
Funny	When we were out to dinner with friends, she had everyone laughing.
Hardworking	Last weekend, she painted both bedrooms.

5. Now go back to your list of criticisms. Look at the first negative behavior on your list. Close your eyes and visualize your partner doing that behavior. When you have it clearly in mind, release the image and then bring to mind a positive be-

havior your partner has done that you do like. (Look at your list of positive traits for suggestions.) Hold the positive image in your mind and note how you feel. Do this for all the negative words on your list.

6. Use the Imago Dialogue to discuss with your partner what you learned about yourself doing this exercise. (This is not a time to talk about what you don't like about your partner. You are sharing self-discoveries.)

7. In the next few days, when you have a negative thought about something your partner has done, release it and think of something he or she has done that you do like.

8. In the next few days, make it a point to tell your partner about only the positive things he or she has done that you appreciate. If you have a negative thought or memory, release it.

9. When your partner does or says something that you wish hadn't happened, refrain from criticism. Instead, use the Behavior Change Request Dialogue (exercise 14) to make a request for a positive change in behavior.

EXERCISE 17: ZERO NEGATIVITY AND RECONNECTING PROCESS

(*review chapter 11*)

Time: Approximately 15–30 minutes.

Purpose: The purpose of this exercise is remove all negativity (criticism, shame, or blame) from your relationship.

Comments: This exercise should be done together.

Important Note: Signing the Zero Negativity Pledge means that you agree to refrain from any put-downs during your thirty-day commitment. It does not mean that you cannot express your needs and deal with your issues. On the contrary, it means that without the contamination of negative exchanges, you will be able to deal with your issues.

Keep in mind that the pledge is to keep your relationship free of negativity. You will be assessing your relationship, not each other.

Directions:

1. Read out loud together the pledge below and agree to commit to Zero Negativity for the next thirty days by signing the pledge:

> We understand that *negativity* is any transaction that ruptures our connection, whether intentional or accidental.
> We pledge to make our relationship a **Zone of Zero Negativity** for thirty days. To that end, we pledge to avoid any transactions that could be experienced as a "put-down," thus rupturing our connection.
> If we have a frustration, we will change it into a request and ask for what we want without criticism.
> If we experience a rupture, we will send a gentle signal (bing, ouch, oops, wow!) to communicate that we have experienced a put-down and then begin repairing the rupture by resending the message or redoing the action.
> We pledge to gift each other with three appreciations each day, no matter what!

_____

_____

2. Using a monthly calendar, place the calendar in a place where you can see it, like your bathroom mirror. At the end of each day, you and your partner make an appointment and use mirroring to share whether your relationship got a "negative"

that day. If yes, draw a frowny face on the day. If no, draw a smiley face on the day.

3. Use the Reconnecting Process to quickly repair and reconnect whenever you experience a put-down. Communicate to your partner with a gentle signal (bing, ouch, wow, oops!). Then select a behavior that would restore the connection for you and engage your partner in the process until you feel connected. There are various options to help reconnect:

a. Ask for a *redo*. Take time out, start over, and redo the transaction.
b. Model for your partner how he or she might *resend* the message so it doesn't produce a put-down.
c. Offer a *reconnecting* behavior, a single behavior like an apology, flowers, or a hug.
d. If the put-down needs more attention, ask for an Imago Dialogue.
e. Create your own reconnecting process.

Conclude this reconnecting process with an appreciation.

EXERCISE 18: VISUALIZATION OF LOVE

Time: 1 minute, 3 times each day.

Purpose: This exercise uses the power of visualization to amplify the positive changes you have been making in your relationship.

Comments: This exercise becomes a daily meditation.

Directions:
1. Three times each day, do the following: Close your eyes, take several deep breaths, and visualize your partner. Gradually

refine the image until you see your partner as a connected, spiritual being who has been wounded in the ways you now know about. Hold this image in your mind and imagine that your love is healing your partner's wounds.

2. Now visualize the energy of love that you are sending to your partner coming back to you and healing your wounds. Imagine that this energy flows back and forth between you in a continuous oscillation. When a minute is up, open your eyes and continue whatever you were doing.

Seeking Professional Help

Some of you may want to deepen your understanding of your relationship and gain additional skills by working with a couples' therapist. Fortunately, couples' therapy has lost much of the stigma that it had in earlier years. Years ago, only people who were in great pain or who were very courageous signed up for couples counseling. Now more and more couples are deciding to seek help before irrevocable damage is done. They want to enhance the quality of their lives, and they realize that nothing is more important to them than their primary love relationship. They have the healthy attitude that going to a therapist is no different from going to any skilled teacher: you learn faster and better if you get expert supervision.

One of the main benefits of seeing a therapist is that you will speed up the integration of material from your unconscious. A therapist can help you maneuver around your blind spots and assimilate material from your unconscious that might take you months or years to assimilate on your own. As a result, you will spend a lot less time spinning your wheels.

Another good reason to enlist the aid of a therapist is to give you an added measure of safety and support. When you are working on new material and begin to experience some anxiety, a therapist will help you understand your fears. Given reassurance and insight, you will probably be able to plunge ahead instead of retreating to safer ground. This will prove especially valuable for couples who are experiencing a great many problems.

A final reason for seeking professional counseling is to provide a structured environment for growth. If you are short on discipline or motivation, having a weekly appointment and paying a therapist a good deal of money can give you added incentive.

If you are interested in working with a therapist specifically trained in Imago Relationship Therapy or wish to attend a *Getting the Love You Want* Couples' Workshop, please visit www .ImagoRelationships.org. Certified Imago Therapists have gone through extensive training in the skills and processes listed in this book.

If you are interested in working with a couples' therapist but cannot find an Imago therapist or workshop near you, we have some general recommendations. Our advice is that you look for a therapist whose primary area of expertise is relationship therapy, not individual therapy, so that he or she will be well versed in the complexities of love relationships. Furthermore, we recommend that you look for a therapist who will work with you jointly, in what is referred to in professional circles as *conjoint* couples' therapy. If you see separate therapists or the same therapist at different times, you might inadvertently focus on issues that would help you live more autonomously, not help you live more harmoniously as a couple. Dwelling on matters that are not directly relevant to your relationship may help you as an individual, but there is some evidence that it might not be the best way to strengthen your marriage. When you are seeing a therapist together, you will more clearly see how your personal issues affect the state of your relationship, and both your personal and relationship issues can be resolved together.

How do you go about selecting a couples' therapist? A person professing to be a therapist may be a clergyman, a social worker, a psychologist, a psychiatrist, an educator, or, in some states, simply a person with strong views on love relationships. A therapist's training may vary from years of postgraduate training to none at all. In some states, all that's required for a license as a couples' therapist is a recommendation by someone who already has a license. For this reason, it is wise to choose your therapist on the basis of a referral. Get recommendations from friends or from the minister of a church who has successfully referred a large number of couples. If you are unable to get a referral, look in your phone book under the headings "American Association of Pastoral Counselors," "American Association for Marriage and Family Therapy," "Association of Clinical Social Workers," "Marriage Counselors," or "Mental Health." If you live in a large city, there may be a special referral service that will match you up with an appropriate therapist.

When you have been given the name of a particular therapist, there are a number of things you should check out. First, make sure the therapist is fully accredited by a recognized organization such as the American Association for Marriage and Family Therapy, the American Association of Pastoral Counselors, the American Psychological Association, or the American Psychiatric Association. When you are satisfied that the therapist meets your initial criteria, sign up for a preliminary interview to see if you would feel comfortable working together. (Some therapists will waive the fees for this initial consultation.) Find out the therapist's views on relationship therapy. Most important of all, trust your instincts. You are looking for a therapist who is a caring, warm, sensitive person who gives you a feeling of safety and confidence. Even if you like the therapist, it is wise to interview more than one person so that you have a basis for comparison.

Notes

CHAPTER 1: LOVE, LOST AND FOUND

1. U.S. Census Bureau, Current Population Survey, March and Annual Social and Economic Supplements (2017).
2. Flurrymobile, "U.S. Consumers Time-Spent on Mobile."
3. Bottero, *Mesopotamia,* 102–103.
4. McLean, "Man and His Animal Brains." This is one of several ways of looking at the brain distinguished by an evolutionary perspective. We use the terms *old brain* and *new brain* because of their simplicity and illustrative power.
5. These primary evolutionary defenses are believed to have evolved in the reverse order of the way we have listed them. Fear, considered the primary affect, is followed much later in evolutionary history by the nurturing response. It is believed that self-preservation as the basic instinct preceded the nurturing response by millions of years.
6. Garland and Howard, "Neuroplasticity."

CHAPTER 2: CHILDHOOD WOUNDS

1. A conscious marriage is created by bringing into awareness the unconscious directives and purposes of a romantic or love marriage. A love marriage is defined as a voluntary union of two individuals based upon romantic attraction that is stirred by unconscious needs that have their roots in unresolved childhood issues.

2. Buber, *I and Thou*, 76. The notion that human life includes an awareness of oneness with the universe is endemic in most religions in most
cultures and is often referred to by the term *mystical*. This experience
was reduced by Freud to an "oceanic feeling" reminiscent of prenatal
union with the mother, thus polarizing with Buber. Silverman et al., in
The Search for Oneness, subject Freud's thesis to empirical research and
conclude that "unconscious fantasies of oneness can enhance adaptation if a sense of self can be preserved" (1ff).

3. The English language has only one word for the phenomenon of love,
and that word is used in so many contexts to describe so many emotions
that it has no distinct meaning. We use it to say, "I love New York,"
"I love the movies," "I love sex," "I love you," and everything else about
which we may have positive feelings. Consequently, its meaning is determined largely by its context.

   Until recently, psychology made little reference to love, and it is no-
ticeably absent in most studies of marriage. Theories of marriage and
marital therapy have focused on contract making, conflict resolution,
systems analysis, and restructuring rather than love. Freud and Jung
used the Latin word *libido*, but in different ways. Freud spoke of a libidi-
nal love and a narcissistic love; the first is a generalized sexual energy
directed to others, notably the infant to the mother as a first love object,
and later redirected to others. The second, narcissistic love, was a con-
sequence of psychic injury that resulted in focusing libido on the self.
He called this *primary narcissism*. The resolution of this self-invested
love led to the redirection of libido to another, or secondary narcissism. (See Freud, "On Narcissism.") Jung used *libido* to refer to a generalized life energy. (For a discussion of love by psychoanalytically
oriented psychologists and psychiatrists, see Rollo May, *Love and Will*;
Erich Fromm, *The Art of Loving*; Reubin Fine, *The Meaning of Love
in Human Experience*; Willard Gaylin, *Rediscovering Love*; and Nathaniel Brandon, *The Psychology of Romantic Love*.)

   To avoid the vagueness of the word *love*, we have elected to use three
Greek words: *eros*, *agape*, and *philia*. These words have precise meanings and refer to various phases of one phenomenon. They also make
possible a description of a developmental view of love as a possibility
in marriage. *Eros* is the root of the word *erotic*, which in our culture
has a sexual, even pornographic connotation, but in Greek means "passionate love of the world." (See Bauer, *A Greek-English Lexicon*, 311.)

   The broader meaning of *eros* is "life force," which is directed outward in passionate appreciation of the world. This includes, but is not
limited to, sexuality. It also denotes the sense in which the self and its

demands and needs are emphasized. In our view, when eros is frustrated or blunted by deficient nurturing or excessive socialization, it turns back upon itself in self-absorption and becomes preoccupied with organismic survival. This condition remains until the experience of romantic love, when eros is redirected to another, the romantic partner, in an attempt to restore the original condition of connecting. The failure to achieve the original situation results in the power struggle, which is ultimately a defense against death.

4. Plato, *Symposium*, 143ff.

CHAPTER 3: YOUR IMAGO

1. The reconstruction of the past by selecting a partner who resembles one's parents was originally given the name *repetition compulsion* by Freud. This idea was expanded by Fritz Perls, founder of Gestalt therapy, and given the name *unfinished business*. For Perls, this consists of feelings and memories that are unconscious and avoided but are expressed in behavior. Some view this repetition as an attempt to restore the familiar, thus as a static and nonpurposive process. We side with Freud's view of the purposive character of repetition as an attempt at resolution.

2. See Penfield, *The Mystery of Mind*, 20.

3. In *Webster's Dictionary, imago* means the "representation of a person or a thing," "a copy," "likeness," "a mental picture." The term was used in psychology by Freud. In fact, it was the title of a now defunct journal edited by him. Jung also uses the term in his *Collected Works*, vol. 9, 60ff, to mean the "inner representation of the opposite sex." In this book, we depend in principle upon Jung rather than the "object-relations" school, who would define it as the "significant other." In either case, the image is formed out of the internalization of all childhood caregivers, and its projection generates the feelings of romantic love.

CHAPTER 4: ROMANTIC LOVE

1. The experience of romantic love, an intensely passionate and often sexual relationship between a man and a woman, is among the oldest recorded experiences of humankind. It inflames the relationship between the ancient gods and goddesses (Zeus and Hera), sometimes between gods and humans (Cupid and Psyche), often between famous

persons (Isaac and Rebekah, Franklin D. Roosevelt and Lucy Mercer), and surely among many ordinary mortals who were not recorded in history. Some of these relationships inspired by the fires of eros have changed the course of history (Antony and Cleopatra, Paris and Helen of Troy); others have inspired great literature (Dante and Beatrice, Tristan and Isolde); all constitute the most endearing and enduring stories of humankind, most of which end in tragedy and death (Romeo and Juliet, Samson and Delilah, Lancelot and Guinevere). (See Lynd, *Love Through the Ages*.) Explanations of the source of this energy have ranged from the "infusion of the gods" or a "demon" to the result of a disease. People fell in love because they were struck by Cupid's arrow, were tricked into drinking a magic potion, or happened to be born under favorable stars. In every case, something external, even extraterrestrial, was involved. Today, with the decline in the belief of the supernatural, explanations tend to be more psychological and subjective, with the energy believed to be arising from within the persons.

The forms of romantic love seem to have undergone three changes in history, each reflecting changes in the love relationship, and its fate has been determined by social structure and cultural practices. Prior to the eleventh century, the dominant form of romantic love was called *heroic love*. The major theme in heroic love is the pursuit and capture of the woman by the man. The societies in which this form of love existed were feudal aristocracies in which romantic love was sought and mainly existed either in passionate or extramarital love or in romanticized nonsexual relationships. Contributing factors to this situation were the existence of slavery, the bias of freeborn men against labor, the association of slavery with the functions of the home, and the consequent difficulty of associating love with home. Thus, the fulfillment of love was sought outside the home and outside marriage.

A radical reversal in male-female relationships occurred in the eleventh century with the appearance of the troubadours and their love ballads in southern France. In a short time, heroic love was replaced with what is known as *courtly love*, in which the theme of pursuit and capture gave way to the image of male supplication and entreaty of the female. Images of force and rape were replaced with refinements of courtship. This led to the formation of "courts of love," where the merits of love were debated and where judgments were usually rendered that true love was attainable only outside of marriage and often only if there was no sexual communion. The form of modern love relationships was influenced and developed against this background.

Romantic love as the door to marriage had to await the evolving freedom and rights of individuals to choose their fate and to determine their own forms of government. That and the emerging freedom and equality of women were the forces that led to modern marriage, and its attendant psychological baggage. (See Hunt, *The Natural History of Love,* and Schneider, *The World of Love,* vol. 1.)

2. Quoted in Lahr and Tabori, *Love,* 189.
3. Liebowitz, *The Chemistry of Love,* 37ff.
4. Schneiderman, I., O. Zagoory-Sharon, J. F. Leckman, and R. Feldman, "Oxytocin During the Initial Stages of Romantic Attachment: Relations to Couples' Interactive Reciprocity," *Psychoneuroendocrinology* 37, no. 8 (2012): 1277–1285.
5. Apuleius, "The Golden Ass," 1165ff.

CHAPTER 5: THE POWER STRUGGLE

1. Our first encounter with a full discussion of the unconscious expectations couples bring to marriage was in *Marriage Contracts* by Clifford Sager. Sager has worked out a very detailed analysis of conscious, preconscious, and unconscious contracts.
2. Early-childhood experience also seems to be the source of other beliefs that characterize the power struggle. The intuitive response of parents to childhood stress, especially in the preverbal stage, leads to the belief in the omniscience of spouses: they know what we need without having to ask. We resent our needs not being responded to automatically and having to ask breaks the illusion that our partners know what we need. Another belief is that they have what we need and can satisfy us if they would. This is called the *illusion of partner omnipotence.* Finally, we believe they should always be available to meet our needs and have no needs of their own. This is the belief in partner omnipresence. Their failure to meet our needs creates emotional pain and leads eventually to the belief in the partner as evil and therefore the enemy.
3. The stages of grief in a dying person were worked out by Elisabeth Kübler-Ross and described in her book *On Death and Dying.*
4. The bargaining stage in the power struggle, an expression of the quid pro quo that most couples naturally evolve in their attempt to negotiate their needs, is the stage most couples present to the therapist when they enter therapy. In our opinion, this is the source of earlier methods in marital counseling that attempted to help couples develop contracts and negotiate their conflicts. Therapists responded to what couples were trying to

do and sought to help them do it better. They did not recognize it as a stage in the power struggle and unwittingly helped couples stay in it, rather than helping them move to the next stage, despair, and to the surrender of their illusions. The surrender of illusions is a precondition for the conscious marriage and precedes the final step of acceptance.

CHAPTER 6: BECOMING CONSCIOUS

1. Wendy Palmer Patterson, who is on the Imago faculty, devised the concept and definition of Sender Responsibility.
2. *Imago Dei* is Latin for "the image of God." The concept of Imago Dei is an ancient concept fostered in Judaism and Christianity, which asserts that human beings are created in the image and likeness of God. Thus, humans have the ability to actualize the special qualities bestowed by God, which makes us different from all other creatures. These qualities lay within us, waiting to be developed and expressed.

CHAPTER 7: COMMITMENT

1. The no-exit decision is an adaptation of the "escape-hatch" concept developed by Frank Ernst, a transaction analyst, who conceived the idea of the OK Corral (see bibliography). The purpose of this exercise is to engage the rational mind, the new brain, which can make cognitive decisions not to act on impulses and emotions that would be destructive to therapy, to the self, or to a relationship. Our experience that couples will make this decision and still not improve led to the discovery that they use many noncatastrophic exits to avoid positive involvement with each other.
2. I first learned about the concepts of graduated change from Kurt Lewin, an analytically oriented social psychologist who pioneered in the area of the social psychology of group process and group change. Graduated change is also commonly used in behavioral psychology and social-learning theory.

CHAPTER 9: CREATING A ZONE OF AFFIRMATIONS

1. Stuart, *Helping Couples Change*, 17.
2. We are indebted to Stuart and to behaviorism in general for the idea of a structured therapeutic change process. We were also influenced by

transactional analysis (which talks about giving people permission to want) and by John Whitaker, a Dallas psychiatrist and transactional analyst, who developed the idea of the "want" list.

One key difference between the Caring Behaviors exercise and Stuart's Caring Days exercise is that we ask couples to generate their list of caring behaviors by writing down three different kinds of pleasurable transactions: ones they experienced during the romantic stage of their relationship, ones they are currently experiencing in their relationships, and ones that they would like to experience but have never asked for because of fear of being criticized or rejected. All three kinds of pleasurable transactions tap into unmet childhood needs. The enactment of these behaviors touches childhood issues in the unconscious and creates an environment in which the deeper conflicted issues can later be addressed.

CHAPTER 10: DEFINING YOUR CURRICULUM

1. In earlier versions of this exercise, we did not ask couples like Melanie and Stewart to try to figure out what childhood wounds they were re-injuring. It did not seem necessary in order to benefit from the exercise. All they had to do was identify a chronic criticism, convert it into a fear, then into a desire, and then describe a positive, specific behavior that would satisfy that desire. It seemed very straightforward.

   Now we see it quite differently. We believe that it is important to attach the current frustration to a childhood memory for two reasons. First, it helps the Sender know that his or her frustrations have their roots in childhood, not in the relationship. We use the 90 percent formula. Ninety percent of a person's frustrations are repetitions of childhood wounds and 10 percent are from the current relationship. The partner's behaviors trigger the memories but do not create them. Second, linking the present frustrations with the past helps the listening partner know that he or she is not the ultimate cause of the frustrations, but instead the occasion for it. Knowing that the frustrations come from the Sender's childhood, the Receiver can develop compassion and even empathy for his or her partner's pain.

2. *Agape* is the second word in the Greek language for *love*. It is used to express human love, the love of humans for God, and the love of God for humans. It also refers to a love feast that expresses brotherly love. In every case, it seems to mean a love for another without regard for conditions—unconditional love. It is not dependent upon the worth or

value of the other, and when it is expressed it carries no obligation. It is an unconditional gift. (See Bauer, *A Greek-English Lexicon,* 6.)

In Greek philosophy, agape is one of the forms of love on a continuum with eros and philia. Therefore, it is not another kind of love but a special way in which love is expressed. In this book, we view agape as the act of directing eros, the life energy, away from oneself and toward the welfare of the other. In that sense, it is sacrificial, but what is sacrificed is not the self but preoccupation with the self. Although it is used as a noun, and thus denotes an attitude, it is also used as a verb and thus denotes the way one acts toward another. The merger of these two senses means that agape can be understood as an attitude that is expressed in behaviors. On this basis, we call it the *power of transformation* that directs eros to the other, thus creating a new quality in relationships, called *philia.*

CHAPTER 12: PORTRAIT OF TWO RELATIONSHIPS

1. The focus of this book has been on the power of love for psychological and spiritual healing. Evidence is now being accumulated by research psychologists and physicians on the positive effects of altruistic love on the immune system (McClelland) and on the healing process in general (Siegel). This means that love influences body functions as well as psychological processes such as depression (Weissman). Evidence that marital stress results in psychosomatic symptoms by depressing the immune system (Kiecolt-Glaser) and influences psychological stress such as adolescent suicide, high blood pressure, depression (Folkenberg), and possibly cancer (Levenson) is correlated with evidence that an altruistic lifestyle, a life of loving energy directed to others, improves physical and emotional health (McClelland). The implications emerging from this research indicate the significance of a positive marriage, or the idea of marriage as a passionate friendship, for a general sense of well-being and health. Safety is posited as the invariant and essential component behind mental, physical, emotional, and spiritual health.

2. *Philia* is the root of the English word *filial.* Its basic meaning has to do with brotherly love. But in Greek, "brotherly" is not limited to and does not necessarily refer to kinship. It also refers to an attitude and a quality of relating in which the feelings of care that are experienced between people who are connected by blood are experienced between people who are not blood-related. Such bonding is a desirable human condition, because it would remove the reality of the other as strange

and therewith all attendant threats from the outside or the other. Philia is thus the basis of friendship and refers to love among equals (see Bauer, *A Greek-English Lexicon*, 866).

To distinguish friend from foe is essential for personal and group survival. This polarity is the basis of personal and group conflict, violence, and war. True peace—that is, peace without fear—exists only among friends. Peace with fear can exist between foes, but it is always unstable. Again, this appears to be an old-brain function—to respond to this perceived distinction in the service of organismic survival. The admonition by Jesus in the New Testament to "love your enemies" collides with this old-brain directive, but it is the highest concept humans have been able to develop to deal with the animal residues of evolution.

It is interesting that, in a research project of "happy" couples, the item ranked first by all couples was "we are each other's best friend" (Lauer and Lauer, "Marriages Made to Last"). This form of love between friends is a love among equals that is created through agape, a new quality of relating.

Bibliography

Apuleius, Lucius. "The Golden Ass." In *Love Through the Ages,* edited by Robert Lynd. New York: Coward-McCann, 1932.

Atkinson, Brent J. *Emotional Intelligence in Couples Therapy: Advances from Neurobiology and the Science of Intimate Relationships.* New York: W. W. Norton, 2005.

Barker, Robert L. *Treating Couples in Crisis.* New York: Free Press, 1984.

Bauer, W. *A Greek-English Lexicon of the New Testament and Other Early Christian Literature,* translated by W. F. Arndt and F. W. Gingrich. Chicago: University of Chicago Press, 1957.

Bellah, Robert, Richard Madson, William M. Sullivan, Ann Swidler, and Steven M. Tipton. *Habits of the Heart.* New York: Perennial Library, 1985.

Bergland, C. "The Neurochemicals of Happiness." *Psychology Today,* November 2012. Retrieved from https://www.psychologytoday.com/blog/the-athletes-way/201211/the-neurochemicals-happiness.

Bohm, David. *On Dialogue,* edited by Lee Nichol. New York: Routledge, 1996.

Boterro, Jean. *Mesopotamia: Writing, Reasoning, and the Gods.* Chicago: University of Chicago Press, 2002.

Brandon, Nathaniel. *The Psychology of Romantic Love.* Los Angeles: J. P. Tarcher, 1980.

Buber, Martin. *Between Man and Man,* translated by Ronald Gregor Smith. New York: Collier Books/Macmillan, 1965.

Buber, Martin. *I and Thou.* New York: Charles Scribner's Sons, 1958.

Ellinor, Linda, and Glenna Gerard. *Dialogue: Rediscover the Transforming Power of Conversation.* New York: John Wiley & Sons, 1998.

Ernst, Frank. "The OK Corral: The Grid for Get-on-With." *Transactional Analysis Journal* 1, no. 4 (October 1971).

Fine, Reubin. *The Meaning of Love in Human Experience.* New York: John Wiley & Sons, 1985.

Flurrymobile. "U.S. Consumers Time-Spent on Mobile Crosses 5 Hours a Day." *Flurry* (blog), March 3, 2017. Retrieved from http://flurrymobile .tumblr.com/post/157921590345/us-consumers-time-spent-on -mobile-crosses-5.

Folkenberg, Judy. "Multi-Site Study of Therapies for Depression." *Archives of General Psychiatry* 42 (March 1985).

Fredrickson, B. L. "What Good Are Positive Emotions?" *Review of General Psychology* 2, no. 3 (1998): 300–319.

Freud, Sigmund. "On Narcissism: An Introduction (1914)." In *General Psychological Theory: Papers on Metapsychology.* New York: Collier Books, 1963.

———. "The Instincts and Their Vicissitudes (1915)." In *Collected Papers,* vol. 4. New York: Basic Books, 1959.

Friedman, Maurice. *The Healing Dialogue in Psychotherapy.* New York: Jason Aronson, 1985.

Fromm, Erich. *The Art of Loving.* New York: Bantam Books, 1956.

Garland, E., and M. O. Howard. "Neuroplasticity, Psychosocial Genomics, and the Biopsychosocial Paradigm in the 21st Century." *Health Social Work* 34, no. 3 (2009): 191–199.

Gaylin, Willard. *Rediscovering Love.* New York: Viking Penguin, 1986.

Gottman, John M., and Joan DeClaire. *The Relationship Cure: A 5 Step Guide for Building Better Connections with Family, Friends and Lovers.* New York: Crown, 2001.

Greenberg, Leslie S., and Susan M. Johnson. *Emotionally Focused Therapy for Couples.* New York: Guilford Press, 1988.

Gunzburg, John C. *Healing Through Meeting: Martin Buber's Conversational Approach to Psychotherapy.* Bristol, PA: Jessica Kingsley, 1997.

Hunt, Morton. *The Natural History of Love.* New York: Alfred A. Knopf, 1959.

Jung, C. G. *The Archetypes and the Collective Unconscious,* translated by R. F. C. Hull, Bollingen Series XX. Princeton, NJ: Princeton University Press, 1969.

———. "Marriage as a Psychological Relationship." In *The Portable Jung,* edited by Joseph Campbell. New York: Viking Press, 1971.

———. "Two Essays in Analytical Psychology." In *Collected Work,* vol. 7, translated by R. F. C. Hull, Bollingen Series XX. Princeton, NJ: Princeton University Press, 1969.

Kiecolt-Glaser, Janice K. "Marital Quality, Marital Disruption, and Immune Function," *Psychosomatic Medicine,* in press.

Kübler-Ross, Elisabeth. *On Death and Dying.* New York: Macmillan, 1969.

Lahr, Jane, and Lena Tabori. *Love: A Celebration in Art and Literature.* New York: Stewart, Tabori and Chang, 1982.

Lauer, Jeanette, and Robert Lauer. "Marriages Made to Last." *Psychology Today* 19, no. 6 (June 1985).

Levenson, Frederick F. *The Anti-Cancer Marriage: Living Longer Through Loving.* New York: Stein and Day, 1987.

Liebowitz, Michael. *The Chemistry of Love.* Boston: Little, Brown, 1983.

Lynd, Robert. *Love Through the Ages: Love Stories of All Nations.* New York: Coward-McCann, 1932.

Mahler, Margaret. *On Human Symbiosis and the Vicissitudes of Individuation: Infantile Psychosis.* New York: International Universities Press, 1968,

May, Rollo. *Love and Will.* New York: W. W. Norton, 1969.

McClelland, David C. "Some Reflections on the Two Psychologies of Love." *Journal of Personality* 54, no. 2 (June 1986).

McLean, Paul. "Man of His Animal Brains." *Modern Medicine,* February 3, 1964.

Mitchell, Stephen A. *Relational Concepts in Psychoanalysis: An Integration.* Cambridge, MA: Harvard University Press, 1988.

Mitchell, Stephen A. *Relationality: From Attachment to Intersubjectivity.* Hillsdale, NJ: Analytic Press, 2000.

Penfield, Wilder. *The Mystery of Mind: A Critical Study of Consciousness and the Human Brain.* Princeton, NJ: Princeton University Press, 1975.

Perls, Frederick S. "The Rules and Games of Gestalt Therapy." With Abraham Levitsky. In *Gestalt Therapy Now,* edited by Joan Fagen and Irma Lee Shepherd. Palo Alto, CA: Science and Behavior Books, 1970.

Plato. *Symposium.* In *The Portable Plato,* edited by Scott Buchanan. New York: Viking Press, 1948.

de Quincey, Christian. *Radical Knowing: Understanding Consciousness Through Relationship.* Rochester, VT: Park Street Press, 2005.

de Rougemont, Denis. *Love in the Western World,* translated by Montgomery Belgion. Garden City, NY: Doubleday Anchor Books, 1957.

Sager, Clifford J. *Marriage Contracts and Couples Therapy: Hidden Forces in Intimate Relationships.* New York: Brunner/Mazel, 1976.

Sagi, Y., I. Tavor, S. Hofstetter, S. Tzur-Moryosef, T. Blumenfeld-Katzir, and Y. Assaf. "Learning in the Fast Lane: New Insights into Neuroplasticity." *Neuron* 73, no. 6 (2012): 1195–1203.

Shafir, Rebecca Z. *The Zen of Listening: Mindful Communication in the Age of Distraction.* Wheaton, IL: Quest Books, 2000.

Scharff, David E., and Jill Savege Scharff. *Object Relations Couple Therapy.* Northvale, NJ: Jason Aronson, 1991.

Schneider, Isidor, ed. *The World of Love,* vols. I and II. New York: George Braziller, 1948.

Siegel, Bernard. *Love, Medicine and Miracles: Lessons Learned About Self-Healing from a Surgeon's Experience with Exceptional Patients.* New York: Harper and Row, 1986.

Siegel, Dan J. *The Mindful Brain: Reflection and Attunement in the Cultivation of Well-Being.* New York: W. W. Norton, 2007.

———. *Pocket Guide to Interpersonal Neurobiology: An Integrative Handbook of the Mind.* New York: W. W. Norton, 2012.

Silverman, Lloyd H., Frank M. Lachmann, and Robert L. Milich. *The Search for Oneness.* New York: International Universities Press, 1982.

Stolorow, Robert D., and George E. Atwood. *Contexts of Being: The Intersubjective Foundations of Psychological Life.* Hillsdale, NJ: Analytic Press, 1992.

Stolorow, Robert D., George E. Atwood, and Donna M. Orange. *Worlds of Experience: Interweaving Philosophical and Clinical Dimensions in Psychoanalysis.* New York: Basic Books, 2002.

Stuart, Richard. *Helping Couples Change: A Social Learning Approach to Marital Therapy.* New York: Guilford Press, 1980.

Sullivan, Harry Stack. *The Interpersonal Theory of Psychiatry.* New York: W. W. Norton, 1953.

U.S. Census Bureau, Decennial Censuses, 1890 to 1940, and Current Population Survey, Annual Social and Economic Supplements, 1947 to 2017.

Weissman, Myrna M. "Advances in Psychiatric Epidemiology: Rates and Risks of Major Depression." *American Journal of Health,* in press.

Wilber, Ken. *Integral Psychology: Consciousness, Spirit, Psychology, Therapy.* Boston, MA: Shambhala Publications, 2000.

Yerkovich, Milan, and Kay Yerkovich. *How We Love: A Revolutionary Approach to Deeper Connections in Marriage.* Colorado Springs, CO: Water Brook Press, 2006.

About Imago Relationship Therapy

Imago Relationship Therapy, originating in the partnership of Harville Hendrix, Ph.D., and Helen LaKelly Hunt, Ph.D., integrates the seminal interpersonal insights of major Western psychological systems, behavioral sciences, and spiritual disciplines into a uniquely comprehensive theory of primary love relationships. Developed from the exclusive study of couples and the integration of the relational implications of various psychological and spiritual systems, it presents an approach that builds on previous efforts to understand intimate partnerships and extends those efforts to create a relational theory and therapy that mirrors the view that the basic characteristic of the universe is connectedness.

Imago Relationship Therapy (IRT) is an expression of the new paradigm of relationality that includes and transcends the traditional paradigm of the individual. In the individual paradigm, all things are separate and relationships have to be constructed. The focus is on the intrapsychic. In the relationship paradigm, all things in the universe, from particles to galaxies to persons, constitute an unbroken connectedness. The focus is on the intersubjective, or the "between." This means that couples are essentially connected, although they experience themselves as separate. In conflict, they lose their awareness of connection and experience isolation. IRT utilizes a variety of clinical procedures to help couples—and singles desiring an intimate union—understand that the unconscious forces that influence partner selection and the inevitable power struggle that follows represent an unconscious attempt to restore connections that were ruptured in childhood. The goal of therapy is to help couples achieve a *conscious partnership*. This includes assisting them in identifying and interpreting their defenses against intimacy, which precipitate the power struggle, as a paradoxical yearning for connection, and helping couples restore connections within themselves, between themselves, and with the universe. The process of the therapy includes identifying frustrations rooted in primitive and illusory ideation of one's love partner; recognizing the failure of archaic behavior to gratify needs and achieve self-completion; and perceiving one's partner as an "other" without the encumbrance of one's own unconscious projections. Other aspects of the Imago process involve learning new skills and changing hurtful behavior, in the course of which partners consciously aim to meet one another's needs and thereby restore the lost and denied parts of themselves and recover their wholeness. The core skill is a three-part dialogue that helps couples make contact by breaking out of defensive and symbiotic relating and promoting differentiation from each other, compassion and empathy for each other, and connection and communion with each other. Therapy is ultimately made obsolete as each partner becomes a skilled advocate and "container" for the other's growth process. The Imago process, when consistently applied in any relationship, has the potential to be a transformational journey toward mutual healing, emotional maturation, and spiritual evolution. Creating healthy intimate partnerships and healthy children ultimately transforms society.

Imago Contacts

Imago Relationship Therapy is available in over fifty countries from more than 2,500 Imago therapists. If you are interested in working with a couples' therapist specifically trained in Imago Relationship Therapy or wish to attend a *Getting the Love You Want* or *Keeping the Love You Find* workshop, visit the website www.ImagoRelationships.org.

PROFESSIONAL TRAINING

Imago Relationships International is dedicated to providing the very best resources for therapists. Its international faculty consists of over twenty-five members worldwide, with trainings offered regularly on five continents.

Imago trainings are designed for therapists at all levels to develop proficiency in the Imago approach to working with couples and individuals. The Imago Clinical Training will provide you with an overview of the theory and essential skills for working with couples. For more information on clinical and educational training opportunities, visit the website www.ImagoRelationships.org.

Safe Conversations Leader Training was developed to support the movement toward an exciting and thriving relational culture, all over the world. The Leader Training Program will develop community leaders to teach Safe Conversations in diverse formats, designed for maximum sustainability in communities, schools, companies, and places of worship. For the Safe Conversations Leader Training Program, please visit www.RelationshipsFirst.org.

Additional Relationship Resources

Become the most connected couple you know!

For additional resources, including books, DVDs, audio-tapes, videotapes, and other educational opportunities, please visit www.HarvilleandHelen.com.

- Discover writings, podcasts, and invitations to special events including live teleseminars with Harville and Helen.
- Find updates on Harville and Helen's workshop and lecture schedule.
- Explore Imago resources, including workshops and educational programs for couples and singles, Certified Imago Therapists, professional training programs for qualified therapists and educators, and related products.
- Participate in a global mission of creating healthy relationships.

www.HarvilleandHelen.com

Index

repetition compulsion, 72, 291n
repression, 29–30, 63, 70, 145, 177, 185
requests, 175
  Behavior Change Request Dialogue (Exercise 14), 12, 161–75, 176–77, 198, 221, 239, 272–76
  SMART, 163, 166, 198
resistance, 144, 172–74
reunification, in romantic love, 47, 48
romantic love, 42, 43–58, 94, 133–34, 241, 291n
  brain and, 32, 45, 47–48
  chemistry of, 45–46
  commitment in, *see* commitment
  denial in, 52–55, 63
  enduring truths about, 4–5
  expectations and, 59–60
  heartache in, 4–5
  historical forms of, 292n
  Imago and, 36–42; *see also* Imago
  love marriage defined, 289n
  necessity in, 47, 49
  power struggle and, 59, 75; *see also* power struggle
  projections in, 55–56, 79
  Psyche and Eros myth and, 56–58
  recognition in, 46
  re-romanticizing, *see* re-romanticizing
  reunification in, 47, 48
  subterfuge in, 50–52
  timelessness in, 46–48
  unconscious mind and, 46–48
  universal language of, 46–49
Rumi, 130

sacred space, creating, 176–200
safety, xxi, xxii, 10, 12, 117–18, 138, 144, 176, 177, 187
  Imago Dialogue and, 117, 121, 127
  Space Between and, *see* Space Between
Sager, Clifford, 293n
Sai Baba, Shirdi, 176
Search for Oneness, The (Silverman et al.), 290n
self-care, 13
self-love, 151–52
semantics, 115–16
Sender, 118, 121
Sender Responsibility, 82, 118–19
serotonin, 45
shame, 187, 205
shock, in power struggle, 73–74
SMART requests, 163, 166, 198
socialization, 26–30
sorrow, 177
Space Between, 12–13, 69, 72, 81, 83, 119, 143, 144, 176, 205
spirituality, 205–6
"Still Face" experiment, 20–22
Stuart, Richard, 135, 294n
Sullivan, Harry Stack, 96
superego, 30
Surprise List (Exercise 11), 141–43, 144, 145, 269
symbiosis, 18
Symposium (Plato), 30–31, 48

Tao of Physics, The (Capra), 204
target behaviors, 140–41
ten-session timeline, 248–50
  see also exercises
therapy
  psychotherapy and psychoanalysis, 134
  see also relationship therapy

About the Authors

Harville Hendrix, Ph.D., and Helen LaKelly Hunt, Ph.D., married in 1982 and became partners in life and work. They co-created Imago Relationship Therapy and developed the concept of *conscious partnership*. Their partnership and collaboration has resulted in ten books on intimate relationships and parenting.

Harville is a clinical pastoral counselor, couples therapist, and author who is known internationally for his work with couples. A graduate of Mercer University in Macon, Georgia, in 1957, his alma mater awarded him an honorary doctorate of humane letters in 1989. He holds a bachelor of divinity from Union Theological Seminary in New York and a Ph.D. in psychology and religion from the School of Divinity at the University of Chicago. Dr. Hendrix is the recipient of several honors, including the Outstanding Pastoral Counselor of the Year Award (1995) from the American Baptist Churches, the 1995 Distinguished Contribution Award from the American Association of Pastoral Counselors, and, jointly with Helen, the Distinguished Contributors Award from the Association for Imago Relationship Therapy. He is a Diplomate in the American Association of Pastoral Counselors and has been a clinical member of the

American Group Psychotherapy Association and the International Transactional Analysis Association and former board member of the Group Psychotherapy Foundation.

Dr. Hendrix began his career as a therapist and educator at the Pastoral Counseling Center of Greater Chicago in 1965, where he was clinical director. In 1968, he became a member of the faculty of Perkins School of Theology at Southern Methodist University in Dallas, Texas. After teaching for nine years, he entered private practice. Following his divorce in 1975, he began a study of couples in order to better understand his own divorce and to search for the ingredients of a successful marriage. Since 1977, he has conducted couples' therapy and couples' workshops, taught Imago Therapy to clinical professionals, lectured on marriage to the public, and written books with Helen on primary relationships.

Helen is nationally known as an activist in the women's movement and holds two master's degrees from Southern Methodist University, Dallas, Texas. One master's degree was in Counseling and she went halfway through a Clinical Psychology Degree. She also has a Ph.D. from Union Theological Seminary in New York City and honorary doctorates from Christian Theological Seminary in Chicago and Southern Methodist University in Dallas. She is the sole author of *Faith and Feminism: A Holy Alliance* and *And the Spirit Moved Them*. In addition to being founder of the Sister Fund, she is also cofounder of the New York Women's Foundation, the Dallas Women's Foundation, and the Women's Funding Network. Helen is honored to be an inductee in the National Women's Hall of Fame, in Seneca Falls, New York.

In 1984, Harville and Helen founded Imago Relationships International—a nonprofit cofounded with Imago therapists to train therapists in the Imago process and to develop workshops for couples and singles. The organization has trained over 2,500 therapists who practice Imago therapy in fifty-three countries, and nearly two hundred workshop presenters conduct workshops around the world. Imago Relationship Therapy was featured on *The Oprah Winfrey Show* seventeen times, one of which won for her the "most socially redemptive" award for daytime talk shows, and Dr. Hendrix's second show was included in *O* magazine's "Oprah's Top Twenty Shows" in 2005. He has also been featured on many other major television shows and in countless radio shows, newspapers, and major magazines, and he continues to conduct professional trainings and appear as a public lecturer.

In addition to *Getting the Love You Want: A Guide for Couples,* a *New York Times* bestseller which has sold more than 4 million copies, Harville and Helen are the authors of the two other bestselling books, *Keeping the Love You Find: A Personal Guide* (written for singles) and *Giving the Love That Heals: A Guide for Parents.* They have also authored and coauthored *Receiving Love, Making Marriage Simple,* and *The Space Between,* three workbooks and three meditation books. Their work has been translated into more than fifty languages. Harville and Helen were also executive editor and producer, respectively, of *Getting the Love You Want: The Home Video,* which has been seen on more than three hundred television stations.

In 2010, Harville and Helen created a think tank called Relationships First. In collaboration with their peers, they decided to take the insights of the relationship sciences from the clinic to the public and initiate a relational revolution. The think tank evolved into a nonprofit organization by the same name, and became the vehicle for launching a global movement from a Dallas, Texas, base. They developed and streamed an intervention called Safe Conversations to more than one hundred countries and launched a training program with leaders now active globally. Their goal is to promote a shift in the cultural value system from a focus on individualism to relationships and ignite a global movement in the service of creating a relational culture.

Harville and Helen have a blended family of six children, including two from their own marriage. They also have six grandchildren. They live and work in New York City and Dallas, Texas, where they are busy writing new books, launching old ones, giving lectures at various conventions, training therapists and movement builders, managing Relationships First, planning the expansion of Imago processes into the larger community, and creating a relational civilization.

Imago

Ongoing Support for Your Relationship from Imago

Imago Relationships International was cofounded by Harville Hendrix, Ph.D., and Helen LaKelly Hunt, Ph.D., to help couples and individuals create strong and fulfilling relationships. We offer the following:

- Weekend workshops based on *Getting the Love You Want* are available at many locations in the United States and internationally. Thousands of couples take this workshop each year.
- More than 2,500 Certified Imago Therapists are available in more than fifty countries. They can guide you through the Imago process and help you achieve the relationship of your dreams.
- A monthly email newsletter, with stories from couples and a look at Imago in practice.
- A range of audio and video programs based on Imago, including *Through Conflict to Connection*, an introductory DVD showing three couples using Imago Dialogue, that features Harville Hendrix and Helen LaKelly Hunt.
- Information on training programs for mental health professionals, coaches, and educators that can help you work more effectively with couples and families.
- Workshops for individuals as well as parenting programs.
- Training in delivering the Safe Conversations workshops and seminars.

For information on these and other Imago programs, please visit our website: www.ImagoRelationships.org; www.Relationships First.org; and for Helen and Harville's personal schedule of presentations including workshops, go to www.HarvilleandHelen .com.

Email: Info@ImagoRelationships.org

In addition, you can find information about the Imago program for religious groups by visiting www.CouplehoodStore.com.